DELIVERANCE OF THE SPELLBOUND GOD

Also by Marie-Laure Valandro

Camino Walk
Where Inner & Outer Paths Meet

Letters from Florence
Observations on the Inner Art of Travel

DELIVERANCE OF THE SPELLBOUND GOD

An Experiential Journey into Eastern and Western Meditation Practices

MARIE-LAURE VALANDRO

Lindisfarne Books | 2011

2011
Lindisfarne Books
An imprint of Anthroposophic Press / SteinerBooks
610 Main St., Great Barrington, MA
www.steinerbooks.org

Cover & book design: William Jens Jensen
Cover image: Varanasi, India, by Marie-Laure Valandro
LIBRARY OF CONGRESS CATALOGING-IN-PUBLICATION DATA

Valandro, Marie-Laure.
Deliverance of the spellbound God : an experiential journey into
Eastern and Western meditation practices / Marie-Laure Valandro.
   p. cm.
Includes bibliographical references (p. 220).
ISBN 978-1-58420-100-7
1. Meditation. 2. Steiner, Rudolf, 1861–1925. 3. Occultism.
4. Valandro, Marie-Laure. 5. Spiritual biography. I. Title.
BL627.V35 2011
204'.35092—dc23
[B]
                                                    2011029459
        Print edition: ISBN 978-1-58420-100-7
        eBook edition: ISBN 978-1-58420-105-2

Contents

"So began the great cosmic drama in which the initiand's life was engulfed. The drama consisted of nothing less than the deliverance of the spellbound God." —RUDOLF STEINER [1]

MYSTAI, MYSTES, MYSTERIES

Dedicated to all seekers

The West:
I think, therefore I am not,
I think, therefore I am dead.

The East:
Satyam jnanam anantam brahma
Anandarupam amritam bibharti
Shantam shivam advaitam
Om, shanti, shanti, shanti

Truth, wisdom, immeasurability, O God,
Blessedness, eternity, beauty,
Peace, blessing, indivisibility
On me (Aum)
Peace, peace, peace

One of the basic principles of true esoteric science is that those who dedicate themselves to it must do so in full consciousness. As students, we should undertake nothing, nor engage in any exercises, whose effects we do not understand. An esoteric teacher, when giving advice or instruction, will always explain what the effects of following the instruction will be on the body, soul, or spirit of the person striving for higher knowledge. [2]

---

1   Steiner, *Christianity as Mystical Fact and the Mysteries of Antiquity*, p. 14.

2   Steiner, *How to Know Higher Worlds*, p. 108.

It has now become possible to describe the way of initiation that can be traversed so that the soul will not need to go through certain experiences that are likely to lead it into catastrophes and revolutionary events. Thus far, it is possible today to speak in public of the path into the higher worlds. But it must be stated that even now, if one desires to go still further, the path into the higher worlds is bound up with a burden of suffering and pain, entailing special experiences that can no doubt take disconcerting and revolutionary hold upon the human life, the preparation for which one must first be brought to a certain maturity.... Naturally, the path into the higher worlds is nowhere closed, and if one passes a certain stage and wants to go even farther, this requires a special degree of maturity if it is to be achieved without a shock in the soul life—not merely superficially but with real inner convulsions of the soul. Even these pass quite naturally over the soul when the whole course of initiation is carried out correctly. Nevertheless, it is necessary that it should occur in the right way.[3]

These rules are written for all disciples: Attend to them. Before the eyes can see they must be incapable of tears. Before the ear can hear it must have lost its sensitiveness. Before the voice can speak in the presence of the Masters it must have lost the power to wound. Before the soul can stand in the presence of the masters its feet must be washed in the blood of the heart.[4]

If you were ever to take part in the Mysteries, you would feel ashamed at having been born a mere human.[5]

3   Steiner, *The Mysteries of the East and of Christianity*, pp. 8–9 (trans. revised).

4   Collins, "Light on the Path," in Rudolf Steiner, *From the History and Contents of the First Section of the Esoteric School, 1904–1914*, p. 403.

5   Emperor Julian, quoted in Steiner, *Christianity as Mystical Fact and the Mysteries of Antiquity*, p. 82 (trans. revised).

Dedicated to
Dorothea Sunier-Pierce and Janny Mager
for their devoted attention

↓

EAST: PREPARATION

"One-pointedness, can you tell me what that means again?" I asked this of my friend R, who had brought me to this Catholic high school in the center of Montreal, where we were about to begin a ten-day course in a Buddhist form of meditation called Vipassana. Although I had many questions on this August day in 1979, this was not my first introduction to Eastern disciplines. At twenty-nine, like many of my contemporaries, I had been reading Buddhist texts for years and found them fascinating.

I had also studied martial arts in Boston with Okinawan masters since age sixteen. My choice of karate actually began earlier, when I lived in Algeria from the age of nine until I was twelve. My father, a policeman and soldier, used to take me, his eldest daughter, to judo practice at his compound headquarters, where I would watch the men practice judo and imitate them, as children do. Seeing my enthusiasm, my father suggested, and I agreed, that I should study karate, which he thought a better choice than judo for a woman. I was small, and with karate I would not be required to have close contact with or throw my partners to the ground. It was a good choice. My karate masters were gentle, strong as steel, and from their beautiful brown eyes came stories of untold wisdom and love.

I remember one Saturday morning when I was eighteen. I had gone to the library at Boston University to find books about the East in an effort to understand what my karate masters were teaching me, and to fathom the mysteries behind the martial arts. I was steeped in French, Spanish, and English literary studies at the time, but I had not found the books I was looking for, because what I was looking for could not be found in books. I was practicing it, but I did not know I was. In the dojo, being for a long time the only girl among boys and men, I was learning control of my body, control of my thoughts, gentleness,

1

strength, memory, discipline, confidence, fearlessness, clarity, meditation, emptiness, speed, respect, community—all that and much more. But my intellect wanted answers to why, what, and where. Like all good Westerners, I wanted to understand things intellectually. I was born with a question in my mouth: Why? I was definitely not the dumb Parcival who did not ask questions, but a Michaelite, as some call ourselves, after the Archangel Michael, whose name *Mich-ael* means question.

I had been a bookworm since age eleven, when someone gave me a real book with no pictures, because, I imagine, she felt sorry for us poor kids playing on dirt piles with little plastic cars found in Camembert boxes, making roads and cities in front of our apartment building in Annaba (formerly Bône and, before that, Hippo) in northeastern Algeria. Because my father was not exactly rolling in money, we did not have toys or books, so we played with nothing but beach sand, water, dirt, oranges, frogs—the opposite of an intellectual upbringing. After that first book, however, I read everything I could lay my hands on.

Nonetheless, I did not limit my experience to the printed page. I had met my friend R, the expert who had practiced Vipassana meditation, in 1977, while I was living and traveling for several months in India. I had ended that trip with a one-month trek with him in the K2–Annapurna range in Nepal, walking in the intoxicating scented groves of blooming rhododendrons. The sense of humor of this handsome québecquois captivated me, so we kept in touch.

Then there was a subsequent trek to a Mt. Everest base camp in the spring of 1979, after I had spent the winter skiing and living in a tiny village in the Alborz Mountains of Northern Iran, studying Buddhist scripture and Sufism, among other things, and writing a book while a revolution was going on in Tehran. Two important things suddenly dawned on me during that trip: I needed to study with a Buddhist master, and I wanted to have a child—sooner rather than sometime in the future.

Perhaps it was because the mountains there are so high and closer to the heavens that messages can be heard more clearly. As I was walking in that hauntingly beautiful setting, the message was clear: *get yourself a Buddhist master and study real meditation.* I can remember the distinct moment that this thought came to me. It was quiet; the horizon was filled with tall, granite fortresses, blue skies, quiet, and peace. Yes, a master. Then the other thought, just as powerful: *this world is beautiful and I will have children to show them its beauty.* Up until that moment, I had not wanted to be a mother because I did not want to lose my freedom to roam the world. But then the decision was made. When the time came, I would take these future children everywhere. That was my task: to show them how wonderful this Earth is, and in that respect I have not failed them.

In the spring, I flew back to the US, and upon returning home (at that time Vermont, when not in Iran), I contacted R., who was living not far away in Quebec. I asked him about a Buddhist master. He told me to attend a course taught by his master, a real Buddhist master named Goenka, who had studied with Burmese Master Sayagyi U Ba Khin in Burma. They said his was supposedly the purest technique, descended from the Buddha 2,500 years ago and handed down from master to master in an unbroken line, untainted, pure, powerful.

Goenka had taught his first ten-day course outside of Burma in 1969 to his Bombay relatives in India. This was barely ten years after he began spreading the Dharma from Burma after Sayagyi U Ba Khin died. This course would be held within just a few weeks in Montreal, also close by. It was good timing for me that the master teacher Goenka would be on this continent when I was here as well. A real master would cross my path.

My story, until this turning point, like everyone's story, is complex, and the pages you have just read could be several books in themselves. There is much ground to cover in only a few sentences.

↓

INITIATION

To comprehend merely the things of the world around, leads only to a denial of God. On the evidence of the senses, God does not exist any more than he does for the intellect that interprets sensory experience. God lies spellbound in the world. To find God requires a power from God himself. That power must actually be awakened in the candidate for initiation, it was stated in the ancient teaching.

So began the great cosmic drama in which the initiand's life was engulfed. The drama consisted of nothing less than *the deliverance of the spellbound God.*[1]

These are beautiful words: "the deliverance of the spellbound God." But as my drama was about to begin, my intellect was not about to give up without a fight. It seems that the intellect kept the God spellbound, chained to its dead thoughts. The mighty was well hidden.

On that day in August 1979, I was extremely nervous about the retreat, even though my life up to this point had not left me completely unprepared. Being a thorough intellectual, however, and a French one at that, I still thought I needed to know the terminology with my *intellect*—terms such as one-point-edness, impermanence, non-self, mindfulness, and so on. So here I was, swimming in jargon and wanting last-minute information from my friend R.

The course was held in a rented Catholic high school dorm. There were more than three hundred people coming from all over the US and Canada and everywhere else, and the Indian community living in North America was heavily represented as well. R did answer my question about one-pointedness, using words I did not really understand, and then it was time to begin.

---

1   Steiner, *Christianity as Mystical Fact*, pp. 13–14 (italics added).

Everyone was very excited as we gathered in the big hall and said goodbye to one another. We were not to look our friends in the eye, as that was considered disturbing. I took my seat in the middle, toward the back of the room, ready for instructions. Being a good and eager student, I observed all the rules, once in a while glancing at friends scattered here and there. And so we began our very perilous ascent into the unknown territories of the mind, the first-timers without a clue as to what we were getting into. We thought we were going to do a little meditation, like clearing the mind, and just sit there as on a cloud.

Goenka, our teacher, entered the room with his wife, a very quiet, devoted presence who never spoke but stayed at his right side, as she would for the whole ten days. Everyone bowed. I did not because, being a modern human being, I did not see why I should bow to someone whom I did not know. Never a follower, I was the only one who did not bow. As a Westerner, it was not natural for me to do so at the beginning, but it wasn't long before I did. I resisted until he actually became my teacher and I gave him my trust. That, in fact, took only a day. Without that trust, I would not have been able to survive the experience ahead. We had to give ourselves up to the *Sangha*, the *Dhamma*, and *Buddha* for protection, and I did as everyone else did because we were about to enter states of consciousness in which there was nothing to keep us all together—no ego, so something, someone, had to do that job for us. *Sangha* is the community of believers; *Dhamma* the body of rules; and *Buddha* our protector. I had an ego, a strong one at that, but I had to relinquish that ego force within me and give it to the teacher. I gave him my trust and took refuge in the *Dhamma*, the *Sangha*, and the *Buddha*. "Taking refuge" could also be another whole book in itself.

So, in the ancient language of *Pali*, we repeated:

> I take refuge in the *Dhamma* (3 times)
> I take refuge in *Sangha* (3 times)
> I take refuge in *Buddha* (3 times)

…which, when I look back, *meant absolutely nothing to me.* Okay, "I take refuge." Fine. But why? Taking refuge from *what*? And what is a refuge anyway?

Why am I saying this? These thoughts were going through my mind. And, I was just about to learn the answers.

We followed, of course, the Noble Eightfold Path:

1. Right view, *samma ditthi*
2. Right aspiration, *samma sankappa*
3. Right speech, *samma vaca*
4. Right conduct, *samma kammanta*
5. Right living, *samma ajiva*
6. Right effort, *samma vayama*
7. Right mindfulness, *samma sati*
8. Right concentration, *samma samadhi*

The mood in the hall was profoundly solemn, somber, and dark—serious business, nothing to laugh about. This was very different from the atmosphere surrounding my québecquois friends, who were forever joking and laughing about nothing in particular.

Then Goenka gave us our first instructions. The first three days would be dedicated to *Anapana*, and we were told to pay attention to the breath entering the nostril at the tip of the nose; not inside, just the tip of the nose—constantly, for three days. We all fought the pain of sitting in a very uncomfortable position, not moving for hours on end, excruciating pains shooting into the legs and everywhere else. We moved very slowly when the body could not take it, but we increased our ability to bear the pain, to observe it, and mostly not to react to it. With reaction came much more pain, but when I observed the pain it dissolved; rather than multiplying, it melted. By letting go of the physical pain, this, too, shall pass—sometimes it did. Then we had mental anguish of all sorts, depending on our own little bag of problems. We also observed daydreaming and fantasizing. We observed the chakra centers acting up, or opening up, and our own bewilderment; this on my part, since I really did not know anything about chakras except through my reading. Experiencing these centers is quite another story, and I observed that, too. At that stage, I had a new mantra, which was *observe, observe*, back to the breath, and observe, and sometimes observe that I was observing. I thought that my meditation was nothing but this little word *observe*. I became a *witness*, to myself.

Our concentration increased as the hours passed, and body, soul, and mind were starved. We starved ourselves through denying our senses and lived on breath and the beautiful words in the ancient, beautiful Pali language coming from Goenka's warm voice as it echoed in the darkness of the hall. The mantras he recited kept us sane and gave us the energy to keep going in this more-than-arduous task of living with ourselves. We had absolutely nothing to hold on to as we plunged into the unknown hidden corners of the psyche while the soul was swimming in soothing mantras.

Many educated people today find the repetitions in the Buddha's discourses difficult to understand. But once we embark upon the esoteric path we learn to enjoy dwelling on these repetitions with our inner senses. For these repetitions correspond to certain rhythmical movements in the ether body. And when we surrender to the repetitions in perfect inner peace, our inner movements blend harmoniously with them. When we listen to the word-melodies of the Buddha's teaching, our life becomes infused with the secrets of the universe. For the movements of Buddha's word-melodies mirror cosmic rhythms that also consist of repetitions and regular returns to earlier rhythms.[2]

In the gymnasium, which was the "temple," we were lined up like sardines, women on the right, men on the left, sitting on our meager cushions from early morning until late at night. The room was kept dark like a cocoon, a womb where we would all retreat deep within ourselves for days. Our schedule went as follows:

4:00 a.m.: wake-up call
4:30–6:30: meditation in hall or residence
6:30–8:00: breakfast break
8:00–9:00: group meditation in hall
9:00–11:00: meditation in hall or residence per the teacher's instructions
11:00–12:00: vegetarian lunch
12:00–1:00: rest
1:00–2:30: meditation in hall or residence
2:30–3:30: meditation in hall

2   Steiner, *How to Know Higher Worlds*, p. 137.

3:30–5:00: meditation in hall or residence as per the teacher's instructions
5:30–6:00: tea break
6:00–7:00: group meditation in hall
7:00–8:30: teacher's discourse in hall
8:30–9:00: group meditation in hall
9:00–9:30: questions in hall
9:30 p.m.: retire to own room, lights out

Besides this grueling schedule, men and women were separated at all times.

Here are some of the other rules we had to observe:

Abstention from killing
Abstention from stealing
Abstention from all sexual activities
Abstention from telling lies
Abstention from intoxicants
Abstention from taking food after 12:00 noon
    (exception for health reasons; hot lemon water allowed; first-
    timers could have a small meal)
Abstention from sensual amusements and bodily decorations
    (no jewelry or perfumes)
Abstention from using high and luxurious beds

These rules were not difficult for me to follow, as I had followed them without much trouble in my own personal life. But the most stunning for me was this one: students must observe "Noble Silence," from the start of the course until 10:00 a.m. on day ten. Noble Silence is silence of body, speech, and mind. Any form of communication, whether by physical gesture, written notes, sign language, or any other means was prohibited, although students were allowed to speak to the teacher when necessary. I had never spent days on end without talking to anyone except when hiking in the mountains, where one is silenced by the awesome scenery; my work as a teacher was certainly anything but quiet. We ate in silence in the communal dining hall, walked in silence, took showers in silence, slept in silence. Neither could we practice yoga, dancing, movement, rites or rituals, prayers of any sort, other meditation techniques, reading, writing, or taking notes. Basically, nothing was allowed except sitting, sleeping, a little eating, and following the meditation instructions given every day.

And so, through rhythm and discipline we moved through the stages of our journey. Here is what Mathieu Boisvert (from the québecquois Vipassana group I was hanging around with) has to say:

> The second step (the first is to follow the precepts) is the practice of concentration. At the beginning of the course, our mind is very agitated, so to calm it down, for the first three days we use our breath as the object of our meditation *anapana-sati* (breath-awareness). This is not a breathing exercise; we do not try to control the breath, but just observe it as it is. The entire technique consists in moving from a subtle to a subtler field, from the conscious to the unconscious level of the mind.... The breath can be a tool for us to introspect the unconscious field. It is the only function of the body that works both ways, intentionally and unintentionally. We can control our respiration to a certain extent, but if we leave it on its own, it will continue to function normally. When a negativity arises at the mental level, two things happen at the physical level; the breath deviates from its normal rhythm and certain biological changes occur in the body; these changes are experienced as sensations. So by observing the breath objectively, we not only gain control over the mind, concentration, but also obtain purification of the mind because the breath is related to our defilements. Thus by observing the breath, indirectly, we are observing our defilements. The first three days of the retreat are fully devoted to *Anapana* meditation because at the beginning the breath is easier to observe than the sensations, and at the same time we develop more concentration to enter the subtler field, the field of *Vipassana*.[3]

Here is what Goenka has to say on this subject:

> The next step is to develop some mastery over our wild mind, by training it to remain fixed on a single object: the breath. One tries to keep one's attention for as long as possible on the respiration. This is not a breathing exercise; one does not regulate the breath. Instead one observes the natural respiration as it is, as it comes in, as it goes out. In this way one

---

3   Ahir, *Vipassana*, p. 118.

further calms the mind, so that it is no longer overpowered by violent negativities. At the same time, one is concentrating the mind, making it sharp and penetrating, capable of the work of insight.[4]

After observing the breath for three days, on the fourth Goenka had us moving our concentrated attention to the top of the head very slowly and deliberately. By this time, many of us had acquired acute concentration and we knew by the formality of Goenka's directions, his very slow speech and his extreme seriousness, that things were about to happen. Listening to Goenka's measured voice, every single meditant moved his or her intensely focused attention to the top of the head. In that instant, I felt an opening, an opening into another space where there was no space, no right or left, up or down. Even the sound was special, a popping sound. I felt suspended somewhere, with no attachment to anything, floating. It was a bit bewildering to me: Where am I? What is happening? My self was there, but my body was not; it had become transparent, it seemed, and I was in suspended animation. I opened my eyes ever so slightly and was back in my body just to check things out, but then I closed my eyes again and entered this alternate space, noticing that all was fine. So, holding on for dear life to Goenka's deep voice leading us, very slowly now, we were entering the second part of the retreat which is called Vipassana. Every time I entered this spacelessness, I said to myself, *Here I go again; hold on; we are swimming now in liquid space.*

I became objective, seeing and becoming aware of this new space, trying to find balance where there was no balance. Balance as we know it is in the physical world and this was not the physical world, so it had rules pertaining to other phenomena which are the opposite of the physical world. Through the strong forces of my ego, I kept myself together (the ego I was supposed to let go of or melt down). I also never lost my sense of humor, even though the experience was extremely difficult to bear.

In the middle of the night, I was strangely aware of happenings, because at night most of us, of course, were not sleeping at all. Trying to quiet our minds during the day, for me at least, made for little sleep at night. My body was in

---

4   Ibid., p. 21.

a state of rest, but the mind was busy. So, by the third night, the opening that had happened during the day as a lifting of my consciousness into another nonspace-space—or to use anthroposophic language, entering the etheric world, or elemental world—this entrance, or opening, became something else.

During the night, it became the other side of the coin. It was the opening of the unconscious, and I saw all that was there, literally spilling out from this deep well of the unknown, instincts foaming out. It was difficult to observe, but I did observe it. By this time, observing was becoming easier, since we had done little else for days. And what a world came out; it was like the medieval world of Hieronymus Bosch's paintings or like Milton's *Paradise Lost*. It felt extremely good to have that hidden well opened, emptied, with all that was unconscious out in the open for me to look at, experience, and view in awe. Or we could call it a descent into some kind of hell; nothing pleasant there, but since I was an observer and not a participant, it was a sight to behold. I never asked Goenka about this, but kept it to myself. He always reminded us that whatever happens, let it go; do not hold on to whatever it is, as it will pass. Those words kept me together. Observe, observe, observe. This, too, shall pass.

I entered deep meditation; there was no going back into the intellectual jargon. This was experiential, overwhelming knowledge about myself and the world. My concentration had been sharpened like a sword, light penetration, and was doing its job only *too well*. I guess I was a good student. Perhaps being a bad student would have been better. At some point after three or four days, a woman sitting next to me, who had just had enough, spoke to me: "I can't sit like you people. You can do that; I just can't bear it." She simply gave up the practice as too much pain, too much to ask. She said, "You're strong; I'm weak," and blamed herself. I did not understand her or why she gave up.

Now we had entered the subtler field of Vipassana meditation. The word *Vipassana* is a compounding of the prefix, *upasanna*. "Vi" used as the preposition and the root word *passana* from the verb *passati*, to see... The prefix has been applied to carry the vigor of Insight, Clarity, Distinctness, Accuracy, Rightfulness, etc., to the Act of seeing or Perceiving. Thus the word *Vipassana* as a whole may be rightfully explained as "to see or to perceive," correctly and accurately or to go Positive into the Insightness. Insightness of what? And what is to be perceived or to be seen? It is the Insight or discerning of all the material and mental phenomena or the happenings of the living beings with Rightful understanding. In other words, *Vipassana bhavana* stands for the insight system of meditation. By Insight, one should mean, the clear and correct perception of the true nature of things as they really are. In other-wise, the insight means understanding of the Reality itself, that is, the conditioning and the unconditioning of the material phenomena.[5]

Mathieu *Boisvert* again:

Having begun with gross reality (breath), we move toward a subtler and subtler one, and on the fourth day, *Vipassana* is given and we plunge into the ocean of sensations, the gateway of wisdom. From the top of the head to the tips of the toes, we observe with increasing equanimity all the sensations we come across, in every part of the body, without craving for the pleasant ones, nor rejecting the unpleasant ones, just seeing things as they are.

Here the meditator, when feeling a pleasant sensation understands properly, "I am feeling a pleasant sensation"; when feeling a painful sensation, he understands properly, "I am feeling a painful sensation"; when feeling a neutral sensation, he understands properly, "I am feeling a neutral sensation."

Now his awareness is firmly established in the present moment. This awareness develops to the extent that there is mere observation and mere understanding, nothing else, and he dwells in a state where he does not grasp anything, and there is nothing for him to grasp in the frame-work of the body. This is how a meditator dwells observing bodily sensations in bodily sensation itself (*sattipatthana-vedanaupassana*).

When we start our observation of the sensations, it might be difficult to develop sensitivity of the mind, but with a continuous practice, and with a strong equanimity, we calm our mind, and thus increase our awareness which enables us to feel sensations which were always there—in the parts that were blind before. Once we feel sensations everywhere on the surface of the body, we direct our awareness inside, and through the same process, start feeling sensations deep inside. As we proceed

---

5   Ibid., p. 29.

through the ten day course, we can go much deeper in our observation of the body. We will reach a stage where we understand the composition of the body.[6]

Goenka always mentioned that this process was like peeling an onion—the top layer is exposed, then the next layer, and so forth until we reach the core. That core is the "spellbound God."

Part of the ten-day course, besides the once-a-day discourse with full details about the practice and detailed explanation of the exercises, was a few minutes meditating in front of the teacher, alone in the huge hall. To me that was a real ordeal because I did not know if I was practicing correctly. Because of my extreme nervousness, thoughts drifted through my mind; I sit quietly, and he sits quietly. What is he doing? What am I doing? How can he know what I am doing?

I believe this experience taught all of us how to remain cool and collected on the outside. At that stage, I had no real concept of the fact that I was in front of an accomplished master; the word *master* had no meaning to me whatsoever. I had read great beautiful books full of wisdom, but a *living* master was another thing entirely. Looking back, I see myself as a naïve, intellectual idiot. I was definitely born in France's land of the "I think, therefore I am" duality—me here, that there. I was about to learn that "me here, that there" can melt into "one," but not without a very good fight. I was very far from where I wanted to go. "Understand the word *this*, and you are in the right place; you need no further instruction."[7]

The days went on, one more arduous than the next, as we practiced observation of the sensations throughout our bodies, repeatedly, in the same order, over and over, observing them from head to toe, not skipping any parts, not dwelling on any areas longer than any other. Blind spots opened up and the body became more transparent to our witnessing, the layers slowly peeling, one after another through our piercing, concentrated minds. I became able to sit for one-hour sessions with more ease, and some of the pain melted away.

---

6   Ibid., p. 127.

7   Kühlewind, *The Light of the "I,"* p. 64.

Observing what came was difficult at times, but I kept going through the rough moments steadily by not getting involved in the pain, lust, joys, and so on. By not speaking one became intensely aware of others, of their presence.

Goenka's evening speeches were always a blessing, full of jokes to release our tension and small anecdotes to help us go on our spectacular ascent into the fortress of the mind/body. Here is one of my favorites:

↓

A young professor was on a boat journey. He was extremely well educated with many higher degrees to his name, but he did not have much down-to-earth experience of life. Among the passengers on the boat was a very old, illiterate sailor. Every night, the old sailor came to the young man's cabin to listen to his dissertations on various subjects. The old man was very much impressed by his vast knowledge.

"Old man, have you studied geology?"

"What is that, sir?"

"The science of the Earth."

"No sir, I never went to school. I have never studied anything."

"Old man, you have lost a quarter of your life."

The old man felt bad, and went to his quarters. "If someone like this learned young man tells me I have lost a quarter of my life it must be true," he thought sadly. The next evening, the old man was just leaving his cabin, when he met the young professor.

"Old man, have you studied oceanography?"

"What is that Sir?"

"The science of the sea."

"No Sir, I have never studied anything."

"Old man you have lost half your life."

The old man left once more, even sadder. "I have lost half my life this learned man says."

The next evening, again the young professor asked the old sailor, "Old man, have you studied meteorology?"

"What is that sir? I have never even heard of it."

"Well, it is the science of the wind, of the rain, of the weather."

"No sir, as I have told you, I have never gone to school so I do not know anything."

"You have never studied the science of the Earth on which you live; you have never studied the science of the sea on which you work; you have never studied the science of the weather which you meet every day on the high seas. Old man you have lost three quarters of your life."

But the next day it was the old man's turn to question the young professor.

"Mr. Professor, have you studied Swimmology?"

"Swimmology? What do you mean?"

"Do you know how to swim sir?"

"No old man, I do not know how to swim."

"Mr. Professor, you have lost all of your life. This boat has hit a rock and is about to sink. The ones who can swim have a chance to reach the distant shore; the others who cannot swim will perish. I am very sorry, Mr. Professor, you have certainly lost your whole life."

One can study all of the "ologies" of this world, but if you do not learn how to swim, all your studies are totally useless, vain. You can read or write books on swimming, you can enter debates on the subtle theoretical aspect of swimming, but how will this help you if you refuse to enter the water? You must learn to swim.

↓

You can see why I like this one. We were all in that hall, definitely swimming in deep water. Actually, we were drowning most of the time, able to take a bit of air from the surface and then dive down again amid tall waves, tsunamis of our own making. We were drowning in endless desires, fantasies, dreams, illusions, pain, lust, fears, daydreams, good emotions, bad emotions, future, past—every day for ten days.

On the last day, we practiced a new technique called *metta*. Goenka gave us one last memorable talk, asking our forgiveness that he was responsible for our pain, our awareness. Then he sent us loving kindness, told us to remember all our friends and family, and taught us how to send feelings of love to all of them. I became very upset with myself, because I noticed that my power of love was almost nonexistent. I did what I was told, but there was not much substance to my *metta*. The thought was there, but it felt like nothing. I thought to myself, *I will try sending my love to all my friends and family, but compared to Goenka's love, mine feels like a meager, emaciated love thought that will never get where it is supposed to go.* It was a very half-starved love thought, and I needed to do much work on it. Once again I was experiencing the old duality; the thought is *here*, and I am *there*. It did not register one bit that a thought is a reality; it has substance. My intellect did not *get it*.

But my heart did. With my heart I did send loving thoughts to all my friends, relatives, and students; it was a long list. But my intellect was there fighting all the way. Where is the thought? How does it get there? I just can't muster love power like that; mine is so weak. And so it went. I guess I am a fighter. My painting teacher says that people who have very curly, unmanageable hair were warriors in their past lives, and I think there is something to that.

As Mathieu Boisvert observes:

After ten days of diligent practice of awareness and equanimity, we learn a new meditation technique called *metta* meditation, or *loving kindness*. Since the beginning of the retreat, we have been digging out our accumulated stock of negativities and on the tenth day, naturally, we feel much more lightened and feel like sharing our peace and harmony with others. With the fruits we have gained, we generate thoughts of boundless love, compassion and peace toward all beings. These thoughts will not only affect our minds, but will affect our environment and eventually our minds as well. By practicing *metta* meditation, we generate vibrations of pure love which will *metta* not only the surrounding atmosphere, but also the persons toward whom the *metta* is directed. After this meditation of loving kindness, we break the Noble Silence and start chattering with other meditators. It is only the next day that we return home. This small gap between *metta* and departure is essential to get used to the gross level of reality again before going back in the society.[8]

The ten-day retreat ended, and all the participants were elated, feeling lighter and more peaceful, including myself. We all departed, and I stayed with some québecquois friends in a small house in the woods for a few days. But the result of the ten-day retreat for me was just beginning. I was to suffer for several weeks because of that intense practice.

---

8   Ahir, *Vipassana*, p. 130.

ADJUSTMENT

It took years to understand what happened to me during those retreats in which I participated for several years; this book is the result. Many former practitioners over the years have asked me to share these experiences, but it has taken me thirty-two years to decide that I should do so in writing. It has proved most important to share my understanding of these events, and it has provided another journey that is just as full of surprises and unexpected discoveries as were the experiences themselves. When I write, I travel in different realms, one more exciting and rewarding than the next. I never know where they will lead. It is like going to a foreign country, with the reader as my companion in a world of discoveries that are full of life and wonder. Like many journeys, it has steep, difficult, and sharp rocky ascents, as well as easy paths, deep valleys, ocean depths, and wide meadows.

This book is not written like other books; rather, it is an experience for the reader to go through—a living experience. It is imperfect, and I have learned to accept and live with my imperfections. I can only do the best I can, which is to share my experiences here.

Because I was such a devoted and good (meaning I did what I was told) student, the powerful technique produced results within me, which were almost instantaneous. The opening of the head, the opening of the unconscious, and the opening of various chakras, force centers, are all experiences for which I was totally unprepared at some level. But of course, on another level I was prepared by my other "incarnations," which I knew nothing about yet; otherwise I would not have been led to such an experience and to such a powerful teacher. Vipassana is also called the "short road," or the "direct road to enlightenment." There is no question that it produces immediate results. But most people who are interested in Buddhist meditation do not choose Vipassana, because it is so difficult; most prefer the other techniques. I believe I was led to it by my karma with my québecquois friend R.

During the strenuous days following the retreat, I consciously experienced the separation between my physical body and my astral-feeling body. It was on the third day that I suddenly felt I was floating in the air. I was living then in my etheric body with no attachment to my physical body. The other meditators called this an out-of-body experience. Of course I could come back into my body just by focusing, but I was practicing the exercises, as Goenka instructed. Whatever happened, I observed it—weightlessness, suspension in nothingness—but without understanding it. Out of body? In body? These words did not really match what I was feeling. I felt these experiences, but they did not register in words. So, when someone spoke about their experiences and said, "I was out of my body," I would think to myself, *What are they talking about? Out of body? What does that mean?* It did not register in my mind that I was experiencing *that*.

Once the course ended, I observed other very disturbing effects of my experience. I felt like a stone. I could not write well anymore. My hand was not obeying my conscious will, because there had been a separation of my physical body and feeling body. My mind was way out in the universe and my body was here with no one in control. So I saw myself doing things I would not ordinarily do—nothing outrageous, but sometimes disconcerting. However, I was in the company of friends, so I was under protection; but they were worried about my state of mind and body and how I was going to go home in this condition.

At one point, I went into a coffee shop filled with men having breakfast. They looked at me and I heard one say, "Here comes the Virgin Mary." I was so embarrassed that I totally ignored them, but I wondered what it was that they saw within me, these regular, uneducated, Catholic men, full of repressed sexuality.

For long nights, imaginations assailed me, pictures coming one after the other. These were not dreams, but Christian visions, some having to do with the life of Christ, playing like a film. They were just there, like tableaux, dozens of them present within my mind, playing, vivid and clear. Now I cannot remember them, and I have lost my notes.

My relentless, intensive practices caused a break. I felt as though I was surrounded by beautiful beings, and all was peaceful. Music was incredibly beautiful, and I could feel it was coming from a heavenly world. The Earth was sublime. However, it was time to go home, so I went to the Montreal bus station, where someone was to pick me up to go back to Vermont. In that bus station, the incredible experiences were coming to me more and more, again as a result of the techniques that had opened up new dimensions. At one point, I went outside the station and spoke perfectly in the Creole language to a group of Haitians gathered there. They were stunned and so was I. I know that I have a gift for learning languages—but instantly? Inexplicably, their language just came out of my mouth and they understood me.

I went back inside, had some food, and observed how fast everything seemed to be moving. After the pace of the ten-day retreat, it was extremely painful to see the speed of life, and I tried to slow it down. Eventually it was too painful, so I went outside again and a young woman who noticed my bewilderment said to me, "Look at the dove," and I did. As I observed the dove by the sidewalk, peace came suddenly, a beautiful peace. That woman acted like a guardian angel I think. I went back to the waiting room and a feeling came upon me as I was sitting down on a plastic chair looking up at the day's date printed on a large board: my body became full of light. This was probably for only a split second, but it was like an eternal moment, something that cannot be described. I stayed in that ocean of light and felt blessed.

As I read the date printed above me, I felt: "This is the first day of my life." After that intense moment passed, I went to every single individual in that large waiting room and blessed everyone. I saw that my actions were absolutely, completely out of the ordinary to say the least, but I still did it. My rational mind was working, but something else was present, something beyond my rational intellect, something much more powerful. Whatever it was that went out through me was a blessing, and that is all I can say. As I was going around the room, I glanced at a young man whom I recognized from the course. He looked at me, said nothing, and went on his way. There were many women with children waiting for the bus that day, and they and the other individuals in that room showed no sign of surprise at my actions, as if bestowing blessings were absolutely normal. Still, to this day, it is a mystery to me.

When I went back to my seat I had more experiences. My face felt like it was transfigured. Later I pondered this for some time, but "transfigured" is the only word that fits this experience for me. It was in the middle of another powerful experience of feeling light and dark within me that my ride came.

The driver was very upset to see me in this state. He had no knowledge of meditation, let alone other states of consciousness. I stepped into the car and felt extreme discomfort. The car seemed full of beings, and not nice ones, and I was unable to accept them. Nevertheless, as I was taught, I proceeded to observe these experiences. But halfway into Vermont, I felt like I was dying. Autumn was approaching in full color, and I felt I was dying, too, so I asked my friend to take me to the emergency room because I was not going to live another moment. These, of course, were all experiences of the soul for which, again on one level, I was not prepared, hence the intense suffering and danger.

My friend did take me to the emergency room, where an Indian doctor was in attendance, to whom I explained that I had gone to a meditation retreat. As an Easterner, he understood what had happened. So I stayed in the hospital room, lying down for a bit. I could feel things happening and the presence of beings, and I said to them in thought: *Please leave my mind, my intellect, intact. Do not touch my mind, my intellect, my "I," my Self. It has taken me many years to come to this; please help and do not take them from me.* Whatever was happening at the spiritual level, I was aware of having to give up my brain, my mind, my thinking apparatus, my intellect, and was asking supernatural beings up there in the spirit world to please be careful.

Soon there was silence and total trust. My fear dissipated. The doctor prescribed some pills, which I took for a couple of days. I went back home where, little by little, I came back into my body until I felt normal again.

A few months after that episode, I traveled back to the East, to Iran, and resumed my teaching life, but something had happened to me at a very deep level, though I had no understanding of it whatsoever. Since I did not really understand it, I kept up my practice by meditating one hour in the morning and one hour in the evening, and I kept the experiences I had in the deep recesses of my mind. It is only now that I have allowed myself to return to them, but with more understanding thanks to twenty-three years of studying the work of Rudolf Steiner very intensively. His large body of writings and lectures are the only work that I know that explains those experiences in a direct, no-nonsense way. As I continue here with more stories of my Vipassana experiences, I will bring insights from Rudolf Steiner. I did, in fact, practice Vipassana for years afterward and took more ten-day courses—one in England when I was five-months pregnant; another in Igatpuri, India, with my three-year-old son; and another in Massachusetts a couple of years later. All these courses were accompanied by deep changes within my psyche.

Goenka had told us never to talk about our experiences. They were personal, and another person might get upset if they did not have the same experiences. They are all individual, he said, so there should be no attachment to them. You might think you are enlightened but that, too, will pass, and you might deny yourself more important experiences if you think you have arrived at the top. I believe this to be very wise, so I kept my inner experiences to myself and kept going. This, too, shall pass; *observe*.

But my other teacher, Rudolf Steiner (through his books), wrote that it is good to share our experiences nowadays. Of course, we have to live with them, digest them, and not speak about them casually. People learn only from others who have lived something, not from people who talk about what they do not know. Many people who talk about meditation have never actually meditated; they may write books and speak of Buddhism without having ever meditated—a tragic state of affairs. The ones who know usually do not talk.

The cause of suffering among intellectuals today is not because these don't really know. They know a little. But what they know is not their own knowledge, and that is why they suffer. A little or partial knowledge is always dangerous, like partial truths. A partial truth is not truth at all. So is the case with partial knowledge. The wise directly perceive truth. The sage who did not even know the alphabet of any language would always remove my doubt. Systematic study under a self-realized and competent teacher helps in purifying the ego, otherwise scriptural knowledge makes one egotistical. He who is called an intellectual man today only collects facts from various books and scriptures. Does he really know what he is doing? Feeding intellect with such knowledge is like eating a food with no value. One who constantly eats such a food remains sick and also makes others sick. We meet many teachers and they all teach well, but a student can assimilate only that which is unalloyed and comes directly from self-experienced teachers.[9]

I love the quote, "Feeding intellect with such knowledge is like eating a food with no value. One who constantly eats such a food remains sick and also makes others sick." One of the main reasons for sharing these experiences is to give *real food* to the hungry reader. After that experiential overload, I truly knew what was meant by meditation, and Buddhist meditation language took on new meaning for me because I had lived it.

---

9   Swami Rama, *Living with the Himalayan Masters*, p. 78.

Persevering on the Eastern Path

I took on my second Vipassana course when I was five months pregnant in the fall of 1980. I was living in Vermont, my adopted home when not traveling in the East. I wanted to do another ten-day retreat because, if you are a practitioner of the *Dhamma*, it is advised to do such a retreat once a year in addition to meditating every day for one hour in the morning and one in the evening. That is the way to preserve purity of thoughts, feelings, and actions. Since I am a devoted student, I tried to go by the rules. I flew to England, where there was a course given by a Burmese woman who was a student of Sayagyi U Ba Khin, as Goenka had been. Vipassana had a center in a beautiful brick house in the country, and there I went. I began the course with a small group of other students, but after a few days, I started bleeding and had some cramp-like contractions, so I went to the local clinic. Since I was pregnant, I was afraid of losing this child, whom I wanted very much and had foreseen in the Himalayas a year earlier. The doctors told me not to panic, just to relax and do nothing; so I stopped the meditation and stayed at the center and practiced a little bit here and there. After the course was over, a few of us went sightseeing to Bath and beautiful Celtic sites and mounts, and enjoyed some of England's old sacred places. Some meditants among us were priests, artists, and those who could see auras. I listened to their experiences, since nothing like that had happened to me. But my experiences held treasures of their own. Goenka was right, we all are different, and sharing our experiences can be bewildering, but when we meet others in their uniqueness, we learn other facets of life through them.

I flew back to the US and prepared for the birth of my son in the beautiful mountains of Vermont, Robert Frost country, among friends in a gorgeous, wood-heated mountain home I had rented for the winter. I skied downhill and cross-country until one day I fell in the middle of nowhere on cross-country skis and could not get up because my nine-month belly was in the way. I decided it was not safe to ski cross-country, but I continued downhill skiing. I read a lot of poetry, including the work of Blake, and seafaring books, including the books of Tristan Jones, the famous adventurer and sailor. I know my son wanted me to read such tales right up until his birth. Now twenty-nine, he is a sailor and professional fisherman, loves being at sea and loves music. I was glad that I had done my meditation work prior to the birth so that I could be in tune with the person the spiritual world was sending to me.

Goenka always mentioned that before one decides to have a child, one should meditate even more. The mother and father become a receptacle for a wondrous being who chooses them and the more they meditate, the more developed will be the being who will come to them. At least in that realm I had done the best I could.

As a mother, I kept up my practice and went back to teaching languages in high school full time. I practiced a bit of Vipassana in Barre, Massachusetts, during the summer. Mothers and their children were not allowed in the vicinity of the campus, so a group of us stayed a distance away from the center. We took care of the children and went for a session one hour here and there and enjoyed one another's company, not really knowing why this rule was enforced. Now, of course, I understand only too well why children should not be there at all. Let us say that children are extremely opened little beings, and everything we feel they feel. So one can imagine what a poor little soul would experience if we were all together facing our dark sides as we entered deeply into the meditation practice. It is no place for children.

My next session was in the winter of '83 to '84, when I returned to Iran so that my son could meet his father. In December, during my winter break from teaching at a small embassy school for kids whose parents were diplomats from Africa, Holland, and other places, I decided that I needed to participate in another course. My life at home with my husband was unbearable. All was a disaster, and I needed to focus and strengthen myself to face up to this failure and take care of my son, who was now two-and-a-half. So my son and I flew from Tehran—which by now was an Islamic state where I was obliged to wear the chador, or rather, the "classic manteau" over my clothing—to Bombay.

On that busy December morning in 1983, it was freeing to enter the busy life of India. I went straight on by train to Goenka's Vipassana headquarters in the small town of Igatpuri. There I asked permission to do a course. Goenka said that they would see if someone could take care of my son during the 10 days. Friends from my québecquois gang at R and his wife's house, Francis Boisvert and his brother Mathieu Boisvert, were there meditating. They took care of my son which, as Mathieu told me later, turned out to be a very difficult task. He said he had never done anything so difficult as taking care of a two-and-a-half-year-old boy. He said he'd rather do meditation than take care of a child. I must say my son was willful, more than a handful.

So I started the course, again full of wonder, very thankful that someone was taking care of my son for 10 days. I would sometimes look to see if I could catch a glimpse of him playing outside the compound, but I did not want to disturb him. I felt like I was abandoning my child, but I needed to have some time to myself after living in Iran under very difficult personal and political conditions.

I deepened my concentration, and felt more at ease with the practice. I remember one instance when I could communicate by mind reading and did not have to talk. It happened with a young German woman I wanted to speak with, and the words came silently. We spoke without speaking; it was awesome.

At one point in the middle of a session I looked at the sun and realized that there were beings in it. It was not just the sun, but a place for beings. That was a huge revelation for me. As usual, everything was very much alive, and becoming more and more so due to the intense concentration and meditation exercises. The group meditating there was large and I made friends from France, the US, Canada, Germany, Australia, and India of course, among others. After the retreat I went to say goodbye to Goenka, and he gave me a candle. As usual upon leaving the retreat, I was bewildered as I entered the etheric field and came back to my body, especially so with a small child full of energy. That was an extreme challenge, more so because we were in India. A couple of French people who were meditants accompanied me to the train station. My son still remembers how, when he was walking through the village with Mathieu, the small children would play and touch his blond-white hair and would not leave him alone. He hated that part of it.

I noticed that, as soon as I left the center, the two French meditants immediately started talking about drugs. I noted that it did not take long for these two to get right back into their bad habits, and I wondered if they were really practicing, as they were bombarded, in a way, by bad thoughts. Why spend all this time meditating (these guys were doing a one-month course) if they could not keep their bad thoughts at bay? What was going on? Were they meditating or just hanging out? I concentrated and told myself that I would not let myself be affected by these bad thoughts. I probably should have gone alone to the train.

Once in Bombay, I took my son on a boat trip to the sacred Buddhist caves just off the coast. When we arrived at the site and followed the other tourists, I was stunned to smell the aura of monks as they walked by. I had developed clairalience, or smell-clairvoyance. I could smell the sanctity of these holy monks, a refreshing, soothing smell like gentle flowers. Other tourists, such as an older ugly English couple, had a meat-eating stink to them that I could hardly stand. That, too, was a surprise to me, as smell had not affected me as much before. Because of my intense practice, however, I had gone into increasingly subtler levels of consciousness.

On the boat back into Bombay, I was the only foreigner among a group of Muslim pilgrim men from Pakistan. One of the younger men told me that I should wear the *hijab*, because my husband was a Muslim. I told him that he had to do the real *hijab* himself by controlling his sensual thoughts, and then there would be no need to wear a *hijab*. It was his responsibility, not mine. The young man thought about it, and then asked me, "Why don't you come with us into the mountains of Pakistan and become our Mother?" I was stunned, surprised, and told him that I was married. How could I leave? But he did not care. I was to go with them and be their mother. I was thirty-five and they were grown men. That was an intense experience, and I was extremely thankful for his unusual offer.

Back at the hotel in Bombay, I had more incredible experiences in different states of consciousness. I remember going deeper and deeper, becoming quieter and quieter, and then a big black raven came to the hotel windowsill. The window was open with no screens, and I watched his orange beady eyes as he sat there. I asked him, "What are you doing here? What message do you have?"

More imaginings came later that night, disturbing ones of whole cities burning and Iran going off on its own tangent in some other sphere. Fractions of the future. I could hear an incredible harmonious musical sound, sometimes called "music of the spheres." It was indescribable; the closest comparison I can make is that of monks singing in the Middle Ages. What was I seeing and hearing? Hell in the making? Paradise?

On the flight back to Tehran, cages of parrots were sitting in the first-class seats. Back at the family compound, I sat in the green garden and tried to get back into my body as quickly as possible. The green plant life helped me to reenter my physical body. The family took care of my son, as they saw that I was not really ready to do it myself. This lasted for a few days until I was again ready to teach the children, whose energies I experienced as wonderful and healing. The small embassy school where I taught was owned by the Vatican. It had a small Catholic church on the grounds, and I noticed that the priest there was having a terrible time. He was in the church by my classroom, and he looked gloomy, dark, and was obviously fighting his own dark side. I sent him warm thoughts and went on with my classroom duties, hoping my *metta* had acquired more substance.

Being in a totalitarian state was nearly unbearable after the Vipassana course, and I could see much ugliness, pain, and suffering in people. But thanks to skiing in the beautiful mountains north of Tehran with friends, I was able to finish the year. In June I flew back to southern France with my son to visit friends and family and to try to forget this sad episode of my life.

After France, I return to the United States and found a job as a high school language teacher in Connecticut, where I taught for three years. After one very busy year teaching Spanish full-time and taking care of my son, I felt that I needed to meditate again, so I enrolled in my next course. It was the summer of 1985. I went back to the center in Barre, Massachusetts, to take another ten-day class under Goenka's instruction. My husband and I were together again, as he had recently left Iran and emigrated to the US. He took care of our son and studied from morning till night to pass his medical exams.

They dropped me off in Barre, and I began what was to be my last course. This time I had my own little tent, and I was happy to have some time to myself after a year of full-time teaching, full-time mothering, full-time wage earning, and being a full-time wife. I was also excited because, again, I was about a month pregnant. I worked hard at the intense practice and of course went deeper and deeper into states of consciousness as before. I remember going into the kitchen and actually living with the minerals and all the grains used in the cooking: I *was* the oats, the silverware, the flowers, everything. I was very much alive, with nothing between me and nature—I was all. I was the words, and duality had flown out the window. I was really out of my body this time. No more me here, object there. I was the object, or the object was me, whichever way you wished to look at it.

I remember one exceptional moment in my little tent during the night when I saw a very cute skunk by the tent door and I did not dare move in case he sprayed the whole area of little tents. I suspended my breathing and politely said, "Please, go away where you belong." And he did, much to my relief.

I also remember seeing Goenka going by the tents and I felt a bit bewildered by what was happening to me. He had caused it all—in my mind. I had a talk with him about my experiences, and he told me to let go of them, that what I was experiencing were impurities of the mind. I felt that it was not enough for me to hear about impurities in my mind.

When the last day came, I had ventured so far out of my body that the administrators were worried about me and tried to help me. Of course, I still had no idea about anything; I was undergoing experiences with all the courage and strength I could muster, but I still could not understand anything that was happening. Nothing made sense.

And this is the reason for writing this narrative, telling it as I lived it. At that time I knew nothing about these unknown states of being that were brought on by intense exercises. It was before I began my deep studies in Anthroposophy, the work of Rudolf Steiner, and met my many teachers working through Anthroposophy with whom I had a chance to study.

I was lying down. An older French woman was sitting by my feet, trying to get me to focus on my feet, which might get me back into my body. My husband and son had come to pick me up, but I could not take my son's intense lively energy. I was out of my body, but did not really know it. I finally got into the car, and we went home, where more intense experiences awaited. I saw myself doing karate because I had studied it for several years, but now I could feel something different about the karate; life forces were flowing through me, or I was aware of the life forces. I remember thinking what our karate master had told us about mastering *qi* force. That is what it was all about. When this subsided, I tried to get back into my body by taking baths.

My husband, bewildered by what was happening to his wife, called the hospital without telling me. They took me to the local psychiatric center by ambulance, and I was given some very powerful drugs to take me out of what they considered "unusual" behavior. My behavior had not been outrageous; actually it was very peaceful. I remember the psychiatrist asking me some very stupid questions, but they had given me drugs so I could not answer them, as the drugs had affected my speech. That's medicine for you.

Moreover, I was pregnant. I spent a few days at the psychiatric center with other people, including drunks and drug addicts, while all the time wondering what was happening. I had only gone to meditate and I was now incarcerated against my will. However, I did not protest. I went along with it and began knitting baby clothes. Finally I came back into my body, but then had to figure out how to get out of the institution. The fear was gone; it had been another experience that taught me a lot. One of the men who was there for drinking problems wondered what I was doing there. I said "spiritual work," and he answered, "Of course, I understand. That can be dangerous."

I was very upset and called the retreat center. I wanted to speak to Goenka to explain all of this. I told the person who answered that I had done meditation work, followed the advice, schedule, and agenda of the program and this is where I ended up. What had I done wrong? I was an excellent student, wasn't I? He said that it was not recommended that I practice Vipassana meditation; it was not for me. My inner response was, "Well, thank you very much. I wish you could have told me this before I became fully trusting, with admiration and wonder and excitement for the teachings. Now I am in a psychiatric hospital, not knowing what I did wrong."

But there was nothing wrong, although no one said that to me at the psychiatric center, where they had no understanding of spiritual work. This rampant ignorance is true of the medical field in general.

> But there is another way of relating to the world, incomprehensible though it must remain for those who cling to the "reality" we have just described. It comes to certain people at some moment in their lives, overturning their whole way of looking at the world. What they call "real" are the images that surface from the spiritual life of the psyche, and they ascribe a lesser degree of actuality to the sense impressions of hearing, touching, and seeing. They are aware that their assertions cannot be proved. All they can do is to tell of their new experiences, knowing that they are then in the position of someone with eyesight addressing the blind. If they nevertheless try to communicate their inner experiences, it is in the conviction that others may be around them who, though their spiritual eyes are yet unopened, may be able to understand through the very power of what they have to convey. For they have faith in humanity and wish to open the eyes of others. They can offer only the fruits gathered by their own spirit. As to whether the visions of the spiritual eye are understood by others, that depends on the degree of their understanding.[10]

I finally managed to explain to the psychiatrist that I wanted to go home, and she had the nerve to tell me, "How did you know you could leave?" So they sent me home. I guess they would not make any more money from me.

That was the last time I went to a Vipassana course. My Western body was not meant to undergo such a regimen of intensive Eastern meditation techniques. It was not made for Eastern practices, but I did not know it. Thank goodness, the *Dhamma*, the *Sangha*, and *Buddha* were there protecting me, along with all the sacred Buddhist *pali* writings that had been chanted all day long.

What I lacked was just a little, a tiny bit, of explanation about the effects of these powerful exercises. I am being sarcastic, but it seems no one really asked these questions. Was I the only one with an inquisitive mind, a mind

---

10   Steiner, *Christianity as Mystical Fact*, p. 3.

that wants to know what it is doing and practicing, instead of blindly accepting everything?

I took the medicines prescribed for me and, because of my intense practice, I could feel them working into my body. I felt the lithium go into the spinal cord and apply some weight there so that there was no movement, a weight that remained sitting on the spinal cord, kind of preventing me from going into the etheric realm and helping me stay in the physical body. Lithium is close to lead, and lead is a protection for forces coming from the outside. That is what I experienced in my body, and to me it was a gift to be able to perceive the effect of substances at that level. My body had become transparent to me.

It is ironic that I had worked so hard to develop my concentration through meditation, and now I was given something to suppress the result of those intensive practices. I experienced all of this because no one, including me, had any knowledge of what was happening.

I was pregnant and decided I had to abort the five-week-old fetus because the child would not be right after I had taken such heavy doses of the drugs for several weeks, and I would not forgive myself if I had injured the tiny being. I went to the clinic in tears and had the abortion. This was definitely my lowest point, the bottom. The curly headed little girl I had seen while hiking in the Himalayas dissolved into nothingness and I was heartbroken. I had trusted those exercises and now I did not understand why it was all happening. Why, if I fully trusted someone with my life, was this happening to me? I was not looking for Nirvana, but just wanted to know what Buddhism was really about, the real thing. I did receive knowledge, but at an immense cost—the life of my child. I was angry about it for many years, but that, too, eventually dissolved.

I started teaching again in the fall, and the high school students, as usual, helped me through this very challenging time. Time healed everything, and I grew to be thankful for that experience in the hospital. I had learned a lot through my pain, and I abandoned the practice of Vipassana, also with much pain, and focused instead on raising my son, spending time in nature hiking, swimming, wind surfing, traveling in South America, skiing, and getting back into my body. During the Christmas season of 1985, I became pregnant again, and my daughter was born in October 1986, on my birthday. After a full day of teaching and a meeting that lasted until 10:00 p.m., I went to the hospital at 5:00 a.m., and she was born—a wonderful gift. Today, she still resents the fact that, as she put it, she came into the world so late. "I should have been born earlier" lies behind her words. "I should have been born a *lot* earlier Mom," means a great deal to me.

Life had returned to some kind of order, and in the spring of 1987, we all moved to our new home in New Hampshire, where I taught in a Waldorf high school. There I met the work of the seer, scientist, and teacher Rudolf Steiner. Thanks to his large body of work, I finally understood what had happened to me. But this happened only after having studied much of his work, which comprises more than 350 books and lectures. It has taken me more than twenty-three years of intensive study and meditative work. Not exactly the fast-track to knowledge, but the opposite. I followed the fast track first and then the slow track.

In the beautiful granite mountains and lakes of New Hampshire, I was now spending my time raising my children. I quit teaching and studied Anthroposophy full-time, and I have never stopped. One door had been closed to me, slammed in my face in a grandiose fashion; "This kind of meditation is not for you." But, there is another kind of spiritual work, meditative work that is right for me. As the sayings go, destiny has its ways of meeting a person; another door always opens when one closes; the pain that comes from one path, leads to another. I am thankful for all these experiences, even the painful ones. And Goenka was right, I do have impurities in my mind like everyone else. But there are different ways of meeting and dealing with these impurities.

WEST: DISCOVERING RUDOLF STEINER

N ow that I have related some of my experiences, I will refer to them again with additional insights gained by my studies in Anthroposophy. I will explain what happened to me during those years of meditation and will describe my recent journey to India. Telling about a life means weaving several stories into one. It is an arduous and exciting task, as well as a daunting one. Nevertheless, I must attempt to do it despite all my weaknesses. Fortunately, help always comes when there are difficult tasks.

Growing up in Northern Africa, my family lived first in Rabat, Morocco, and then in the shadow of St. Augustine in Bône, or Annaba. Annaba is a city on the coast of Algeria, where one of the most famous Christian churchmen lived centuries ago. I remember as a nine-year-old being fascinated by the name *Augustine*. It was not very French. We used to go to church there, to catechism, and I did not much enjoy it, but I did enjoy the church atmosphere, with its incense, rituals, and strange phrases like *"le fruit de vos entrailles"* (the fruit of your womb). Those words fascinated me, even though I could not understand them, but I would live into them, trying to fathom their mysterious meaning. Yes, it was another world to which I belonged, in the Arab world, in which I was perfectly comfortable.

Because this city was so famous and important in church history for the Vatican, they used to send their important delegates and high officials to us—in this far-flung corner of the planet—whenever there were confirmation rites or the *communion solennelle* rite, for which I and the other girls dressed as brides. To me that experience was absolutely real. I was a bride, and the ceremony was extremely serious. For my Communion, the bishop, who would become the next pope, officiated during the ceremony, as my mother tells it. In this big cathedral, with great Christian fanfare, I became, as many of us did, the bride of Christ. I was very much affected by it.

When I returned to France at the age of twenty-three to study at the Sorbonne, I visited as many churches in Paris and France as I could. I spent many hours lying on the steps in the middle of Notre Dame and listening to concerts. For some reason, I loved the Basilique Saint-Denis, one of the oldest churches in northern Paris and very important historically. I also loved Notre Dame. I simply loved to sit in the cathedral atmosphere. I quit the boring Sorbonne after Christmas, and walked in regularly on the nude sittings at the "Beaux-Arts" to practice drawing. I partied with the snobbish *artistes-intellectuelles* scene, posing for famous painters and plainly having fun.

During my year in Paris, I had become an atheist, an atheist who was visiting lots of churches in her spare time. I had missed these beautiful old cathedrals when I lived in Boston, so now I bathed myself in them for the entire year. I did not attend services during this time, but liked the peaceful atmosphere of the churches themselves.

Life is full of wonder. From my love of cathedrals I plunged into the world of the East, the Arab world, and left the Western Christian world. I did not understand the Christian world at all, not through my Catholic upbringing, not through going to church, not through the rituals, not through sitting in cathedrals. So I went to the East. I was born into the "intellectual-consciousness soul," as Rudolf Steiner termed it, but through the East I understood my own Christian background, which is what this story is about. My task in this lifetime has always been to make a bridge between the East and the West, including the Arab world into which my karma has thrown me. I did this by living it; by the time I was thirty, I had spent a third of my life in the Arab world, a third in Europe, and a third in the Americas.

I spent many years studying philosophy in college and graduate school, delving into the work of Pierre Teilhard de Chardin, Henri Bergson, Jean-Paul Sartre, Simone de Beauvoir, Claude Lévi-Strauss, Bertrand Russell, Paul Claudel, and many other great writers through centuries of Spanish, French, South and North American, English, Russian, and Soviet literature. I had a facility for reading difficult philosophical works.

During the many years of studying Steiner's works on my own and sometimes in groups, I attended many conferences led by talented anthroposophists in various places, including New York State and Maine. At one of those gatherings, I had familiar experiences that I recognized from my Vipassana retreats. It happened in 1993 during a talk in Chestnut Ridge, New York, by Georg Kühlewind. Listening to this very talented older man, I felt that he was an eagle flying high above us. My imagination was correct. I still remember the content of his heartfelt and powerful talk. It was about the meaning of *creativity* and the word itself. The audience was full of poets, artists (I had taken up watercolor painting for the first time since college), sculptors, housewives, and writers, and we were all mesmerized by this short, powerful man. He said something like this: All the work that we do as artists—the poems we write, the paintings we paint—all our creative work that no one ever sees is what is most important. This is not the work that is praised by our materialistic society, which honors making lots of money, investing funds, selling things, and making useless items cheaply. What counts is our creation, what comes out of nothing, and what has no meaning to society. He said that society really does not care if we write a poem, sing a song, write a song, or finish a beautiful wooden sculpture. Society does not really need those things and considers them "extras." But the future of humankind badly needs our "rejected" creative works. It will be thanks to them that we have a future. After we listened to his words (more or less these words), the whole room felt lighter and the atmosphere changed from gloomy (because the world didn't care about our creation) to enthusiastic. We were all ready to go back to our studios to work. He had spoken directly to our hearts.

Here is what Steiner said from another perspective, which adds even more power to Kühlewind's words:

> Everything that human beings create today in terms of technical apparatus and machines will come to life in the future and oppose them in a terrible and hostile way. All that is created out of a purely utilitarian principle, through individual or collective egoism, is the enemy of future humanity. Today, we ask much too much about the *utility* of what we do. If we really want to foster evolution, then we must not ask about utility, but rather we must inquire about whether something is beautiful and noble. Everything that people do today to satisfy their artistic needs, out

of pure love of beauty, this, too, will come to life in the future, but it will contribute to the higher development of the human being. But today it is terrible to see how many thousands of people are kept from knowing any activity other than those done for the sake of material utility; they are cut off from all that is beautiful and artistic in their lives. The most wonderful works of art should hang in the poorest elementary schools; it would bring boundless blessings to human evolution. Human beings are building their own future. We can get an idea of what it will be like on Jupiter [the far-future evolution of Earth] if we clearly understand that today there is nothing absolutely good and nothing absolutely evil. Today, good and evil are mixed in every human being. Good people must always say that they have only a little bit more good than evil within, but that they are not wholly good. On Jupiter, however, good and evil will no longer be mixed; rather human beings will divide themselves into the entirely good and the entirely evil. And all that we cultivate today in terms of the good and the beautiful serves to strengthen the good on Jupiter, and all that happens only from the perspective of egoism and utility strengthens the evil.

So that human beings in the future are a match for the evil powers, they must gain mastery of the most inner power of their "I."[11]

Georg Kühlewind was an eagle able to teach people how to reach the heights, but without the dangers of Vipassana. His work is deeply Christian, and he meditated for years on St. John's Gospel. He was from Budapest, and his background was one-hundred-percent Jewish. He had survived the Holocaust, so had gone beyond pain, race, blood ties, ritual, language, and religion. He was a free man. To me, he was another master crossing my path, and for years I attended a working group that gathered around Kühlewind each year for a few days in various places. It was a great gift to me to once again meditate. I had missed the meditative group life of the *sangha*. But here, once a year, I joined a group of people with whom I had much in common. We meditated together under the advice of this great teacher and human being. Georg Kühlewind had studied the work of Rudolf Steiner backward and forward, and we benefited from his incredible mind, his knowledge, and especially his

---

11   Steiner, *Esoteric Lessons, 1904–1909*, p. 247 (trans. revised).

practice. He developed his own exercises, which he gave to us with patience and love. He passed away in 2006, but we still meet once a year and meditate together in the same spirit. Many of us feel his presence, once in a while, like a breath of fresh air, a gentle cool wind.

The following is a passage that I love, written by Michael Lipson, a talented meditation teacher in his own right and master student of Kühlewind. He beautifully describes who this teacher was:

> "Beware when the great God lets loose a thinker on this planet," wrote Emerson. He might almost have been speaking of Georg Kühlewind (1924–2006), the Hungarian chemist, linguist, philosopher, and mystic who shocked heavenward all those fortunate enough to meet him.
>
> There was always something a bit dangerous about Georg's presence. It was not ill will: no one could be more compassionate. It was not a dark mood: no one could have a lighter wit, even in the face of horror. It was nothing unbalanced: no one could draw on healthier psychic roots. Yet there was a sense of things on the move, of discoveries that might take you who knows where, of having to put down your baggage and for once run free. Freedom: that was the danger in Georg's presence, threatening to everything in us that wants stasis and self-protection.[12]

So after years spent practicing Vipassana and having been left out, I finally had found a path on which I could undergo spiritual development that would not injure me. Between the many books written by Steiner, which I studied dutifully every day, and my Kühlewind-style meditation, as well as the help and insights of other talented teachers, I was well taken care of by the "upstairs," as I call it—*upstairs* meaning the good spirits who are ever ready to give a helping hand when we need it.

And I learned that we are never given more than we can handle, even though at times life's challenges seem impossible to face. That is the time when things happen.

---

12   From the introduction to Kühlewind, *Wilt Thou Be Made Whole?*, p. 7.

↓

Understanding My Buddhist Practices

The insights that follow include passages that are difficult to read and understand, and they should be read several times. You can skip some and revisit them later; it is easy to grasp.

The following passages explain what I went through in my Buddhist meditative practice and are like a balm to me. They have allowed me to understand what was happening to my soul, my spirit, and my body at that time. Without that understanding, I would not be where I am now. I owe everything to it, and I am forever thankful to the great seer and larger-than-life human being, Rudolf Steiner. I also do not forget that, without Goenka's gentle directions, nothing would have happened. So I have become thankful over the last thirty years for all the suffering I went through. It was, after all, my chosen karma.

> The flames are nearing—nearing with my thinking
> from distant cosmic soul-shores of my being.
> A heated battle nears—and my own thinking
> must battle with the thoughts of Lucifer;
> within another soul my thinking fights.
> Hot light is wafted—out of fierce dark coldness—
> It flashes lightnings, this hot light of soul—
> the light of soul—in cosmic fields of ice.

The memory of the experience that can be expressed in such words.... What, however, the soul has to feel to have such a memory of the cosmic midnight must also lie in one's earthly life, for here the human soul goes through events that bring to it the moods of inner anguish, inner resolve, inner dread.... Indeed, one has to have felt that the individual self tears itself away from what one generally calls the inner life; that the power of thinking, with which one feels so confidently connected in life, tears itself out of the inner being and seems to go off toward the far, far limits of one's field of vision; and one must have found alive in oneself as soul presence what is expressed in such words—though, naturally, these will seem complete nonsense, overflowing with contradictions, to the sort of comprehension limited to the outer senses and bound to the brain. One must first have experienced the feeling of one's own self moving away, of one's thinking moving away, if one is to live through the memory of the cosmic midnight again in complete calm.[13]

These words particularly express what I felt after my first ten-day course as I lay in the small clinic in Vermont thinking that I was dying, truly dying. It was an actual fact. My driver got off the main road and took me to the emergency room. The tearing away of my thinking, my thinking leaving me, other beings whom I thought were taking my thinking away, caused such incredible anguish, fear, death. I thought, "I can't have my thinking; it does not belong to me. How could it be, no brain, my ego, me?" I had entered the spiritual world, meaning that there were spirits there, and thinking is left behind when one enters that world. The brain no longer functions there, and when one realizes that, it is more than overwhelming. We are there but then we are not, and others are there as well.

> The memory of real sensory existence between birth and death stays firmly present in the soul between death and rebirth. But if we penetrate to the true "I" after having become clairvoyant, we come to realize that a decision, a spiritual act is necessary. It can be said of it that this must be a strong, determined decision of the will, to root out, to forget the memory of what we have been, in all its detail.... But one stands, in the fullest sense of the word, at the abyss of existence when making the decision in true freedom and energy of will, to blot out and forget the self.
>
> All these things are completely true of all human beings; nevertheless, people are unaware of them. Every night we are required to blot ourselves out without being conscious of it. But it is an entirely different matter to give over, in full consciousness, to destruction and to forget one's remembering "I"—to stand in the spiritual world as a nothing on the edge of the abyss of nothingness. This is the most shattering experience a person can have; we must approach it with great confidence that

---

13 Steiner, *Secrets of the Threshold*, pp. 6–7 (trans. revised).

the true "I" will be brought to us out of the cosmos. And this is indeed the case.[14]

This is a feeling of approaching death as one must give way to this experience. Then somehow, we go through with the fearful give-away, and we are still there.

It is not just people who think only about the world and the everyday affairs of life who would have to admit that they are nothing. Scientists and philosophers would have to admit the same. After all, philosophy, too, considers and judges the world only according to the characteristics of the human soul. But such a way of judging cannot merge with the suprasensory outer world. It will be rejected by it. This is why all that one was previously is rejected. To enter the suprasensory world, you must look back at your whole soul, your "I," as something to be cast aside.

Until you enter the suprasensory world, however, you cannot avoid taking this "I" to be your true nature. Your soul *must* see the true human essence in this "I." You say to yourself, "Through this 'I' of mine, I must make ideas about the world. If I lose this 'I,' I shall lose myself as a being." Your soul's strongest desire is always to guard the "I," for it does not wish to lose the ground from under its feet. But as soon as you enter the suprasensory outer world, your soul will no longer feel what it feels in ordinary life. Your soul must step across a threshold, leaving behind not just this or that treasured possession but its very own being. It must be able to say that it now sees that what it once valued as its most powerful truth may—on the other side of the threshold of the suprasensory world—appear as the greatest error. . . .

Until we ourselves approach the threshold, however, we are protected from those experiences. Even though we may hear accounts of them from those who have approached or stepped over the threshold, we remain protected. In fact, such accounts can serve us well when we do approach the threshold. In this case, as in many others, it is better to undertake something when you already have an idea of what awaits you than to approach it without that knowledge. But what a traveler in the suprasensory world may gain in self-knowledge remains unchanged by such prior knowledge. Therefore, the assertion by clairvoyants, or

---

14 Ibid., pp. 120–121 (trans. revised).

those intimate with clairvoyance, that we should not speak of such things to those who have not resolved to enter the suprasensory world is not true. We now live in a time when we must become increasingly familiar with the nature of the suprasensory world if our soul lives are to be adequate to meet life's demands. The spreading of suprasensory insights, along with knowledge of the Guardian of the Threshold, is one of the tasks humanity must undertake now and in the future.[15]

As a rule, we cannot enter the spiritual worlds without passing through a deep upheaval in our souls. We have to experience something that disturbs and shakes all our forces, flooding our soul with intense feelings and sensations. Emotions that are generally spread out over many moments, over long periods of living, whose permanent effect on the soul is therefore weaker—such feelings are concentrated in a single moment and storm through us with tremendous force when we enter the esoteric worlds. Then we experience a kind of inner shattering, which can indeed be compared to fear, terror, and anxiety, as though we were shrinking back from something in horror. Such experiences belong to the initial stages of esoteric development, to entering the spiritual worlds. Just for this reason, great care must be taken to give the right advice to those who would enter the spiritual worlds through esoteric training. We must be prepared so that we may experience this upheaval as a necessary event in our soul life without its encroaching on our bodily life and health, and insofar as the body is included, it must suffer a like upheaval. That is the essential thing. We must learn to suffer the convulsions of our soul with outward equanimity and calm.

This is true not only for our bodily processes. The soul forces we need for everyday living, our ordinary intellectual powers, even those of imagination, of feeling and will—these, too, must not be allowed to become unbalanced. The upheaval that may be the starting point for esoteric life must take place in far deeper layers of the soul, so that we go through our external life as before, without anything being noticed in us outwardly, while within we may be living through whole worlds of shattering soul experience. That is what it means to be ripe for esoteric development: to be able to experience such inward convulsions

---

15   Steiner, *A Way of Self-Knowledge,* pp. 29–30, 31–32.

without losing one's outer balance and calm. To this end, those striving to become ripe for esoteric development must widen the circle of their interests beyond everyday life. They must get away from the things that otherwise keep us going from morning to night and reach out to interests that move on the great horizon of the world.[16]

As the reader has noticed, I was thoroughly unprepared for all these upheavals, and they went right into my physical body, disturbing my everyday life for at least three weeks after the first retreat I attended, because prior to the retreat no one explained anything about the work and what it was we were really doing. Perhaps no one really knew. We were to eradicate suffering, follow the footsteps of the great Buddha, and attain enlightenment. Did I ever think seriously about what I was doing?

Of course not. I was interested in Buddhism, and wanted to study with a master. That was all. There was no thinking about what it meant to study with a master. What is a master anyway? A master of what? What is he teaching as a master? Of course I had read of truth, love, wisdom, and so on, and the end result was to attain wisdom, become wise, and follow the rules. That was as far as I looked: wisdom would be there. Never did I realize until I went through the results of the practice that reaching wisdom was nothing like I had envisioned—becoming old and wise. Rather, it meant intense suffering. To escape suffering, I had to undergo suffering, or bring more suffering to myself.

Thinking of suffering reminds me of an experience I had when I was sixteen or seventeen, just after my family emigrated from France to Boston. I was distinctly aware that I received some kind of instructions or knowledge when I was sleeping. It dawned on me that I was not just sleeping, but that nighttime is as important as daytime. How, I did not know. The thought that came to my mind was: *How can I be happy when there is such misery everywhere? How can I ever reach happiness while others are miserable?* That was a huge question for me, and with that question came the realization that I might as well not even try to be happy, because there is so much unhappiness that I can't do anything about. I cannot be happy if someone near me is miserable.

---

16 Steiner, *The Bhagavad Gita and the West*, pp. 112–113.

Then it went further. I made vows that I could stand suffering myself. I was strong enough to take the suffering, but under no circumstances could I cause any kind of suffering in others. So I made a commitment at that age never willingly to cause someone else suffering. I could not bear the thought of that. Again, I was quite young.

The bodhisattva vow is that, after one receives enlightenment, one must return and help others. Not until all have received enlightenment do you allow yourself to be totally free. In other words, not until everyone is happy can you be happy.

Just prior to the retreat I attended in Igatpuri, India, I had a talk with a young European woman, who said categorically to me, "I am meditating, and I am staying here until I am enlightened." I was stunned by that statement. How can one be so stupid as to say that? I had done numerous retreats, and it never occurred to me that I was practicing Vipassana to be enlightened. Don't ask why I was practicing; in this I was the stupid one. I needed some space, peace, and so forth, but I certainly had no intention of becoming enlightened; that was too presumptuous. As for the others who wanted to attain nirvana and never come back to Earth, I thought they were simply mad. Nirvana? Where is that? That was my frame of mind. I was practical and idealistic, but not a dreamer. The harsh realities of having lived in Northern Africa and then moving back to France and being treated as a non-French person woke me quickly, even at twelve years old, from my dreamy temperament. Welcome to racism and darkness; gone were the sunny beaches of North Africa.

I had a love for the Earth and all its diverse human beings, animals, plants, mountains, everything. The last thing I wanted to do was go to Nirvana, some place, somewhere, floating in the clouds. I was far too practical to float in the clouds. So there was always a deep gulf between me and the other people attracted to meditation. They wanted out; I loved being here. That is why the break into the spiritual world was so intense for me—I did not really want to go there. But I did. And for what?

When I was sitting in that little hotel room in Bombay after the retreat and the big black raven came to sit on the windowsill and calmed me down, I thought that he was a messenger from "upstairs." The raven is a wonderful animal, which Steiner mentions in his lectures as sacred. It was important to me to see a huge black raven as I was going through these difficult, soul upheavals with my two-and-a-half-year-old son. It sort of woke me up or gave me inner strength.

> The mystery schools were not institutions like churches or schools in an external sense; rather, they were educational as well as cultic centers where people learned wisdom, devotion, and faith that was both a gnosis of facts and deep insight into reality....
>
> The greatest moments in the evolution of humanity may be compared to the experiences of people who are born blind, but are given sight through an operation—an entirely new world opens up for them. The eyes of the spirit are opened for initiates. In light and color, a world of spirit reveals itself—an entirely new and much larger world than the physical, a world full of beings and inhabitants....
>
> There were seven...steps of initiation. The "raven," which mediated between the world of spirit and the external world was on the first step. In the Bible, we hear of the raven that came to Elijah. Legends speak of the raven of Wotan.... We find the esotericists on the second step, such a person was admitted to the inner sanctuary. The third step was that of the "fighter." Those who achieved this stage were allowed to intervene in the external world on behalf of spiritual truth.
>
> Initiates who achieved the fourth step were called "lions." Their consciousness had expanded beyond their own individuality to the consciousness of their entire tribe.[17]

Then we have the Persian, the Sun hero, and the Father on/at the seventh step of initiation.

> In the ancient mysteries, people were made into wise human beings and truly cultured. They became those who could take the spiritual realm seriously. They had to go through seven stages, with only very few reaching the highest stage. Those seven stages had names that we must come to understand if we are to know what those who reached them had to do.
>
> If we translate what a person had to do when first admitted to the mysteries, we come to the word *raven*. Those of the first stage thus

---

17 Steiner, *The Christian Mystery*, pp. 26, 29.

were the Ravens. Admitted to the mysteries you became a Raven. What did Ravens have to do? Primarily, they had to maintain communications between the outside world and the mysteries. They did not have newspapers then. The first newspapers came only thousands of years later when printing was invented. The people who taught in the mysteries had to gain information by sending out trusted individuals who would observe the world. The Ravens may be said to have been confidential agents of the people who served the mysteries. And this was something you had to learn first, to be someone who could be trusted.... Those employed as Ravens in the mysteries were accepted as confidential agents only after being tried and tested. Above all, they had to learn to take the things they saw seriously and report on them truthfully. To begin with, however, it was also necessary to learn what truth means in human beings. I am sure people were no less deceitful in antiquity than they are today. Today, lying and deceit come into everything, whereas in those days one first had to learn to be a true human being. This was what you had to become during the years of being a Raven: a confidential agent of the mysteries.[18]

---

18   Steiner, *Beetroot to Buddhism ... Answers to Questions*, pp. 40–41 (trans. revised).

DRAWING UPON MOTHER INDIA

In 2009, thirty years after my first experience with meditation, I decided it was time to write about it. I chose to return to India and settle in Benares to write for a couple of months. It felt like the right place, and I have loved Mother India ever since I traveled there for the first time in 1977, and twice after that, in 1979 and in 1983 to 1984.

Thus, I began my fourth visit to India, flying direct from Chicago to Delhi in the fall, with the specific intention of writing about my meditation experiences. I arrived late at night and took a taxi to a hotel in Old Delhi that I had found on the Internet. I almost never used the Internet, but this time I had not looked for a place to stay in the usual way, which I had done by reading backpackers' manuals and their comments, as they are always truthful and to the point.

Even late at night the city was full of noise and traffic. The taxi left me in a depressed area of the broken-down old city. I had clearly forgotten what India was like, and I could not get my bearings. The hotel workers were all men, of course, with no women in sight; there were only very young men sleeping on couches and in empty rooms. I seemed to be the only woman around, certainly the only Western woman. The room was worse than awful, even for me, with dirty sheets, no real locks on the door, and we won't even talk about the bathroom. So I said to myself, *Hey, you are no longer twenty-five. Perhaps you should be a bit more careful in the future.* I was carrying, as always, enough cash to last the whole trip. Where I go, there are no banks.

I hardly slept; the whole area was full of noise. Women were screaming, men yelling in the street, dogs barking. I meditated on dissolving my fears and embracing faith. *You will be fine,* I said to myself. *This is India, and this is the way people live here. You have forgotten. It has been a long time since your last visit.* Although my meditation worked, at 5:00 a.m. I bolted out of the place

Delhi, India

and asked for a taxi to the airport so I could catch my plane to Benares. I got out of there. Fast.

I arrived safely at the airport in Benares and took a taxi into the biggest, messiest city I have ever encountered. With my backpack, a suitcase full of books, and my small laptop, I walked through the narrow streets of old Benares until I found my hotel. After a few days of sightseeing, I was so taken by India and its problems, and once again trying to straighten out my personal life, that I did not feel like writing a single word. So, I just enjoyed Mother India for *who she is*, tumultuous atmosphere and all, and postponed my writing for later. One can have all sorts of plans, but if the time is not right, then one must go on with the flow and change. I had waited thirty years to write about my spiritual journey; I could wait another few with no problem.

India's population is rapidly approaching that of China, which is more than one billion and one hundred million people. The stress on the country is visible everywhere. During this visit, I was appalled by the intensity of its problems—the fumes, the lack of water, the multitude of people in rags, the overcrowded trains that are prone to crashes, bombings, and sickness. I pictured potential uncontrolled diseases and famine that could affect the country because of this sad state of affairs. One can do nothing to remedy these problems, which are so overwhelming that nature will surely take its course.

Nevertheless, I love this surprising place. Along with my inward journey, I will share some stories and insights from my visit there. I went to various sacred sites that I had not seen on my previous trips: Deer Park in Varanasi (Benares), the center of Hinduism; Bodh Gaya, the center of Buddhism; Rishikesh, which I call the meditation capital of India; and Sikkim, a little kingdom in the Himalayas.

As mentioned before, I had stopped Vipassana meditation around 1985, and this time in Bodh Gaya I went to sit in the many Buddhist temples that have been built there. I especially enjoyed the Japanese temple, which had a meditation sitting at five o'clock every evening. A few of us sat there with a young, austere monk in attendance. We all enjoyed the serene atmosphere and the master's gentle touch on our shoulders with his stick if we were not attentive. It was as if I had never left. I could sit for an hour and time flew by. No pain this time.

I found deep delight in sitting at the Bodhi Tree, where hundreds of people come to sit from all over the Eastern world, because this is the place Shakyamuni sat and became the Buddha. It was wonderful to see Buddhists from Vietnam, Korea, China, Cambodia, Thailand, Japan, India, Tibet, Sikkim, Nepal, Burma, and other places, all of whom had come to celebrate the enlightenment of the Buddha Shakyamuni.

People from the Eastern world can fly directly from Bankok to Bodh Gaya. The reverence of those people added another dimension to this holy site, which is very much alive. The center of the world for the Buddhists, it is said that all the buddhas have awakened here and that all future buddhas will awaken here.

The place was full of monks in deep-red and gold robes. The child monks were having fun poking and pulling each other, being children, while their elders recited the *sutras*. The beautiful prayer printed on the cloths blew in the wind and, as the wind breathed through the prayers, the words were sent into the world. I sat for a few hours next to a housewife from Japan, who was effortlessly reciting the *sutras* aloud to the world, messages of peace and love. I sat quietly, taking in this sacred atmosphere that is still alive after 2,500 years.

I also traveled and hiked in Sikkim, the land of many Buddhist monasteries perched atop mountains. In one of the monasteries, called Pemiyatse, I met the abbot and invited him for tea at a deluxe hotel next door, and he graciously accepted, along with two others. He was very concerned about peace in the world and said he often travels to Bodh Gaya with the children and the monks for celebrations. He also had the responsibility of teaching quite a few youngsters at another place, and he requested I stay and teach there for a few months, but I had made other plans. After an enjoyable couple of hours we were ready to depart, and he put his forehead against mine, grasped my hand and said goodbye. I will never forget that affectionate farewell and the infinite love there was in those few moments shared by two human beings from different worlds.

Back in Bodh Gaya, I took a trip to the cave where Buddha sat for many years in ascetic practice. Going to the village was an experience in itself, as it is as poor a village as can be—no running water, no toilets, no wells, no sewers, children in rags or naked and playing in dirty mounds of garbage, women in

The Mahabodhi Temple, Bodh Gaya, the site where Gautam Buddha attained enlightenment

The Vishal Buddha in Bodh Gaya

rags, sick babies carried by sick children—real poverty. There were only a few gardens on the outskirts, owned by the wealthier. And amid all this, twenty kilometers down the road, hundreds of new Buddhist monasteries were being built by groups from different countries in the Eastern world, literally millions of dollars worth. The people who lived within a few kilometers of the sacred city had nothing. It seems that the message of Shakyamuni to help neighbors has not gotten through. While thousands of monks and individuals spend time sitting, these local villagers are dying each day.

I was deeply affected by all the misery and by my own powerlessness to help, but I was also very lucky to meet an extraordinary human being as I was on my way back to Delhi. This man was sleeping under my berth on the train. He looked Indian but was Scottish and educated at Eaton. He had used all his wealth to build clinics, schools, and training centers around Bodh Gaya. A very tall emaciated man, he must have weighed no more than 130 pounds. We chatted, and he showed me his projects on his laptop computer, hundreds of pictures of what he was doing. He said that he was not a religious man at all, but just wanted to do something for others, and he loved the challenges. Life is so full of mysteries. One person prays all day for years and does not seem to do anything at all, while another never prays and does not particularly believe in anything but devotes all his waking hours to countless projects that help men and women survive. I received an email from him in January 2010 from Bodh Gaya. He wrote that it is extremely cold there this year and that children go to school with no shoes and no clothes (in that village they are lucky to have a school, as schools are not generally functional in India in the smaller localities). Two women had just died in childbirth, and he and a team of local Indian helpers he had hired had to teach the two widowed men how to take care of their infants.

I felt bad when I reflected upon myself, living in luxury compared to where he is, writing a book on my experiences in meditation—that is, I thought, sitting and doing nothing. But in truth, meditating is far from nothing, even though it looks like it is; that much I know. But still one wishes one could do more. I sent him a check to sponsor a clinic, which is something I can do and am glad to do. But meeting him was a message: everyone has their little part. Although I cannot do more at this time, someone else is now ready to pour all his enthusiasm (being with God), his love, energy and funds into helping others, especially the women and children. I felt it was a gift to have met this very reserved, unassuming human being. And of course it was not by chance. There are 7,000 trains daily in India, and I had chosen just that particular one, that seat. Life again is full of wonder, mystery, and awe.

I also spent some time in Rishikesh, in the foothills of the Himalayas, and there I met many foreign tourists from all over the world, many retired women, men, young men and women, traveling and looking for the spiritual life. As I was walking on the many paths along the sacred river Ganges, I wondered how many of these young and old souls would have to go through experiences that they did not understand at all. Many were doing ancient yoga practices of all kinds, intensive practices using breathing, postures, and so on. I wondered how many of them lost their way because there was no explanation of what the soul goes through when put through these intensive practices.

As I was sitting and eating a wonderful curry lunch in one of the hundreds of hotels in Rishikesh, I struck up a conversation with a Hindu couple in their thirties and their parents. They had come to attend a ten-day retreat with one of the famous gurus; there are many, many gurus in India. The woman said to me after I had told her that I had done Vipassana meditation myself in retreats, "Yes, there are many paths, aren't there? But they reach the same goal."

I agreed completely. In this land of India, *Mother India*, where the spiritual life is still present and where the everyday sensory world is considered *maya*, I was enjoying the thousands of people flocking there for retreats. There are ashrams everywhere, and both young and old were present in the ashrams, chanting, singing, praying, doing yoga, and playing music. I wanted to stay in one of the hundreds of centers, but this one was full. There were 3,000 people meditating with this holy guru for his retreat, coming in from all over India by train, of course. It was mobbed and that was just one place along the river. It was overwhelming to feel the strength of people's beliefs in God, in the afterlife and the reality of the world of the spirit. No wonder no one paid much attention to everyday problems such as lack of good drinking water, toilets, bathrooms, and starvation.

Attaining a glimpse of God was a priority for all who came to this famous sacred spot. What do we have in the West to equal this massive interest in the world of the spirit? What we have in the West is belief in shopping, buying, selling things, making money, making more money, investing money, losing money, and everything material.

Thank goodness we have these great interchanges between East and West. The East comes to the West and imports its spiritual practices, and the West—people like my Scottish friend in Bodh Gaya—goes East to build toilets, wells, and clinics and address the material needs of the people. Somehow we will come to the middle, and as long as individuals want to see the world, we will have this exchange.

> Esoteric, or inner, development gradually leads individuals to the steps of their *own* knowledge.... When we reach the pinnacle of knowledge, when we stand on the peak of a mountain, then we have an unhindered view in all directions. As long as we are merely on the way, until we attain the peak, we do not have an unhindered view. The more we climb, the more we know, but a great deal remains concealed by the mountain. This picture of a mountain fits very well with inner development. Every single individual wanting to ascend the steps of higher knowledge must start from a point appropriate for him or her. This means that people are different on the Earth, different in relation to their physical, etheric, and astral constitutions.[19]

I walked through Rishikesh and enjoyed watching all the different people who had come there. There were a lot of backpackers on their way around the world spending a few days here, many of them smoking pot and just hanging out, enjoying their days in a beautiful setting, ready for the next city or town or country. These backpackers, or older travelers (who get insulted if you take them for tourists), stay in the same area at mostly cheaper places and give one another hints about where to go next. They seem to crisscross India, and the whole planet Earth on a well-determined path and are a motley group: hundreds of Israelis who have finished their military duties and are happy to be in a safe, free country; Australians; New Zealanders; lots and lots of French;

---

19   Steiner, *The Christian Mystery*, p. 161.

English; some Americans (not many as they do not have the funds, unlike the Israeli kids who get their paycheck at the end of their duties—paid for by my US taxes of course); Japanese; Dutch; many Germans; québecquois; Swedes; Norwegians; and Swiss, among others. Couldn't these young travelers be our modern "ravens"? I think so. Just to travel in India or around the world is an arduous task. They must save money, and that means working somewhere and disciplining themselves to save it. Then they get sick, get stuck in terrible bus stations, miss trains, starve when there is no food, get amoebic dysentery, colds and fevers, sleep in terrible beds with bedbugs, go to hospitals, get lost, lose passports, and so on. If that is not a modern initiation brought on by freedom, what is?

All these young and old men and women travel in couples, by themselves, or in groups, and you can meet them repeatedly in various cities. We know where to eat, where to gather for the Internet, and which places to stay in that are clean…or not. And it is wonderful to see that there are people who have not been seduced by materialism. They are free to observe the world and bring home many insights that are worth much more than gold. One hopes that the young people from Israel will bring some fresh air to a country that desperately needs it. But I discovered that those kids cannot escape the vigilant eyes of their elders up north in Daramsala. The Jewish instinct for protecting sends rabbis, some from New York, to make sure their children do not get into trouble, which they invariably do like the rest of the young travelers, as there are too many drugs, too much sex, and too much meditation. So these young kids have an opportunity to attend an evening prayer at a local rabbi's home to reconnect. Here we see how independence is not fostered, but one cannot blame them.

On one of my former trips, I was in the middle of Bombay and traveling in a bus when a relatively young French woman boarded. This was 1976; she was pregnant and skinny, an addict who wanted money. No one was there to protect her from her own freedom. It broke my heart to see a young woman having reached the bottom, the gutter—the Indian gutter. No French Catholic priest was there to take care of this transplanted soul who had lost her way.

During that same journey, as I was eating a vegetarian meal overlooking the beach and the dunes in Goa, I saw another, younger woman lying on the sand, while an Indian man injected heroin into her arm. I could not understand how a soul could fall so deeply into slow death. What I saw made me sick at such suffering, and sicker to see that I could do nothing but bear witness to life's horrible hell on such a beautiful beach. Again, my heart went out to these lost souls who likely died on Indian soil. No priest or pastors or gurus were there to help them, so I can sympathize with the rabbis who truly care about their people's children. Freedom is a harsh reality that can come with a price. I am forever thankful to all the young souls who lost their way and who are still losing their way and dying. That is the price of my freedom, and I have never forgotten them.

On one of the paths leading out of Rishikesh toward the source of the Ganges, a beautiful path with trees and shrubs, small villas, and ashrams, I saw a young Japanese traveler with his backpack, resting on the ground, sitting with an old *sadhu* (renunciate) by a very old tree. The sadhu was looking at the young man's hand and telling his fortune. They were both totally absorbed in the conversation. It could have been one or two thousand years ago, and it would not have changed. I was reminded of many years ago in Calcutta (1977), when an old sadhu dressed in white spoke to me while I was climbing stairs to a holy site, although I had not asked him anything: "You live in the past." I looked at him surprised, then went on. That became for me a kind of mantra. Here is a little story:

> What did I offer my master? I will tell you. When I received my second step of initiation, at the age of fifteen, I had nothing with me, I thought, "All these rich people come with baskets of fruit, flowers, and money to offer to their teachers, but I have nothing to give."
>
> I asked my master, "Sir, what is the best thing for me to offer?" He said to me, "Bring me a bundle of sticks."
>
> He said: "This is the greatest gift that you can ever give me. People want to give me gold, silver, land, a house. These valuables mean nothing to me." My master explained that when you offer a bundle of dry sticks to a guru he understands that you are prepared to tread the path of enlightenment. It means, "Please relieve me from my past, and burn all my negative thinking in the fire of knowledge." He said, "I will burn these dry sticks so that your past karmas do not affect your future. Now

I am giving you a new life. Do not live in the past. Live here and now and start treading the path of light."

Most people brood on the past and do not know how to live here and now. This is the cause of their suffering.[20]

I sat for many hours in cafés overlooking the sacred river, mingling with this international group of human beings and having wonderful exchanges about the world. That spot had a good feel to it, surely because of the hundreds of thousands of people who have gone there for thousands of years to dedicate themselves to reaching the heights. And of course the Himalayas are in the background. This city is on the path that all the sadhu take on their way up to the source of the Ganges, deep into the Himalayas.

Many holy men in their orange clothes were there, living and sleeping outdoors with no belongings. They had matted hair and gnarled fingers, some holding a joint, which is accepted in India for these men. Many of them had a far-away look as they asked for a rupee so they could eat. Many of these wanderers were originally family men with important jobs, but they gave up the world to be with their god. They cross India from one sacred site to the next, walking on the well-trodden dirt paths. A few are authentic while others have adopted this lifestyle and everyone respects them. I would love to see the reaction that these young men and women with this lifestyle would get in the United States. The scorn would be unbearable. No, not in the West. I did see some of the kids in Berkeley, California, living on the street, young people who came from wealthy families who wanted to live like the homeless, but their issue was the rejection of money and materialism and not a deep search for God.

I had a wonderful long conversation with a young French woman from southern France who was doing a three-month intensive in yoga. She was deeply searching for answers and it showed in her beautiful open face. She was here from the hills of Mexico, where she lived with a young German man. Together, they had started a little "farm-retreat" there with gardening and ancient native rituals. She was in India deepening her spiritual life. I told her of my project and

---

20   Swami Rama, *Living with the Himalayan Masters*, p. 52.

Scenes in Varanasi (also called Benares), on the banks of the River Ganges

she was seriously interested in the details of meditative practice—what actually happens to you when you meditate, not just the results, but the actual explanation of the changes undergone by our bodies. These include our different subtle bodies—changes in the physical body, changes in our emotional-feeling body (astral body), changes in our life body (etheric body we have in common with the plants). I said that I would send her the book when it was published. First it must be written. I could not explain much in a morning's talk. I needed a book. And it is for such beautiful human beings that I am writing about this journey. They are constantly in my thoughts. She is back in Mexico and recently gave birth to a delightful daughter named Manon.

She invited me to an evening with local renunciates, sadhu, who perform their *puja* (ritual-thanking) in a tiny temple. She said she had the most amazing evening with these very old, odd fellows. They had accepted her into their little private circle and performed their ceremony in private, away from all the big ashram commotion, tourists, and pseudo-sadhu. I could not attend, as it was too late and I was staying on the far side of Rishikesh. But I could see that the place was teeming with energy by the foot of this river that flows from the eternal snows right through India to join the sea in Calcutta. It was too late in the year to go up into the mountains, as they were snowed in, but I will return to trek into the mountains some other time.

Another evening I sat for hours on the floor of a terrace with a few dozen foreigners and Hindus listening to a concert of classical music and dancing. I loved the sound of the sitar and the small drums intoning melodies from far, far away, sounds that invariably mimicked the sounds of the cosmos. The rhythms, strange rhythms, were not the monotonous rhythms of the West, but complicated sounds. Here religion and music are not separate; they, and the beautiful movement of the dancer, were one. We sat listening and watching, not tired but full of energy and peace. An attractive, tall Hindu man wrapped in the sadhu orange cloth was there. He must have been influential from the way he behaved. He was listening to the music with two older women. At one point he got up and picked up his cell phone. We were on a terrace overlooking the sacred Ganges, and a playful monkey and her two young ones were running past the sadhu, who talked on the cell phone while the music played magically. The sun was setting on the mountains, with the beautiful Ganges flowing by. This was India at its best. Forgotten were the sacred cows wandering everywhere and littering the streets with manure, the old sick dogs, the starving mother and child sitting begging, the stoned hippies, and old emaciated sadhu. We were in another realm, which was the point. But the real question is: How are we to be on Earth and still in that other realm? When we know that, then we can take care of the manure, cows, beggars, filth, and more.

A group of Italians were staying at my strange little hotel, sometimes cooking pizza in the outdoor oven. One was an older paraplegic man, whose friends took him around in a small car. I was impressed by this man's energy to travel so far from home. They spent every evening smoking pot and during the day soaking up the sun on the shore of the Ganges. One evening, there was a *puja* celebration at the ashram next door, which lasted all weekend. Sounds from loudspeakers screamed live music and old mantras twenty-four hours a day for three days. I was exhausted by the cacophony of sounds and screams. I should have packed up and moved on, but remained. I had a room on a terrace and a bathroom with hot water. What else did I need?

As I walked around on both sides of the Ganges, I was pleased to see many women around my age (sixty) who were living in Rishikesh, studying yoga or just hanging out for months at a time. An older Swiss woman lived there full-time. She had abandoned the West and established herself in the town, teaching yoga. She was not the only one to abandon the West. I met an English woman who was living in India several months of the year, helping and teaching children. This holy place still attracts many searching souls. Just down the road toward the plain, a festival was scheduled for early December, and literally millions of people were expected to flock to the area for a sacred ceremony. A fifty-eight-year-old French woman told me she was coming to it with her adopted seven-year-old Indian daughter and would not miss it for the world. She had become a devoted *shivaites*. I met her in Benares and spent a few delightful days with her and her friends.

After spending almost two months traveling in India, my fourth trip to this very old continent, I was once more spellbound by these people who belonged to the world of 5,000 years ago or even more, and to the world of the future, with its atomic energies and new technology. It is not unusual to have a bicycle taxi, a rickshaw, take one around Delhi, while the driver of this ancient mode of transportation talks on a cell phone. The two worlds lived side by side, but I observed that things were not working right. The fully modern metro station stood in the middle of Delhi amid cows, dogs, filth, and women laborers working on the construction site with baskets over their heads filled with bricks, climbing stairs to build a ten-story building by hand while their babies sat nearby on a pile of dirt—modern and ancient. In the West, we have completely lost the ancient traditions, and we can look toward our brothers and sisters in the East for not having lost sight of the "land of the gods," but they have lost sight of living on Earth. Travelers, the modern "Ravens," will always come to the East to reconnect, but we will have to reestablish our connection in the modern way, not the old way. We cannot forget the Earth as we try to assail the heavens. But where did this ancient Indian culture originate?

> We know that the human race in its present state of civilization has by and large descended from the human race that evolved before disaster befell the continent of Atlantis...an area between present-day Europe, Africa, and America that is today covered by the Atlantic Ocean. We know that under the influence of that disaster...the people of that time migrated first in an eastward direction, populating Europe and then Asia as they moved on, and that the European and Asian peoples of the present day are in fact the descendants of the peoples of Atlantis.
>
> The soil of Europe had a different effect on the descendants of the Atlanteans than the did the soil of Asia....
>
> Asian peoples got more into the habit of thinking with their souls; the Europeans got into the habit of thinking more with their bodies. That is in fact the major difference between the civilizations of Asia and Europe. If you want to show up the clear difference that exists between the kind of intelligence apparent in the Vedic writings or Vedantic philosophy and other cultural streams in Asia compared to European culture, you have to say to yourselves: Asians are thinking more with their souls, Europeans more with their bodies.
>
> The people of Asia may thus be said to have taken the intellectual element into a higher aspect of their human nature, with the result that an

advanced civilization developed much earlier. This however was a civilization of the soul that had fewer abstract concepts, a culture that found its own ways to higher things, using the human soul and spirit to reach the soul and spirit of the world without resorting to abstract concepts. That is where the spiritual nature of Asian civilization lies—inasmuch as it is essentially a civilization based on soul qualities. The peoples of Asia largely left their bodies unused when it came to thinking; they merely carried their bodies with them through life on earth. The life of the mind was nurtured entirely at soul level....

Europeans were basing their thinking more and more on the physical body. That is also why the foundations were more strongly laid among them than in Asia for a culture in which freedom can be the central principle. The people of Asia, endowed with intelligence at soul level, still were more part of the whole cosmic organism. The human body specifically isolates itself from the rest of the cosmic organism. Using it as the instrument for our intellectual life we become more independent, though this independence is more bound up with the body than is the case with the people of Asia who have developed intelligence within the soul principle and are consequently less independent.

In the East...the old spirituality is increasingly falling into decadence and decay. It is rotting away. The experience we have of the East is such that we may certainly say: The human being, once perceived as a heavenly, spiritual being, has come to look like a senile old person. This human being still has no understanding for the things of the earth, for the things in which human beings, too, are clothed on this earth. The West understands earthly things only; the East has no understanding of them. Because of this, the heavenly element has grown completely senile....

On the one hand, we must be wary of past elements reaching across from the East, be wary of past elements from the East in someone living in this century, and on the other hand we must be wary of what is only in its beginnings in the West.[21]

The sentence "being wary of what is only in its beginning in the West" is what brings all these Westerners to the East. They feel the dangers of life in the West and are trying to find some answers from Eastern elders. They know about their own deeply materialistic society and the dangers of being soulless

---

21   Steiner, *Polarities in the Evolution of Mankind*, pp. 15, 16–17, 132, 133 (trans. revised).

human beings, people with no feeling, who follow the rules like robots, having lost sight of where they came from through theories such as the one that proclaims that love comes from the brain. So what a relief it is to see these old sadhu who walk thousands of miles across the old continent, carrying nothing, reciting old mantras, wanting to go back to the world of the spirit. One could also say they never left the spiritual world, were never really on the Earth.

Here in Mother India, reverence, or veneration, is a touchable substance. We can smell the devotion everywhere; we can see it. The people live with it, breathe it, and thereby they have not lost touch with the world of the spirit. This feeling of reverence is what the young are looking for.

Rudolf Steiner wrote:

> Our civilization is more inclined to criticize, judge, and condemn than to feel devotion and selfless veneration. Our children criticize far more than they respect or revere. But just as surely as every feeling of reverence and devotion nurtures the soul's powers for higher knowledge, so every act of criticism and judgment drives these powers away. This is not meant to imply anything against our civilization— our concern here is not to criticize it. After all, we owe the greatness of our culture precisely to our ability to make critical, self-confident human judgments and to our principle of "testing all and keeping the best." Modern science, industry, transportation, commerce, law—all these would never have developed without the universal exercise of our critical faculty and standards of judgment. But the price of this gain in outer culture has been a corresponding loss in higher knowledge and spiritual life. Therefore we must never forget that higher knowledge has to do with revering truth and insight and not with revering people.

> Nevertheless, we must be clear about one thing. Those completely immersed in the superficial civilization of our day will find it particularly difficult to work their way to cognition of the higher worlds. To do so, they will have to work energetically upon themselves. In times when the material conditions of life were still simple, spiritual progress was easier. What was revered and held sacred stood out more clearly from the rest of the world. In an age of criticism, on the other hand, ideals are degraded. Reverence, awe, adoration, and wonder are replaced by other feelings—they are pushed more and more into the

background. As a result, everyday life offers very few opportunities for their development. Anyone seeking higher knowledge must create these feelings inwardly, instilling them in the soul. This cannot be done by studying. It can be done only by living.

If we wish to become esoteric students, we must train ourselves vigorously in the mood of devotion. We must seek—in all things around us, in all our experiences—for what can arouse our admiration and respect.[22]

Walking through the paths in Rishikesh, one is assailed by signs everywhere advertising yoga practices of all kinds, motley offerings of new age practices: ancient rituals, yoga techniques, Hindi and Sanskrit language classes,

---

22 Steiner, *How to Know Higher Worlds*, pp. 18–19.

yoga breathing techniques of all sorts, ancient massage, flower essences, aryu-vedic medicine, chanting, dancing, and music. If one were to arrive there and had to choose among this cornucopia of spiritual practice in this very tiny cor-ner by the flowing Ganges, it would be almost impossible to make a decision between one ashram or another, compounds with many buildings, common meditation rooms, cells for practitioners or rooms for families, gardens within walls—all with signs reading "no picture taking here."

The Yoga Path and the Westerner

The French woman who had come to further her knowledge of yoga had many questions about her practice and about what was happening to her psyche. I will try to clarify some aspects of meditation that are not often discussed in actual practice. Failing to understand the work of a practice and what is at stake can lead to suffering for the practitioner, as happened to me so many years ago. In our modern age, we can no longer accept a spiritual practice without asking ourselves some very important questions: What is it that I am practicing? Yes, I want to stop suffering or be happier or see God, but how am I going to do that? It is no longer enough simply to go to an ashram and be told to practice a breathing technique or to recite a mantra without actually knowing how it will affect us. We can no longer be so ignorant. Today, we must be aware of what happens when we practice these ancient techniques with teachers who often do not fully understand what they are doing themselves.

> One of the basic principles of true esoteric science is that those who dedicate themselves to it must do so in full consciousness. As students, we should undertake nothing, nor engage in any exercises, whose effects we do not understand. An esoteric teacher, when giving advice or instruction, will always explain what the effects of following the instruction will be on the body, soul, or spirit of the person striving for higher knowledge.[23]

After having practiced Vipassana, I remember being horrified when I was told that I should no longer practice it, that it was not for me. Later, while reading Rudolf Steiner's book *How to Know Higher Worlds*, I skipped the chapters on the exercises. I did not even glance at these practices in case I would be tempted to try them. I said to myself, "I was caught once, but never

---

23   Ibid., p. 108.

again. Now I need to know what I am doing." It was years before I tried to practice Steiner's specific meditation exercises. By then, however, I had made a detailed study, thanks to the clarity of his instructions, of what it is that I do when I meditate. I did not attempt to practice the exercises until I had a thorough understanding—or as thorough as my abilities allowed, which are limited, but one must start somewhere. Of course, there is always more to understand as one's knowledge deepens. Learning has, in fact, no end. But at least there can be some understanding of some simple laws. Anthroposophy, the work of Rudolf Steiner, has many of the answers to deep questions concerning the various ways to approach the spirit world.

People of the East are constituted differently than those of the West, and that was something I did not know, although it should have been obvious. Again, we must acknowledge that the Eastern, Western, and central paths all lead to the same place, to the same goal. But they are achieved through different paths, ones that are suitable to who we are as individuals.

> The East and the West have always had entirely different ways of initiation that correspond to deeper ethnic characteristics.... All of these paths lead, of course, to the same goal, since truth is here and there, today and yesterday, and in all eternity the same....
>
> We will first consider the Eastern path of yoga. It is possible for the human soul to develop itself so far that it becomes like an eye that can see directly the spiritual, eternal, nontemporal. The path of development taken by an individual of the East is different from that taken by a European. Hindus are not only different from Europeans externally; even their brains and souls have different structures. Therefore, it is clear that a Hindu must take a different path than a European to really reach the intended goal. Indeed, the differences are so great that Europeans would ruin themselves morally and physically if they wanted to take the Eastern path of development. The loneliness and withdrawal of the soul from civilization required by the yoga path is almost impossible in our European culture. We would have to step entirely out of our ordinary lives, indeed, out of our entire culture in order to devote ourselves to our own inner development.
>
> Those advancing spiritually on this path need a spiritual leader, or guru, who can lead them safely through the many possible confusions.

It is impossible to tread such a path without a guru. Furthermore, it requires a complete transformation of the human being, a transformation prescribed by the guru. Such a guru then possesses altogether an unlimited power over the pupil. It is not a matter of indifference what the human being does in life. It is no longer adequate to be a good, decent human being of the ordinary sort, simply to be a person whom society ordinarily deems exemplary.

It must now be possible to completely distinguish and separate body and soul; they must no longer be permitted to interpenetrate as they did earlier. In the future, passions and animals instincts should no longer have to be involved with the soul for as long as they are now; the soul is hindered from penetrating through the fog of the physical world and seeing into the higher, spiritual world. However, when soul and body are separated from each other, the body can assert its passions and desires even as the soul is simultaneously located in a higher life. It is possible then for the soul to transform itself to the point of spiritual vision while the body falls prey to all kinds of wicked traits and possibly perishes because the body's passions and drives are no longer guided to something better by an insightful soul.

We see from this the enormous importance of proper guidance on this dangerous path. In every case, the guru must be obeyed, even when one is disinclined. Gurus are permitted to interfere in the most intimate affairs of the heart and give their pupils corresponding rules for behavior....

A human being acquires the capacity for gaining knowledge of the higher worlds through initiation, which consists in an intimate path of development of the soul. There are various paths to this knowledge for various people, but the truth is everywhere the same. Only after we have achieved the pinnacle of a mountain do we have an unlimited view in all directions. But it would be nonsensical for us, starting from our present location, to take any but the most direct path to the top. It is the same with initiation. When we have arrived at the goal and have truly achieved the unhindered perspective of knowledge, then this knowledge is the same for everyone.

It is, however, not good for us to follow any path of knowledge other than the one appropriate to our nature. Actually there ought to be a special path to initiation for every individual man and woman. But all paths can be traced back to three different types: the yoga path, the Christian Gnostic initiation, and the Christian Rosicrucian initiation. We can travel on any of these three different paths. They are different because there are three diverse kinds of people. Among Europeans we find very few who can follow the yoga path. For this reason it is generally not right for a European to journey the yoga path. In the East people live in an entirely different climate, exposed to an entirely different form of sunlight. The difference between a person of the East and a European cannot easily be proved by anatomy, but there is a deep soul and spiritual difference between them. This difference must be taken into consideration because inner development reaches deep into the soul-spiritual nature of the human being. The finer structures of the brain of a Hindu are not perceptible to an anatomist. But if we were to demand of a European the same thing that can be expected of an Indian, then we would destroy him or her. We can prescribe certain actions for an Indian that would be of no use to a European or could even be detrimental for him or her.[24]

I was well acquainted with how detrimental it was to my own body and soul, which was not suited to such practices, because our Western bodies, unlike the Eastern ones, have become increasingly deadened, hardened, tough, and unbending, unlike the more flexible, softer, and more delicate bodies of our Eastern contemporaries. Just looking at the Hindus one can see the beautiful, fine subtle features of the men and women....

In early times, the human bodies of Europeans were very much the instrument of their kind of elementary intellectual thinking, but then this body gradually began to die. Physical evolution of European humanity until the fifteenth century, and even to this day, involved the physical body becoming increasingly deadened. Our physical bodies are growing denser and more bony. We cannot demonstrate this with the methods of ordinary anatomy and physiology, but it is true. We no longer have bodies as inwardly alive as those of the people who lived in the first, third and even during the tenth and eleventh centuries. Our European bodies of today have grown bony and paralyzed compared to those ancient bodies, which were inwardly alive.[25]

24 Steiner, *The Christian Mystery*, pp. 125–126, 133–134.

25 Steiner, *Polarities in the Evolution of Mankind*, p. 19 (trans. revised).

When we look back to the spiritual paths of humankind in a very distant past, we find among others the one practiced in the East in the culture known later as the ancient Indian civilization. Many people nowadays are returning to what was practiced then because they cannot rouse themselves to the realization that, in order to penetrate into suprasensory worlds, every epoch must follow its own appropriate path.... One of those methods followed is known as the path of yoga.[26]

Many yogic practices involve the breath, and here are some insights into what is involved in this very ancient practice. I am quoting at length, because it is not a simple matter.

In those remote ages of humanity's evolution, human consciousness was in general very different from what it is today. In the present age, we look out into the world and, through our senses, perceive colors, sounds, and so on. We seek the laws of nature that prevail in the physical world, and we are conscious that if we attempt to experience spirit-soul in the outer world, we add something to it through our imagination. It was different in the remote past; then, as we know, human beings saw more in the external world than ordinary people see today. In lightning and thunder, in every star, in the beings of the different kingdoms of nature, people of those times saw spirit and soul. They perceived spiritual beings, though of a lower kind, in all solid matter, in everything fluid or gaseous. Today's intellectual outlook declares that, through their fantasy, those people of old dreamed all kinds of spiritual and psychical qualities into the world around them. This is known as animism.

We understand little of human nature, especially that of ancient peoples, if we believe that the spiritual beings manifesting in lightning and thunder, in springs and rivers, in wind and weather, were dreamed creations woven into nature by fantasy. This was certainly not the case. Just as we perceive red or blue and hear C sharp or G, so those ancients saw realities of spirit and soul in outer objects. It was just as natural for them to see spirit-soul entities as it is for us to see colors and so on. However, there was another aspect to this way of experiencing the world; namely, human beings in those days had no clear consciousness of self.

---

26 Steiner, *The Human Soul in Relation to World Evolution*, p. 106 (trans. revised).

The clear self-awareness that permeates normal human beings today did not yet exist. Though they did not express it, those people did not, as it were, distinguish their self from the external world.... They felt themselves to be members of the whole universe. They had no definite consciousness of their own being as separate from the surrounding world. Suppose an individual of that time was walking along a riverbank. People today who walk downstream along a riverbank, being intelligent, feel their legs stepping out in that direction, and this has nothing at all to do with the river. In general, people of old did not feel like that. When they walked along a river downstream, as was natural for them to do, they were conscious of the spiritual beings connected with the water of the river flowing in that direction. Just as a swimmer today experiences being carried along by the water—that is, by something material—likewise people of old felt themselves guided downstream by something spiritual.... In all their experiences of the external world, those people felt themselves to be supported and impelled by Gods of wind, river, and all surrounding nature. They experienced the elements of nature within themselves. Today, this feeling of being at one with nature has been lost. In its place, people have gained a strong feeling of their independence, the individual "I."

Yogis rose above the level of the masses, whose experiences were as described. They carried out certain exercises, of which I shall speak. Those exercises were good and suited to the nature of humanity in ancient times. Such practices, however, have later become decadent and have been used mainly for harmful ends. I have often referred to those yogic breathing exercises. Therefore, what I am now describing was a method for the attainment of higher worlds that was suitable and proper only for human beings in a very ancient Eastern civilization.

In ordinary life, breathing functions unconsciously. We breathe in, hold the breath and exhale. This becomes a conscious process only when in some way we are not in good health. In normal life, breathing remains largely an unconscious process. However, during certain periods of exercises, yogis transformed their breathing into a conscious inner experience. This they did by timing the inhalation, then holding and exhaling the breath differently, thus altering the whole rhythm of normal breathing. In this way, the breathing process became conscious. Yogis projected themselves, as it were, into their breathing. They felt united with the indrawn breath, with the spreading of the breath through the body, and with the exhaled breath. Thus, they were drawn with their whole soul into the breath.

To understand what is achieved by this, let us consider what happens when we breathe. When we inhale, the breath is driven into the organism, up through the spinal cord, into the brain; from there it spreads out into the system of nerves and senses. Therefore, when we think, we in no way depend only upon our senses and nervous system as instruments of thinking. The breathing process pulsates and beats through them with perpetual rhythm. We never think without this whole process taking place, of which we are normally unaware because the breathing remains unconscious.

Yogis, by altering the rhythm of the breath, drew it consciously into the process of nerves and senses. Because their altered breathing caused the air to billow and whirl through the brain and nerve and sensory system, the result was an inner experience of their function when combined with the air. Consequently, yogis also experienced a soul element in their thinking in the rhythm of breathing.

Something extraordinary happened to the yogis by this means. The process of thinking, which they had barely experienced as a function of the head at all, streamed into the whole organism. They did not merely think, but also experienced the thought as a little live creature running through the whole process of breathing that they had induced artificially.

Thus, yogis did not experience thinking as merely a shadowy process of logic. Rather, they experienced how thinking follows the breath. When they inhaled, they felt they were taking into themselves something from the external world, which they then allowed to flow with the breath into their thinking. With their thoughts, they took hold, as it were, of what they had inhaled with the air and spread through one's whole organism. As a result, arising in them was an enhanced feeling of the "I," an intensified feeling of self.... This made them aware of their thinking, especially in the rhythmic current of air within. This had a very definite effect on those yogis.

When people today are aware of themselves in the physical world, they quite correctly ignore their thinking as such. Their senses inform them about the outer world, and when they reflect on themselves, they perceive at least a portion of their own being. This gives people an image of how human beings are placed in the world between birth and death. Yogis radiated ensouled thoughts into their breath. This soul-filled thinking pulsed through their inner being, with the result that enhanced feeling of selfhood arose in them. However, they did not experience themselves in this experience as living between birth and death in the physical world and surrounded by nature. They felt they were carried back in memory to the time before they descended to Earth—to a time when they were spirit and soul beings in a spiritual world.

In normal consciousness today, people can reawaken experiences of the past. People may, for instance, experience a vivid recollection of some event that took place ten years ago in a wood.... In just the same way, through altered breathing, yogis felt themselves drawn back into the wood and atmosphere, into the whole setting of a spiritual soul world in which they had been as spiritual soul beings. There, they felt quite differently about the world than they did in normal consciousness. The result of that changed relationship of newly awakened selfhood to the whole universe led to the wonderful poems of which the Bhagavad Gita is a beautiful example.

In the Bhagavad Gita, we read wonderful descriptions of how the human soul, immersed in the phenomena of nature, partakes of every secret, steeping itself in the mysteries of the world. These descriptions are all reproductions of memories, called up by means of yoga breathing, of the soul—when it was as yet only soul—and lived within a spiritual universe.... The soul, with enhanced feeling of selfhood, is transported into its past in the spiritual world, relating what Krishna and other ancient initiates had experienced there through their heightened self-awareness.

Thus, it can be said that those ancient sages rose to a level of consciousness higher than that of ordinary people. The initiates strictly isolated the "I" from the outer world. This came about not for any egoistic reason, but as the result of altering the process of breathing, in which the soul dove down, as it were, into the rhythm of the inner air current. This is how a path into the spiritual world was sought in ancient times.

Later, this path was modified. In very ancient times, yogis experienced how in the transformed breathing their thoughts were submerged in currents of breath, which ran through them like little snakes. They felt they were part of a weaving cosmic life, and this feeling expressed itself in certain words and sayings. It was noticeable that one would speak differently when these experiences were revealed though speech.

What I have described was gradually felt less intensely in the breath; it no longer remained in the breathing process itself. Rather, the words were breathed out and, of themselves, formed rhythmic speech. Thus, the altered breathing led, through the words carried by the breath, to the creation of mantras. Whereas, the process and experience of breathing was previously the most important, now the poetic sayings assumed primary importance. They passed into tradition and the historical consciousness of humanity and subsequently gave birth to rhythm, meter, and so on in poetry....

This is not the path through which modern people should enter the spiritual world. We must rise into the higher worlds not by the detour of breath, but along the more inner path of thinking itself. The right path for people today is to transform, through meditation and concentration, the otherwise merely logical connection between thoughts into something of a musical nature. Meditation today should always begin with an experience in thought, an experience of the transition from one thought into another, from one mental picture into another.

Whereas the ancient Indian yogis passed from one kind of breathing to another, modern human beings must try to project themselves into a living experience of, say, the color red. In this way, they remain within the realm of thought.[27]

Here is another explanation of the very delicate breathing processes practiced by ancient Indian yogis:

What is experienced there [when we have risen to inspiration] remains completely concealed from ordinary consciousness. We would be able to perceive it with ordinary consciousness only if we see not only with our eyes, hear only with our ears, and taste only with the organs for tasting, but if the process of breathing in and out were also a kind of perception—if one could also experience inwardly the in and out of the streaming of the breath throughout the whole organism. Because this is so, a certain Eastern school, the school of yoga, transformed breathing into

---

27   Ibid., pp. 107–112 (trans. revised).

a process of knowledge, transformed it into a process of perception. By converting the breathing process into a conscious, though half-dream-like means to knowing, so as to experience something in it like what we experience in seeing and hearing, the yoga philosophy actually develops a cosmology, or insight into how spiritual beings in the cosmos work into human beings and the way they experience themselves as members of the spiritual cosmos. But such yoga instructions do not accord with the form of human organization that present Western humanity has acquired. Yogic exercises such as these were possible only for the human organization of past ages, and what yogis practice today is basically already decadent.

For a particular "middle epoch" of Earth and human evolution... it was appropriate, so to speak, for the human organization to make the breathing process into one of consciousness, or knowledge, through such yogic exercises and in this way to develop a dreamlike but nevertheless valid cosmology. Such knowledge...must be regained on a higher level by human beings today with our present composition of body and soul—not in the half-dreamlike, half-unconscious condition of that time, but with full consciousness.... If Western people were to practice yogic exercises, they would not under any circumstances leave their physical and etheric organisms undisturbed; they would alter them precisely because they would now have a very different constitution. Elements from their physical and etheric organs would enter their process of cognition, and something non-objective would interfere.[28]

I chose these words carefully, because they resonate with my experiences. My body went through the upheavals Steiner speaks about; I lived these upheavals and suffered the grave consequences of such practices. I thank my "protectors" who were there all along and saved me from physical death.

On my last day in Rishikesh, I took a boat to cross the Holy River Ganges and I sat next to a couple my age who had older children. We watched the last rays of the sun go down as we were waiting for more people to come. It was quiet and peaceful and the colors were beautiful. An old sadhu dressed in orange was sweeping the beach with a funny makeshift broom, while cows milled around looking for food. The middle-aged couple started to chat—Hindus

---

28   Steiner, *Philosophy, Cosmology, and Religion*, pp. 46–47 (trans. revised).

At the Sacred Ganges

love to chat—and said they were extremely thankful to be in Rishikesh and were devoted to their spiritual practices. That kind of devotion from a "regular" couple is unheard of where I come from. Where I come from one is more likely to hear, "What should we buy today?" or "Should we redo the kitchen?" I thought that we had a lot to learn from our brothers and sisters in the East who have such a fervent need to be "with God." Their common spiritual practice will secure them a beautiful old age, not like in the West where there is so much divorce and the potential for a pitiful old age in states like Florida or Arizona, which have become parking lots for abandoned and unwanted old men and women.

In the holy city of Benares, the sacred city of Siva, where I began my journey I felt I was part of an unreal adventure, a world of unknown spaces, so full of life that it was overwhelming. Backpackers young and old can only stay a couple of days, because it is so beyond anything we Westerners can imagine. I was fortunate to be there during many celebrations when day and night the banks of the river were teeming with Hindus coming from all over India to worship and celebrate by performing sacred rituals of all kinds. The first weekend was a festival in honor of women. The worshipers came and set up their *puja* (offerings) rituals along the river around 3:00 in the afternoon, to be ready for sunset, and again at 4:00 a.m. to get ready for the sunrise *puja*. Men and women carried mountains of offerings on their heads that they would set up on the shores of the Ganges as it flows through Benares. I saw the locals, hardly dressed, use enormous water pumps to suck the water from the Ganges in order to clean its banks so people could set up their *puja* there. By 5:00 the area was full, with not an inch available as everyone—children, babies, men, women—set up their modest offerings to the gods. The offerings were beautiful, creative masterpieces with banana leaves spread out, fruits of all kinds, lovingly baked cakes, small handmade lanterns, vermilion or bright yellow paste designs on the earth altar, wicks made by hand which would be lit at the right time by the devotees. This spread of beautiful colors was a true feast for the eyes. And everything was done with such devotion that the whole place seemed alive with love. I wandered everywhere and was so filled with the smiles, kindness, openness, attention, and interest of the people there, that I forgot for a while the pollution of the streets and the air, the stench of the garbage, the poverty and hard lives of those who lived there, and the sacred river itself with its floating bodies, the people using its banks as a bathroom, the water buffaloes washing in it—in the same place the locals, pilgrims, and sadhu brushed their teeth.

At sunset, the whole city comes alive and everyone walks on the river banks and celebrates the magical time of sunset, which lasts for hours, while whole families enjoy the *puja* (worship). I saw children handed from one person to another, infinite love shown to all, even though many of the people had very few earthly possessions. They did have what we do not have in the West: devotion, respect, and intense religious practices. What I describe here is but a small *apercu* of the Vedic religion; it is so vast that it is nearly impossible to talk about. One must live in India, breathe the religion, breathe the air, take it in through all the senses.

> There is nothing simpler and greater than this religion, in which an intense naturalism is mixed with a transcendent spirituality. Before sunrise, a man—the head of the family—is standing before an earth altar where a fire, lighted with two pieces of wood, burns. At one and the same time this man is father, priest, and king of sacrifice. "While dawn disrobes," as a Vedic poet says, "like a woman leaving her bath: Dawn who has woven the loveliest of cloths," the leader repeats a prayer, an invocation to *Usha* (the Dawn), to *Savitar* (the Sun), and the *Asuras* (the spirits of life). The mother and sons pour the fermented liquors of the *asclepus*, the *soma*, into *Agni*, the fire, and the rising flame carries to the invisible gods the purified prayer spoken by the patriarch and the heart of the family.[29]

Diana Eck writes in her book *Darsan: Seeing the Divine Image in India*:

> A common sight in India is a crowd of people gathered in the courtyard of a temple or at the doorway of a streetside shrine for the *darsan* of the deity. Darsan means "seeing." In the Hindu ritual tradition it refers especially to religious seeing, or the visual perception of the

---

29   Schuré, *The Great Initiates*, p. 59.

sacred. When Hindus go to a temple, they do not commonly say, "I am going to worship," but rather, "I am going for *darsan*." They go to "see" the image of the deity—be it Krsna or Durga, Siva, or Visnu—present in the sanctum of the temple, and they go especially at those times of day when the image is most beautifully adorned with fresh flowers, and when the curtain is drawn back so that the image is fully visible. The central act of Hindu worship, from the point of view of the lay person, is to stand in the presence of the deity and to behold the image with one's own eyes, to see and be seen by the deity. *Darsan* is sometimes translated as the "auspicious sight" of the divine, and its importance in the Hindu ritual complex reminds us that for Hindus "worship" is not only a matter of prayers and offerings and the devotional disposition of the heart. Since, in the Hindu understanding, the deity is present in the image, the visual apprehension of the image is charged with religious meaning. Beholding the image is an act of worship, and through the eyes one gains blessings of the divine.[30]

When Hindus stand on tiptoe and crane their necks to see the image of Lord Krsna through the crowd, they wish not only to "see," but to be seen. The gaze of the huge eyes of the image meets that of the worshiper, and that exchange of vision lies at the heart of Hindu worship. In the Indian context, seeing is a kind of touching. The art historian Stella Kramwich writes,

"Seeing, according to Indian notions, is a going forth of the sight toward the object. Sight touches it and acquires its form. Touch is the ultimate connection by which the visible yields to being grasped. While the eye touches the object, the vitality that pulsates in it is communicated." ...

Examining the words used in the Vedic literature, Gonda reaches the same conclusion: "That a look was consciously regarded as a form of contact appears from the combination of 'looking' and 'touching.' Casting one's eyes upon a person and touching him were related activities." ...

Sanskrit poets and dramatists convey the subtleties of meaning expressed by the glances of the eyes, not only between lovers, but between husband and wife, whose public conversation was limited by rules of propriety. They communicated in their glances. Writes Daniel

---

30   Eck, *Darsan*, p. 3.

H. H. Ingals, "One must suppose that the language of the eyes was more advanced in ancient India that it is with us."[31]

Besides the large temples on the shore of the Ganges, there are hundreds of little temples tucked away in narrow streets and small very old temples incorporated into new buildings; everywhere one looks, walks, or gets lost, one sees them with a deity inside covered with offerings. There are places of worship everywhere. Sometimes it might be just a huge tree which has garlands around it and some vermilion paste that a woman has spread early in the morning before sunrise, or perhaps inside a building a little nook will house a statue of Ganesh. There is one for every person's taste and the freedom to choose between them. Perhaps one day a person feels like worshiping Siva, and the next day Ganesh. Or one might have a favorite and routinely come to say hello.

For a painter like me who lives deeply in colors, I was assailed by the liveliness of Indian women's clothes, brilliantly colored and worn with joyful abandonment. What a relief from Europe's grey, brown, and black or the Middle East's enforcement of dark fabrics on its female population. What do these dark colors mean?

"Death of the soul" is what it means. Here in India the soul is very much alive. The people live in the colors very intensely, and the colors help them in return. I have observed the women's intense love of colors when they shop at the *sari* store, perusing dozens of *saris*, or Punjab outfits, made from bright color after bright color, deciding which colors they wish to live with. That fall one lady said that the color that was in fashion was apple green. They know the power of colors deep within themselves. They have not lost that, as one can see by their exceptionally creative textile industry.

When I walked through the markets where the beautiful spices are displayed, again the same love of color could be found in the spice displays. These same spices are used very generously on the *puja* altar. By spreading them out on stones in beautiful artistic designs, marketing becomes a creative, artistic act carried out each evening by thousands of householders

31 Ibid., pp. 8–9.

who make these beautiful little displays on the shores, a ritual repeated in the early morning to celebrate the return of the sun. This joyful atmosphere continued the whole time I was in Benares, a celebratory place where souls come to die. Special hostels for old people are devoted to those who deliberately come here to die. It is like a center for entering the spiritual world, and I was spellbound by the ceremony of the burning of the dead on the *ghats*. Acceptance of the world of the spirit, of another realm, was so powerful that the everyday world was ignored, and hence the notably unpolished reality of common, practical everyday life. Such things as toilets were completely ignored. As Rudolf Steiner said, "The Hindu lives in the soul, and the body is a bit left behind. It is not important." Nowhere is this concept more on display than in this holy city.

Since the Hindus live intensively within their souls, they abandon the needs of the body, as they feel they are not especially important. They are not united with their bodies, or in other words, not incarnated totally. We in the West are more united with our bodies; it is in fact all about our bodies. We are so united with them that we have a hard time with our souls, with our feelings. We are so far into our bodies that our materialistic scientists see only our brain and its chemical contents, only the feeling area of the brain, and claim that our soul is in there living amidst the chemicals which foster calmness, ecstasy, and peace—take a pill and chill.

The passages by Rudolf Steiner quoted in the previous pages have helped me see what was distinctly different about the task of the yogi of ancient times. The Hindu had a different task in the past than people in the Western world have. The yogis had to feel themselves within the body through breathing exercises, to feel the "I" emerging out of the sea of the spiritual world, with which they were still united. We in the West have an "I"; we have left the spiritual world. We have been abandoned by the spiritual world, and now we have the task of going back into the spiritual world through our own efforts. It is *not* our task to do so through feeling or enhancing our sense of self, as did the Hindu yogis of former times. If we revert back to those ancient practices of feeling our "I" even more than we do now, we would increasingly end up within ourselves. We will have a stronger sense of self and escape what we are meant to do, which is to return into the spiritual world after having gained the knowledge of living on this Earth. Steiner goes into finite, detailed explanations of the process that one needs to meditate upon and gain one's *own* understanding of these processes.

ANCIENT PRACTICE THROUGH WESTERN EYES

In Benares, I stayed in a small hotel/pension overlooking the river, and there I met R, an older French woman who with her musician husband had fallen in love with the city. She was going to retire there from southern France and buy an apartment. Several years earlier, she had befriended a local man with a small daughter whose mother had died, and she decided to help them. She found them a place to live and sent them money so that the child could be educated. R bought him a boat, and the girl, now eight, was sent to the outskirts of the city to a school started by Italians. She was an amazing little one, and my friend always took the daughter and father to restaurants, swimming at the luxury hotel, and so on. They were all very thankful.

One morning, she invited me to participate in the ritual bath in the Ganges, the famous Ganges.

> The great Indian rivers, especially the Ganga, have also been of symbolic importance. Himalayan pilgrims climb to the source of the River Ganga Gangotri (north of Rishikesh) where the river emerges from under the glacier. The Ganga is called the River of Heaven and is said to have flowed in heaven alone before she agreed to come to earth. Siva caught her in his tangled ascetic's hair to break the force of her fall, and from his head she flowed down through the Himalayas, leaving the mountains at Hardvar, also called Gangadvar, "Door of the Ganga" and from there flowing out upon the plains of India...reaching the sea at Ganga Sagar on the Bay of Bengal. In Hindu hymns, the Ganga is praised as a liquid form of Siva's divine energy, Sakti. Bathing in the Ganga is said to wash away all one's sins.[32]

We left at 5:00 a.m. with her adopted daughter's father, who had deep brown eyes and a beautiful toothless smile. From our hotel he took us on his

---

32   Eck, *Darsan*, p. 65.

boat to the beautiful old temple a distance down the river. We wrapped our long colorful shawls around our warm local clothes and enjoyed watching the city wake up as everyone came down to the sacred river to welcome the Sun Deity's return to Earth. They brought their offerings to the deities and then washed, brushed their teeth and, especially important, bathed in the river as the sun came up. All this was observed by hundreds of tourists from all over the world aboard very large boats from Japan, US, and Europe. One could feel the life, just like opening an anthill, incredible life streaming from the shores. The gradual changes of the colors in the eastern skies (ironically because of the pollution) reflected many warm tones to accompany the sunrise. I had never witnessed such an intense love for the sunrise and sunset; it was magnificent and very powerful. In the West it seems no one even thinks of thanking the sun, or anything for that matter. We have grown thankless, dried up.

We arrived on the shore and R went straight into the river to perform her ritualistic bath. I declined, the river being far too polluted for me. I watched all the others as they bathed with ecstatic looks on their faces, eradicating all sufferings, worries, fears, and letting their burdens drop into the river, which carried all those negative feelings and deeds to the ocean. Their faces became transformed during this powerful ritual. Old worn-out men and women, old skinny sadhu, fat Brahmans, and tiny young women burdened with countless children bathed together. R loved it all. She went behind a small wall where, with other women, she put on dry clothing and then she took me to a famous temple that she adored, the old Shiva temple that was a distance from the shore. I went in with the proper respect and bought some milk from Bubbly, a young woman who sold it near the entrance. Her father was selling tea with milk nearby. We poured the milk as an offering on the *Lingam*, which were in all the little niches of the temple. The main *Linga*, where all were adoringly and ecstatically pouring the milk, was a powerful site. It was full of garland flowers generously offered to the deity.

The Hindus obligingly told me what to do, and I was very appreciative of their inclusiveness. The men and women gently showed me how to walk around the *Linga*, how to pour the offerings, and so forth. I performed my ablutions like everyone else, and observed the sacred writings on the walls and the other many little sacred areas within the temple. It was full of ancient symbols, and I especially loved the enormous circular stone, which had signs of the planets on it that one could walk around. I felt very thankful to be admitted to this old temple, to be present in this fervent atmosphere of gratitude and devotion to the gods. Outside one could see many foreigners who did not dare go into this mysterious lively temple, and some were actually told not to enter.

R had become a total *shivaite*. She loved the energies of the *Linga*, the male creative symbol. Coming from a highly intellectual nation such as France, she had come here to be healed from the "head," from intellectual education, and to live in her feelings. Christianity did not speak to her anymore; it had lost its meaning, its appeal, its truth. Here she had found meaning and truth, was completely in love with it, and I was thankful that she shared it with me.

> The Linga is perhaps the best known of India's aniconic images.... It is primarily in this form that Siva is worshiped in the temples of India. The Linga as it is worshiped in India today is more accurately seen as an aniconic image....
>
> The Linga consists of two parts: the vertical stone shaft, which many have seen as the male component, Siva, and the circular horizontal base, called Yoni or Pitha, which is the female component, Sakti. The wedge-shaped spout is also part of the Yoni and serves as a drain to carry away the water offerings poured upon the Linga. Together the Linga and the Pitha form the Siva-Sakti symbol of divine unity. The one who is commonly called "Siva" is seen in the Linga as both Siva and Sakti, male and female, divine spirit and divine matter, transcendent and immanent, aloof and active. In addition, the shaft of the Linga is often said to have three sections, representing Brahma, Visnu, and Siva respectively. The word Linga means "mark" or "sign," as well as "phallus," and it is in the former sense, as the sign of Siva, Mahadeva, the "Great Lord" that the Linga is honored in the Sancta of the many temples and shrines of India.[33]

In the temple, I could feel the intense energies which lived there. It was a powerful center from which the many devotees received strength and love.

---

33   Eck, *Darsan*, p. 36.

The image of a beehive came to my mind, as so many people walked around the *Linga* in a clockwise, orderly manner, or sat on cold slabs of stone in the many little niches, while performing their deeply religious absolutions, meditating, reciting mantras, or simply cleaning the inner temple when mountains of flowers accumulated as the day progressed. It was a profound experience. If one allows oneself to be non-judgmental, open, and respectful of people's diversity of beliefs, then deep mysteries come in such an opened space.

Many of the holy men gather in this holy city and one can see them lying on the ground by the river in multi-colored garb, often orange, washing their clothes and living there. So many interesting faces that speak of untold hardships, skinny bodies, long unwashed hair full of ash, eyes which look off into the distance as they walk with their sticks and tiny bundles, with not a care for this world. It is as if they have departed this world and live in another. At night one can see them lying down right next to the holy cows, some of them expressing the same contentment as the cow, quietly glimpsing paradise. Here is a story from one of those holy men:

> I regularly visited a swami near Shrinagar over a period of two years. I would serve and wait on him, but he never talked to me and he rarely opened his eyes. His name was Hari Om. For two whole years he never once looked at me. One day I told my master, "I am fed up with that swami. It's like visiting and waiting on a log of wood or a rock."
>
> My master said, "Don't say that. Although you may not be aware of it, he sees you indeed."
>
> I said: "How could he see me? His eyes are closed."
>
> That day when I went to see him, Hari Om smiled and giggled. Then he said, "Am I a log of wood or a rock? Don't you know I am in such great joy that I have no reason to open my eyes? Why should I open my eyes when I am already with that One who is the fountain of beauty and glory? The partial enjoyment which most people seek can no longer satisfy me. That is why I keep my eyes closed. You will have to open the eye of your mind to see that perennial beauty, for the senses have only a limited capacity. They perceive only the limited beauty of limited objects."
>
> I was inspired by his beautiful words. After that when I went to see him, he opened his eyes ever so slightly. When his eyes were a bit open, it

seemed as though wine were overflowing the cup. You could experience the joy flowing from within.

He muttered the Sanskrit verse, "During that which is night to others, the enlightened one keeps awake." Then he explained: "The finest hours are the hours of night, but very few know how to utilize their worth and silence. Three categories of people remain awake at night: the yogi, the Bhogi (sensualist) and the Rogi (sick person). The yogi enjoys bliss in meditation, the Bhogi enjoys sensual pleasures, and the Rogi keeps awake because of pain and misery. All three remain awake, but benefited is he who is in meditation. The Bhogi experiences momentary joy—and with a desire to expand that moment, repeats the same experience. Alas, it can never be expanded this way. In meditation real joy expands into ever-lasting peace.

"Closing the eyes unconsciously, without having any content in the mind, is sleep. Closing the eyes consciously is a part of meditation. A yogi closes his eyes and withdraws his senses from the sense perception. He remains free from the pair of opposites of pain and pleasure. Closing the eyes is for him the opening of the inner eye. Ordinary people see the objects of the world with the help of two small eyes—But do you know that my whole being has become an eye?"[34]

When observing all the holy men, one never knows who is real and who is not. There were so many sadhu that I did not feel like engaging in conversations with any of them. Many wanted money, and the others were oblivious to everything. Some were handsome young men with long dark curly locks surrounding their bronzed faces; some were middle-aged wise souls; some were very, very old with skin like parchment, and I as a woman had to respect their way of life by not being intrusive and disrespectful to them with my Western ways. So I observed them from afar, and sometimes my glance would meet theirs and much would be said without speaking, about ancient wisdom, truth and love, and a common bond would be made.

It is a heartrending experience to see human beings who basically live like the rest of the animals in the city. They have abandoned everything to discover the real world behind our sense world. They undergo much and disdainfully

---

34   Swami Rama, *Living with the Himalayan Masters*, p. 153.

disregard all our rules and regulations in order to remind us that there is another world. India has worshiped them for millennia and feeds, honors, and goes to them for advice.

Fame follows the wandering sadhu, as they are the priests, psychologists, healers, friends, doctors, and psychiatrists to the Hindu people from the very poorest person to extremely powerful men and women. They bathe every morning in the Ganges, watching the Sun rise, absorbed in their own world, which to them is the real world, the world that we all go to after we die, or before we are born.

In the hostel where I stayed, some young men always hung around trying to get money from tourists. One fifteen-year-old boy accompanied me wherever I went. I chatted with him and asked, "Why aren't you in school?" or "What do you want to study?" and so on. I accepted his offer to be my guide. He would fend off all the other children who wanted to help me, which suited me fine.

One day while I was walking through the little winding alleys by myself, I encountered a small temple just large enough for a few people and I entered. There was a young French couple there, and I sat opposite them and a large man of about forty-five, a sadhu or yogi who was being massaged by another young man. The sadhu was lying on the floor eating some kind of nice food while giving advice to the couple as they sat cross-legged before him. I sat and listened, absorbing the whole scene as they talked about diet and meditation. It was a regular little temple for the worship of Shiva, with pictures and statues, but to me it seemed a farce. The big sadhu said that he has all sorts of ashrams around India, and people from the US send him money to sponsor these places, from which his devotees dispense food to the poor and carry out other charity work. He talked on, eating and enjoying the massage. I asked myself how anyone could be gullible enough to take what this man had to say seriously. He asked me if I had questions about meditation, and I said no, my questions had been answered, but I had some questions for him about his practice. I did not need any answers at this time. But he would not consider my questions about his practice; he just wanted to tell me how to practice. In other words, he did not want to share, but to be the master yogi.

I did not need a master yogi; I hoped we could have an exchange. When he simply ignored me, I walked out. The young couple obviously thought he was great. I shared the episode with my young guide later on, and he said yes, there are many sadhu. His mother was going to that one I had visited and she liked him.

From Rudolf Steiner's book *The Boundaries of Natural Science*, I have tried to select a few words which shed more light on our Hindu sages and their practices. Some of what he says is not easy to understand, but we must try and fathom the deep mysteries behind spiritual practices.

One must become aware that in the later stages of life one can advance through self-education to a higher consciousness, just as a child can advance to the stage of ordinary consciousness. The things we sought in vain at the two boundaries of natural science, the boundaries of matter and of ordinary consciousness, reveal themselves only when one attains this higher consciousness. In ancient times, the Eastern sages spoke of such an enhanced consciousness that renders accessible to people a level of reality higher than that of everyday life; they strove to achieve a higher development...by means of an inner self-cultivation that corresponded to their racial characteristics and evolutionary stage....

If one were to characterize the path of development these sages followed, one would have to describe it as a path of Inspiration.... In ordinary consciousness, we live in our thought life, our life of feeling, and our life of will, and we initially substantiate what surges within the soul as thought, feeling, and will in the act of cognition. And it is in the interaction with percepts of the external world, with physical-sensory perceptions, that our consciousness first fully awakens.

It is necessary to realize that the Eastern sages, the so-called initiates of the East, cultivated perception, thinking, feeling, and willing in a way different from their cultivation in everyday life....

As we enter ever-greater participation in everyday life, however, something arises that initially prevents this emancipated soul and spirit from growing into the spiritual world in normal consciousness. As human beings, we must traverse the path that leads us into the external world with the requisite faculties during our life between birth and death....

What arises is threefold. These three things bring us into a proper relationship with other human beings in our environment and govern our interaction with them. These are: language, the ability to understand the thoughts of our fellow men, and the acquisition of an understanding, or even a kind of perception, of another's "I."

These three senses lead initially to interaction with the rest of humanity. In a certain way we are introduced into social life among other human beings by the possession of these three senses. The path one thus follows via these three senses, however, was followed in a different way by the ancients—especially the Indian sages—in order to attain higher knowledge. In striving for this goal of higher knowledge, the soul was not moved toward the words in such a way that one sought to arrive at an understanding of what the other was saying. The powers of the soul were not directed toward the thoughts of another person in such a way as to perceive them, nor toward the ego of another in such a way as to perceive it sympathetically. Such matters were left to everyday life. When the sage returned from his striving for higher cognition, from his sojourn in spiritual worlds to everyday life, he employed these three senses in the ordinary manner. When he wanted to exercise the method of higher cognition, however, he needed these senses in a different way. He did not allow the soul's forces to penetrate through the word while perceiving speech, in order to comprehend the other through his language; rather, he stopped short at the word itself. Nothing was sought behind the word; rather the streaming life of the soul was sent out only as far as the word. He thereby achieved an intensified perception of the word, renouncing all attempts to understand anything more by means of it. He permeated the word with his entire life of soul, using the word or succession of words in such a way that he could enter completely into the inner life of the word....

The Eastern sage in a way disregards the significance of speech, thought, and the perception of the ego. He experiences these things differently and cultivates a different attitude of soul toward these things, because language, perception of thoughts, and perception of the ego initially tend to lead us away from the spiritual world into social contact with other human beings. In everyday physical existence we purchase our social life at the price of listening right through language, looking through thoughts, and feeling our way right through the perception of the ego. The Eastern sage took upon himself not to listen right through the word, but to live within it. He took upon himself not to look right through the thought but to live within the thought, and so forth. We in the West have as our task more to contemplate man himself in following the path into suprasensory worlds.[35]

Here is a delightful story of one of these Eastern sages. In a way, it exemplifies what Steiner said:

Of all the places I have visited in my life I have found none more fascinating than Gangotri. It is a land of the Hamsas, where mountain peaks are perennially blanketed with snow. When I was young between thirty and fifty yogis lived there in small caves along both sides of the Ganges. Most of them did not wear any clothes, and some did not even use fire. For three full winters, I lived there by myself in a small cave where my brother disciple was staying. I rarely communicated with anyone. Those of us who lived there would see one another from a distance but no one disturbed anyone else; no one was interested in socializing. That was one of the most fulfilling periods of my life. I spent most of my time doing yoga practices and living on a mixture of wheat and gram. I would soak the wheat and gram, and when it germinated after two days, add in a little salt. This was the only food I took.

In a nearby cave lived a sage who was widely respected throughout India. His name was Krishnashram. One night at about twelve o'clock I was overwhelmed by a deafening sound as if many bombs were exploding. It was an avalanche, very close by. I emerged from my cave to view what had happened. It was a moonlit night and I could see the other bank of the frozen Ganges, where Krishnashram lived. When I saw where the avalanche occurred I concluded that Sri Krishnashram had been buried beneath it. I quickly put on my long Tibetan coat, took a torch, and rushed to his cave. The Ganges there is just a narrow stream, so I crossed it easily—and found that his small cave was quite safe and untouched. He was sitting there smiling.

He was not speaking at that time, so he pointed upward and said, "Hm, Hm, Hm, Hm." Then he wrote on a slate: "Nothing can harm me. I have to live for a long time. These noises, these avalanches do not

35　Steiner, *The Boundaries of Natural Science*, pp. 87–89, 91–92, 112–113 (trans. revised).

frighten me. My cave is protected." Seeing that he was unharmed and in good spirits, I returned to my cave. In the morning when I could see more clearly I found that the avalanche had come down on both sides of his cave. The tall fir trees were completely buried. Only his cave remained undamaged.

I often visited Krishnashram from two to five in the afternoon. I would ask him questions, and he would answer on the slate. His eyes glowed like two bowls of fire, and his skin was as thick as an elephant's. He was almost eighty years of age and very healthy. I wondered how he was able to live without any woolens, fire, or protection from the cold. He had no possessions at all. A swami who lived half a mile up toward Gomukh regularly brought him some food. Once a day he ate some roasted potatoes and a piece of whole wheat bread.

Everyone drank green tea mixed with an herb called Artemisia cina. The yogis and swamis whom I met taught me many things about herbs and their uses, and also discussed the scriptures with me. Those yogis did not like to come down to the plains of India. Every summer a few hundred pilgrims would visit this shrine, which is one of the highest in the Himalayas. In those days they had to walk ninety-six miles in the mountains to reach there. If anyone wants to see firsthand the power of the spirit over mind and body, he can find a few rare yogis there even today.[36]

In this beautiful story one can see how the holy Sage totally ignored the everyday world, and purposely did not speak or relate to others' thoughts or egos. He went beyond to live within, and he did not stop at the word, or thought, or abstract element, or ego, as Steiner explains. We in the West stop at the meaning of the word, stop at the thought and what it contains, and we meet the other's ego. Our brains reflect and the reflection is where we are in the West. The word has lost its power; it is abstract and separated and no longer holds any life. The Yogis go beyond; they go into life. Times have changed, and we must find other ways of practicing meditation which take us to the same goal but in a more appropriate manner, more suitable for us in the West. We also have to go into the life that is in the word, using a different approach.

---

36 Swami Rama, *Living with the Himalayan Masters*, p. 30.

Why is it that when we awake we become aware of our soul life? It is because the etheric body does not allow us actually to look within it, any more than a mirror allows us to see what is behind it, and for this very reason enables us to see *ourselves* in it. The etheric body mirrors our soul life back to us; and because it does so, it appears to us as if it were the actual cause of our soul-life. The etheric body itself, however, proves to be impenetrable. We do not penetrate into it, but it throws back to us an image of our soul life. That is its peculiarity. Mystics, however, by intensifying their soul life, succeed in penetrating to a certain extent into the etheric body. Mystics sees more than the mirrored image. By working their way into this part of the microcosm, they experience within themselves what in the normal state people experience poured over the outer world. Thus, mystics, through inner deepening, penetrate, to some extent, into the etheric body; they penetrate *below* that threshold where the soul life is, in other circumstances, reflected in joy, suffering, and so on into the interior of the etheric body. What mystics experience in passing the threshold are processes of their own etheric body.... Mystics become aware of this through the fact that they ignore the principle adopted by the ordinary ego of acting in accordance with the brain-bound intelligence and the dictates of the senses, and the impulses for their actions arise from inner feelings coming *directly* from the etheric body, and not, as happens for others, merely reflected by it. The intensely strong inner experiences of mystics arise because they penetrate right into their own etheric body.[37]

---

37   Steiner, *Macrocosm and Microcosm*, p. 26 (trans. revised).

Revisiting My Spiritual Journey

After my first Vipassana retreat, I was puzzled for a long time about the fact that my body had gone through some unwanted changes. I mentioned earlier that I felt like a stone. At this time I was staying in the little house in the Quebec woods, and one day I had to go to the bank. I picked up my checkbook to write myself a check for cash and realized that I could hardly write. I was shocked to find that my muscles were not responding, and it took enormous effort for me to write down the amount on the check.

The intensive exercises that I practiced for hours at a time had shocked my system, which was not used to it. That is the way I experienced it: a shock to my system. One could say that I jumped into the fires of the inner world in ignorance. By focusing on the breath, and then focusing on the whole body with my mind, my body was, in a way, left to itself. My soul had flown away. The following words from Steiner helped me in understanding these experiences, as did other passages I cited earlier that related to this break between the different subtle bodies.

> The brain is so constituted that the human being's inner spirit and soul element cannot pass through the brain. In his brain the human being is not filled with his spirit and soul element. Instead, external perceptions can enter and make themselves felt in the brain through the senses.... Put another way, the constitution of the brain is such today that the eternal aspect of the human being cannot rise up into it. Instead, external impressions can enter....
>
> Think how a shock affects human beings. They are as though paralysed. There can be shocks which bring about the paralysis of the whole human being. A paralyzed person, a cataleptic person, cannot move about because his muscles are rigid. But in a human being who can go about his life in the ordinary way, his body absorbs this eternal aspect. In our blood, in our muscles down below, the element of spirit and soul,

the eternal element, is absorbed. But because of this it cannot be perceived. It cannot penetrate the brain, but lower down it is absorbed. It cannot be perceived, but when the muscles go rigid it steps out freely as a matter of course.

The rigidity of the muscles was brought about by the effect of the shock. As a result, the element of spirit and soul was not absorbed by the rest of the organism—apart from the brain—but was freed. [38]

Here, Steiner compares the old initiation process with the new ones.

The essential aspect of all this, with regard to the spiritual evolution of mankind, is that in more ancient times the physical body was withdrawn from the element of spirit and soul. The working of the brain was counteracted because the brain was softened by the draught of forgetfulness, and the powers of absorption of the rest of the organism were counteracted by the hardening of the rest of the organism by means of the shock. So in these older times the body was withdrawn from the element of spirit and soul.

Today, our aspiration is not to withdraw the body but to draw out the spirit, by strengthening and enhancing our forces of spirit and soul. The opposite of what used to take place must happen now; now the spirit must be drawn out. No changes must be allowed to take place in the physical, bodily aspect. Since the fifteenth century the human being has been organized in such a way that changes in the physical body, of the kind that were customary in those of mystery pupils, would denote a condition of sickness. It would be a pathological condition, which must not be allowed to come about in normal development. [39]

Here is more about this separation of human physical/etheric bodies from the Astral body/"I" being.

People need only to be more attentive to what happens to them as they go to sleep, and they will notice how the inner activity through which they move their limbs and bring movement to the body during the day with the help of the soul begins to flag. People who practice a little self-observation when they are about to go to sleep will feel that they are no

---

38   Steiner, *Old and New Methods of Initiation*, pp. 59–61.

39   Ibid., p. 62.

longer able to exercise the same control over the body. A kind of lethargy begins to overpower them. First, they will feel unable to direct the movement of their limbs through the will; then, control of speech is lost. Next, they will feel the possibility of connecting with the outer world slipping away and all the impressions of the day gradually disappearing.... In this gradual cessation of the inner soul activity we experience our emergence from our bodily sheaths....

Mystical development does not really involve penetrating into the inner world of the physical and etheric bodies by force; rather one first makes oneself fit for the experience and passing through it consciously.[40]

Vipassana, being an ancient method of initiation, does separate the soul and spirit from the body, or in another language, separates the human physical/etheric from the Astral/"I." In this way, the body is affected because it has been abandoned. Or as Steiner explains, it does not enter by *force*, but makes a person fit for the experience by passing through it consciously. In modern times, we have new methods of initiation which are safer and leave the physical body unchanged.

I went through these deep changes of tearing my soul from the physical/ether bodies in a dramatic way. My Western body was not made to undergo such drastic changes, and it wreaked havoc in my physical body, such as becoming unable to write a check. I could not perform a simple task with my muscles and body because my soul had flown out, leaving my body behind. It seems no one had an understanding about these processes; they ignored them and accepted such phenomena as a normal part of the meditation work. I had no understanding at all and suffered the consequences of the practice.

No one in the *Dhamma* centers explained any of this as we, trusting students, prepared for a psychic operation of the mind. Explanation was simply not part of the Vipassana experience. No one really knew what was happening.

The following passage relates to this:

As a rule we cannot enter the spiritual worlds without passing through a deep upheaval in our souls. We have to experience something that

---

40   Steiner, *Macrocosm and Microcosm*, pp. 30, 48 (trans. revised).

disturbs and shakes all our forces, flooding our soul with intense feelings and sensations. Emotions that are generally spread out over many moments, over long periods of living, whose permanent effect on the soul is therefore weaker—such feelings are concentrated in a single moment and storm through us with tremendous force when we enter the esoteric worlds. Then we experience a kind of inner shattering, which can indeed be compared to fear, terror, and anxiety, as though we were shrinking back from something in horror. Such experiences belong to the initial stages of esoteric development, to entering the spiritual worlds. Just for this reason, great care must be taken to give the right advice to those who would enter the spiritual worlds through esoteric training. We must be prepared so that we may experience this upheaval as a necessary event in our soul life without its encroaching on our bodily life and health, and insofar as the body is included, it must suffer a like upheaval. That is the essential thing. We must learn to suffer the convulsions of our soul with outward equanimity and calm.

This is true not only for our bodily processes. The soul forces we need for everyday living, our ordinary intellectual powers, even those of imagination, of feeling and will—these, too, must not be allowed to become unbalanced. The upheaval that may be the starting point for esoteric life must take place in far deeper layers of the soul, so that we go through our external life as before, without anything being noticed in us outwardly, while within we may be living through whole worlds of shattering soul experience. That is what it means to be ripe for esoteric development: to be able to experience such inward convulsions without losing one's outer balance and calm. To this end, those striving to become ripe for esoteric development must widen the circle of their interests beyond everyday life. They must get away from the things which otherwise keep us going from morning to night and reach out to interests that move on the great horizon of the world.[41]

One must read and reread these passages and meditate on them; then a clearer understanding will arise. I can speak only of the processes and my experiences. Readers must enter these phenomena deeply and gain their own understanding, so that it becomes part of themselves.

---

41   Steiner, *Bhagavad Gita and the West*, pp. 112–113.

By concentrating on what happened during my first retreat and focusing on some of the experiences that came to me, we will try to understand how these experiences were born. I will quote the work of Rudolf Steiner again extensively, because to my knowledge this great initiate is the only modern individual who has explained this topic thoroughly and with utmost clarity—nothing dreamy or lost in feelings here. How I remember my experiences is part of who I am, and how I translate them into words is also part of who I am. However, the experiences in themselves are common to anyone who goes through such spiritual practice. My own insights into my experiences arise from studying Anthroposophy, and many may disagree with them, but I can work only with what I experience myself. Others who have more insights than mine must write about their experiences themselves. When one goes through initiatory experiences, it does not necessarily mean that one is an initiate; it means only that one has embarked upon a very long path.

The following words pertain to karma and bring clarity to these mysteries.

To one who surveys the development of humankind with the eye of a seer, this does not appear as it does to a historian—as a level path, at most overtopped a bit here and there by figures accepted as historical. People will not acknowledge that spiritual peaks and mountains exist; it is more than they can bear. But seers know that there are lofty heights and mountains towering above the path for the rest of humankind; such seers are the leaders of humanity. Upon what is such leadership based? It is based on human beings gradually passing through the levels that lead to life in the spiritual world. We pointed out one of those levels...as the most important one—the birth of the higher self, the spiritual "I."... It is evident that what we call the Christ event is the grandest peak in the range of human evolution, and that a long preparation was indispensable before the Christ Being could incarnate in Jesus of Nazareth.

To understand that preparation, we must visualize the same phenomenon on a smaller scale. Let us suppose that a man starts on the path to spiritual cognition in any one of his incarnations—that is, he practices some of the exercises...which render the soul increasingly spiritual, more receptive to what is spiritual, and guide it toward the moment when it bears the higher, imperishable "I" that can see into the spiritual world. A human being undergoes many experiences before that moment arrives. We must not imagine that anything pertaining to the spirit can be rushed, but must be passed through with patience and perseverance. Suppose, then, that a man starts a training of this kind. His aim is the birth of the higher "I," but he succeed only in reaching a certain preliminary stage and then dies. Then, in due time, he is born again. At this point, one of two things can happen; either he can feel an urge to seek out a teacher who will show him how he can rapidly repeat what he had previously passed through and attain the higher stages, or, for one reason or another, he does not take this path. In the second case, too, his life will often unfold in a way different from that of the lives of others. The life of one who has already gone through some part of the path of enlightenment will, of itself, provide something resembling effects of the level of perception he had attained in the previous incarnation. He will have experiences of a different nature, and the impression of these on him will be different from that received by others. Then, he will attain anew, by means of these experiences, what he had achieved previously through his efforts. In his former incarnation, he had to strive actively from step to step; but now that life brings him what he had once acquired through effort as a recurrence, so to speak. This approaches him from without, as it were, and it may be that he will experience the results of his previous incarnations in quite a different form.

Thus, it may happen that, even as a child, some experience can make an impression upon his soul in such a way as to newly engender the forces he had acquired in his previous life. Suppose such a person had attained a certain degree of wisdom in a given incarnation. One is then born again as a child, like everyone else. At the age of seven or eight, however, a painful experience occurs, with the consequence that all the wisdom previously experienced returns to the foreground; one regains the stage reached before, and thus can advance to the next stage. Now we will imagine further that such a person tries to proceed another few steps, and again dies. In the next incarnation, the same thing can happen again, and once more some outer experiences can put that person to the test, as it were, again revealing first, what had been achieved in that earlier incarnation, and then in the one immediately previous. And now one can climb another step.[42]

---

42 Steiner, *The Gospel of St. John and its Relation to the Other Gospels*, pp. 29–31 (trans. revised).

Rudolf Steiner said that the difference between an initiate-seer and ordinary people is greater than that between an ape and a human being. This puts the beginner on the path in the correct perspective.

In the pages that follow, I will discuss my experiences once again, this time in light of the wisdom I subsequently gleaned from Rudolf Steiner's work. Here is a review of the aspects of my experiences that I will highlight in the pages to come:

SOUL EXPERIENCES:

1. the opening at the top of the head—day experience
2. the opening of the unconscious—night experience
3. tableaux experience—pictures like a film going by, one after the other
4. ladder experience—12 steps up—level of consciousness
5. Mary scene
6. dove scene
7. birth—taste of the eternal
8. transformation of light and dark within
9. meeting ahrimanic beings in car
10. death of body, lower self—birth of higher self

PHYSICAL MANIFESTATIONS:

11. word—language spoken to Haitians
12. physical numbness, loss of control over muscle activity such as writing (already mentioned)

Regarding my first soul experience, after three days of the intensive practice of focusing at the nostrils, Goenka asked us to bring our focused attention slowly and deliberately to the top of the head, and taught us the practice of Vipassana, insight meditation.

Using Steiner's insight, here is a description of what the meditation had prepared us for, when we all focused our attention on the top of our heads.

We begin with simple exercises, above all those designed to deepen and spiritualize our powers of reasoning and understanding. Such exercises render our thinking free and independent of all sense impressions and experiences. We concentrate our thinking in one point, so to speak, over which we then have complete control. In the process a temporary center is created for the currents of the ether body. In other words, initially the central point is not located near the heart, but in the head. Seers can perceive it there as the starting point of the above-mentioned etheric movements.

Only an esoteric training that begins by creating this temporary center in the head can be completely successful. If we were to develop the center near the heart immediately, we would certainly still gain a glimpse into the higher worlds at the early stages of clairvoyance, but we would have no true insight into the connection between these higher worlds and the material world of the senses. It is absolutely essential, however that human beings at the present stage of world evolution understand this connection. As seers, we must not become dreamers: we must always keep both feet firmly on the ground.

Once the temporary center in the head has been properly stabilized, further practice of the concentration exercises transfers it downward, into the vicinity of the larynx. The movements and currents of the ether body then spread out from there, illuminating the soul space around us.

Further practice of these exercises will enable us to determine the position of the ether body for ourselves. Before entering esoteric training, the position of the ether body depended upon forces coming from outside and from the physical body. But, as we advance successfully in our development, we become able to turn the ether body in all directions, using the currents that flow roughly parallel to the hands and whose center lies in the two-petalled lotus flower near the eyes. This is possible because the currents flowing from the larynx form rounded shapes, some of which flow toward the two-petalled lotus flower and thence continue on as wave-like currents along the hands.

These currents then ramify and branch out in the most delicate way to form a kind of net. This becomes a sort of membranous network at the boundary of the ether body. Before we began practicing, the ether body was not enclosed. The currents of life flowed in and out from the universal ocean of life directly and unhindered. Now, however, all influences from the outside have to pass through this thin web or skin. *As a result we become sensitive to these outer currents and begin to perceive them.*[43]

---

43   Steiner, *How to Know Higher Worlds*, pp. 134–136 (italics added).

After we had practiced the Vipassana with focused attention through the whole body, experienced the currents going through the body and the awakening of chakra centers for ten days, we were told to practice *metta* (loving kindness), in which we sent loving thoughts from the heart to all. Here again are Steiner's deeply moving words:

> The time has now come to give this complex system of currents and movements a center near the heart. This is done by continuing the concentration and meditation exercises. At the same time, this moment marks the stage of our development at which we receive the gift of the "inner word." Henceforth, all things have a new sense and meaning for us. They become, as it were, spiritually audible to us in their inmost essence; they speak to us of their true nature. What happens is that the currents described above put us in touch with the inner life of the cosmos to which we belong. We begin to participate in the life around us and let this life reverberate in the movements of our lotus flowers.
>
> With this, we enter the world of spirit. We become able to understand the words of the great teachers of humanity in a new way. The Buddha's sermons or the Gospels, for example, work upon us in a completely new way. They stream through us, permeating us with a bliss we never imagined before, for the melody of their words harmonizes with the movements and rhythms we have formed within ourselves. Now we can know directly that beings such as the Buddha or the writers of the Gospels do not voice their own revelations but only what flows into them from the innermost essence of things....
>
> Many educated people today find the repetitions in the Buddha's discourses difficult to understand. But once we embark upon the esoteric path we learn to enjoy dwelling on these repetitions with our inner senses. For these repetitions correspond to certain rhythmical movements in the etheric body. And when we surrender to the repetitions in perfect inner peace, our inner movements blend harmoniously with them. When we listen to the word melodies of the Buddha's teaching, our life becomes infused with the secrets of the universe.[44]

During the whole retreat, we were bathing in Buddhist scriptures recited in Pali, which, as I mentioned, were a lifesaver for me in my bewilderment.

---

44   Ibid., pp. 136–137.

They felt comfortable, a point of reference (along with the continuous exercises) in otherwise very unsettling circumstances.

If I had known what I was actually going to be doing, I would have run away. My naïve trust and thirst for knowledge led me to the practice. The atmosphere of the retreat was always very somber, and no one from the public was allowed on the premises once the course began. It was shut off from the outside world, just like the ancient practices in the old Mystery centers.

> An atmosphere had to be created that did not exist anywhere in the outer world. That atmosphere in which the *mystai* could breathe was to be found in the temples of the mysteries. There took place the awakening of the slumbering powers within, and metamorphosis into a higher, creative and spiritual being. The transformation of the *mystai* was a delicate process, unfitted to the harsh light of common day. But if they stood the test, they became a rock founded on the eternal, defying all life's storms. They had simply to accept, however, that they could not communicate directly to others what they had been through on the way.[45]

Goenka always compared the courses to a hospital; when meditants did not feel like going home and preferred to remain in the cocoon, he reminded them that one does not stay in the hospital forever. After having undergone the psychic operation, which is what came to my mind when the experience arose during the night of the opening of the unconscious, I was very enthusiastic. This was what I wanted to do myself—to be trained so that I could do it, too, to help others; but my body had other plans.

During that very special moment when we gently and slowly focused on the top of the head under the master's direction, I was literally thrown out of my body, hanging in a non-spatial dimension. The hall filled with 300 people was "breathless," quiet beyond quiet. That night, the opening became the entrance into the unconscious mind, or entrance to the land of the shades, the underworld, a world full of indescribable happenings. The lid had come off, and boiling instincts emerged, infused with sharply focused attention. But I observed it all with equanimity.

---

45   Steiner, *Christianity as Mystical Fact*, p. 11.

In testimony of what happened to them in the mysteries, we have the account of the initiates themselves. Menippus relates how he traveled to Babylon to be taken to Hades and brought back by the followers of Zoroaster. He says that, in the course of his wanderings, he crossed the great water, and that he passed through fire and ice. We hear that the *mystai* were struck with terror by a drawn sword, that blood was caused to flow. Such words are made intelligible by a knowledge of the stages leading from lower to higher cognition. It does indeed feel as though everything solidly material and perceptible has dissolved into water. The ground is taken from beneath us. Everything living has been put to death. The spirit has cut through the life of the senses like a sword through the living flesh; we have seen the blood of sensuality flow.

But life springs up anew. The initiate reascends from the Underworld....

Everyone who lives only in the world of the senses bears this spirit occultly, deep within. Everyone who has pierced through the illusion of the sense-world bears the spirit within as a manifest truth.[46]

Of course, Goenka, who knew the deep sacredness of his work, at the end of the course had great compassion for all of us for what he had "performed" or started. His warm, loving voice asking for our forgiveness went straight to my heart. I knew what he was asking forgiveness for.

That is why to speak of the mysteries is at the same time to tell of dangers. Is not leading someone to the door of the Underworld mean robbing that person of happiness, of the very meaning of life? A terrible responsibility is incurred by such an act. And yet the initiates had to consider whether they could shirk that responsibility. They considered their knowledge to be related to the ordinary soul life of the people as light to darkness. An innocent happiness is contained in that darkness, with which the *mystai* would not wantonly interfere. Indeed, what would be the result if the *mystai* betrayed their secret? Their words would have been just that—empty words. The experiences and emotions needed to evoke the shock of the spirit out of the words would have been lacking without the preparation, the exercises, and ordeals, the total transformation of perceptual life. Lacking this, anyone who

---

46 Ibid., pp. 5, 9.

heard would be thrown into emptiness, nothingness, deprived of happiness but receiving nothing in return. In reality, of course, nothing could be taken away. After all, empty words have no power to alter our experience of life. Actual experience would still be limited to feeling, mediated by the senses. Nothing could come to such a person except a terrifying, paralyzing uncertainty—which it would be criminal to impart. This is no longer completely valid for the attainment of spirit knowledge today. Such knowledge can be conceptually understood because modern human beings have a conceptual ability that ancient humanity lacked. Today one can find human beings who have knowledge of the spiritual world through their own experience; and others they meet can understand conceptually what they have experienced....

A God comes to meet you—either it is everything, or nothing; nothing if you make the encounter in the spirit of the humdrum tasks of life, everything if you are duly prepared and attuned to the experience. As to what it may be in itself, that does not concern you; what matters is whether it leaves you as it found you or changes you. And that depends entirely on you. Training and development, both intimate and intensive, must have prepared the person so that the encounter with the god may kindle and release the powers within. What you receive in the encounter depends on what you bring to meet it.[47]

Vipassana, again, means "insight meditation."

To attain insight is to unfold a new organ, an event comparable to a plant unfolding the color of its blossom out of its former green and leafy state. The ability to produce flowers was always there in the plant, but it was hidden, and became manifest only with the blooming of the flower. Even so, the divine spiritual forces lie hidden within sense-dominated human beings, and become manifest truth for the first time in the *mystes*. That is the nature of the Mystery "transformation."

Through inner development, the *mystai* bring to the world, as it formerly existed, something radically new. The world order known to the senses had formed them as natural human beings, and then abandoned them. Nature's role is then fulfilled, and her deployment of creative forces in humanity comes to an end. But the forces in humanity are

---

47   Ibid., pp. 6, 7 (trans. revised).

not themselves exhausted. They lie as though *spellbound in the natural human being and await their release*. Unable to release themselves, they ebb away unless human beings take hold of them and transform them—unless they awaken to real existence their hidden potentiality.[48]

As I mentioned before, after the retreat, I spent a few days with other participants in a small cabin deep in the woods of Quebec, where we all tried to reenter the rough world of the senses. It was not easy.

During the night my body was sleeping, but I was not. I was having more experiences. One of them was a series of "tableaux," or pictures, emerging as a kind of film, one after the other, many of them Christian from the life of Christ, the Virgin, and others. I do not recall them now; they are vague images in my mind, and I lost all my notes. But these poignant experiences, these pictures flowing in my consciousness, were as clear as daylight at the time.

Human beings strive for occult knowledge and may attain it through their human faculties. But occult knowledge has a greater significance for the world than it has merely within the human soul. In the world around us, we can distinguish various substances and materials, through which its various phenomena and manifestations are expressed. All creatures and things of the Earth and of all worlds are rooted in that primal principle that can hardly be expressed in human language. In the physical world, individual instances of this primal principle are expressed in the substances of earth, water, fire, the ether, and so on.

One of the subtlest substances accessible to human efforts is called "akasha." Beings and phenomena manifested in the akashic substance are the subtlest of all those accessible to human beings. What people acquire for themselves in esoteric knowledge not only lives in their souls but is also impressed in the akashic substance. When we bring an idea from esoteric science to life in our soul, it is immediately inscribed in the akashic substance. It is significant that such impressions, which are significant for the general development of the world, can be inscribed in the akasha only by human beings.

It is important for us to note a special characteristic of the akashic substance. Between death and a new birth, human beings live in that

---

48   Ibid., p. 9 (italics added).

substance, exactly as we, for example, live here within the atmosphere on Earth.[49]

The tableaux experience ended and left me in a questioning state: What is this that I am experiencing? Is this my life or something else? It was a puzzle for my logical, intellectual mind to grasp. As Goenka told us, however, let all these experiences go and do not form any attachments to any of them. So I did as he suggested and left them hidden until Anthroposophy shed some light on what I had experienced within my soul.

I also went through something I call the "ladder" experience. I concentrated somewhere in the deeper recesses, in the middle of my mind, and discovered a ladder, which meant for me different states of consciousness. Twelve is a number I remember. Going up the ladder was going through different levels of consciousness by concentrating. I understood the ladder, but the different states of consciousness I did not understand at all—only the fact that there was a higher and a lower and I could move my attention from one level to the next, though only in the lower levels. I am reminded of Dionysus the Aeropagite, the student of Paul who writes about the hierarchies beyond humankind.

> So that God can enter us, we find an organ by drawing a vertical line from the mid-point of the head through the brain, and another line (horizontal) from the "I"-point at the root of the nose backward. Where these two lines intersect we find the pineal gland.
>
> The human being comes into contact with God himself through this organ.[50]

I experienced this ladder, which exists at that point, the pineal gland, but could not make head nor tail of exactly what I was doing and experiencing until I read the work of Rudolf Steiner.

The other experience that stands out in my mind was when I was having breakfast early one morning after having spent a night without sleeping in a hotel and waiting for my ride to Montreal. I was sitting quietly, simply

---

49   Steiner, *Approaching the Mystery of Golgotha*, p. 2 (trans. revised).

50   Steiner, *Esoteric Lessons, 1904–1909*, p. 112.

eating my breakfast, and some québecquois men who were sitting together were staring at me, saying sarcastically in French, "Here comes the Virgin Mary." I was stunned and wanted to disappear into a corner like a mouse. I left quickly and was very upset with what I saw as the cruelty of men's astral bodies, their lower needs to attack, and the fact that I had to reenter the crude world. They were living in their lower selves, while I had risen to other states of consciousness, and the only way they could experience that was by snickering in a nasty way, comparing me to Mary, Mother of God. Something within them could discern a change deep within me that I was not aware of myself.

> The third stage is the crowning with thorns. This experience tells us that we should not lose our inner firmness, our inner balance, even when we encounter great pain, even when our most sacred feelings and convictions are persecuted with derision and mockery. Symptoms of this stage include aches and pains in the head and a vision of one's self with a crown of thorns on the head.[51]

This experience was brought upon me because I had worked so fervently on my "astral" feeling body in order to purify it, by following the stringent rules during the course which I spelled out at the beginning of the book and, of course, by doing the exercises.

> The farther we advance in soul development, the more regularly structured our soul organism becomes. This organism remains confused and unstructured in a person whose soul life is still undeveloped. Yet, even in such an unstructured soul organism, a clairvoyant can still see a form that stands out clearly from its surroundings. The form extends from the inside of the head to the middle of the physical body. To the clairvoyant it looks like an independent body, containing certain organs. These organs...may be seen spiritually in the following areas of the physical body: the first, between the eyes; the second, near the larynx; the third, in the region of the heart; the fourth, in the neighborhood of the pit of the stomach; and the fifth and the sixth, in the lower abdomen, or reproductive region....

---

51 Steiner, *The Christian Mystery*, p. 130.

Because they resemble wheels or flowers, esotericists call these formations *chakras* (wheels) or "lotus flowers."...

One of the first things to occur when an esoteric student begins practicing the exercises is that the light of the lotus flowers intensifies; later the flowers will also begin to rotate. When this happens, it means that a person is beginning to have the ability to see clairvoyantly. These "flowers" are the sense organs of the soul. Their rotation indicates that we are able to perceive the suprasensory realm.[52]

In earlier centuries, I would have been in a convent, but this was the twentieth century, without the protection of churches, monasteries, and other such institutions. Even then, as now, we must do it all ourselves the best we can. I was in Sherbrooke, Quebec, sitting on a footstool, stared at by Catholic québecquois men.

No one is allowed to imagine that he or she is good—as if we could even do that, as if we could do that for even a moment—or that he or she is much better than other people. We must be completely filled with the thought that we cannot be much better than another. What have we done, for example, if we make people happy while at the same time, because we live the way we live, we are making many unhappy? Ignorance is the root of suffering in life. We are ignorant, as is so often the case, that we have sharpened the knife for those who use it for evil.

Only the strong are able to kill it. The weak, however, must wait their growth, their maturation, their death....

In the course of human evolution the external world around us will become increasingly hostile. Increasingly you must learn to set your inner power against the world pressing in on you. But in so doing, fear must disappear. And especially for those who are undergoing an esoteric training it is necessary, unavoidably necessary, that they free themselves from all anxiety and feelings of fear. Fear has a certain justification only when it makes us aware that we should make ourselves strong; but all of the unnatural feelings of fear that torture people must disappear completely. What would happen if human beings still had feelings of anxiety and fear, and Jupiter consciousness arrived? Then the external world would be set opposite the human being in a much more hostile and terrible way. A

---

52   Steiner, *How to Know Higher Worlds*, pp. 109–111.

human being who does not cease to fear here will fall into one frightening horror after another there.[53]

When I spoke to the group of Haitians outside the bus station, I was as surprised as they were to be understood. That experience, too, I left buried for awhile and have since gained some understanding of that surprising phenomenon. I know the answer deep within, but I must put it into words. I quote Georg Kühlewind, who came to my rescue in trying to grasp this mystery. When I first started participating in Georg's meditation group, I was very often unwilling to speak, as words did not come to me easily. I preferred to say nothing and just listen to others. I still do not speak much, and must force myself to voice my opinion. So I asked Georg, "Why must I speak? Why must I voice my opinion? I understand, isn't that enough?" He replied, "When you speak, or try to articulate something from deep within, you are Christianizing, spiritualizing the word, and that is very important for the world." How did I imitate the language so well that the Haitians understood me? I spoke the language unconsciously, but I was perfectly conscious of speaking in a foreign language I had never spoken before. I was perfectly aware of this mysterious capacity.

> In the speech acquisition of children we have come to know a new quality of consciousness. It might be called a superconscious ability, for the ability to speak grammatically with proper syntax, to mimic words and sounds as they are heard, and to understand wordlessly what has been said is definitely a faculty, a capacity, an *ability*, and not a *knowledge*. Words only play a role in understanding after they have already been understood themselves....
>
> The term *superconscious*, therefore, is appropriate. The superconscious is always an ability, a capacity, not a habit.[54]

Note that in the next quote, Georg Kühlewind refers to "the separating robe." Robe means the habits, dependencies, passions, and egoism from the "flesh" as the source of sins, or, in other words, what makes up the lower self.

---

53 Steiner, *Esoteric Lessons, 1904–1909*, pp. 13, 246.

54 Kühlewind, *From Normal to Healthy*, p. 29.

From the preceding chapters, we can see that in the absence of the separating robe, or if it were not to develop at all, human beings would live in a consciousness common to all. This is evident in small children, as well as in archaic people who, as reports indicate, can communicate among themselves at a distance without signs. In the Bible, the cessation of this ability is portrayed in the story of the Tower of Babel. Silent, signless communication, directed by the attention—ceases, and there remains only the languages of the different peoples, which were already present (Genesis 10) but through which the various peoples could not understand one another.

The original signless (or "direct") communication is even active today, behind our words and signs. Words can never be unambiguous. . . . What allows for mutual understanding is "good will," or "feeling connected," or "you already know what I mean"—in short, the realm of intuitive, common meaning in which the higher self always lives.

Through the temporary dissolution of what separates us, which is called "freedom from sins" or "faith," the sick person, or a representative, gets lifted into the realm of signless understanding, where the Healer is also present. The primary state, still untouched by errors, is reproduced for a time. People then live in their higher being, independent of the lower being, and are therefore capable, with the Lord's help, to have a healing effect on this lower being. . . .

To a limited, partial extent, the higher being has an effect on all the communicative activities of the body, above all in speaking. The movement of the speech organs, the emergence of speech intention (still superlinguistic), the finding of the corresponding words and the manner of expression—all these are supraconscious, i.e., the being or the activity of the higher self.[55]

To grasp this mystery, we can go even further and meditate on these words about meaning and ultimate communication by Rudolf Steiner as quoted by Georg Kühlewind:

Outwardly, Jesus Christ had to express himself in the language of those who were listening to him. But what he had before his soul in the way of an inward word did not correspond to the way words in a

---

55 Kühlewind, *Wilt Thou be Made Whole?*, pp. 48, 49.

language are formed outwardly. Rather, it had within it the lost power of the Word, the undifferentiated power of speech. We need to form an idea of this power, which is independent of the various differentiated languages, and which lives in a human being when the Word completely permeates our spirit. Otherwise we cannot rise to the level of the power that lived in Christ, nor can we know what it means to speak of Christ as the "Word." It was with this that he had completely identified, and it was through this that he worked when he did his healings and cast out demons. This Word had to be lost, as part of human evolution since the Mystery of Golgotha. But now the Word has to be sought again. For the moment, however, we are in a period of development in which it does not seem likely that we will find our way back to it.[56]

These words are helpful to me as I again recall this incredible experience and try to live in its meaning.

The next experience that stands out in my mind is the frustration of feeling rushed, everyone rushing everywhere. I had slowed down my system, and the rapidity of life was painful. I was outside by the sidewalk where others were sitting because it was a warm day, and a young girl saw my deep frustration and told me to look at the dove that was on the ground. I did and I felt peace as understanding came over me and the dove gave some tranquility to my soul. In Christian esotericism, the dove is the sign of the Holy Spirit. The young girl was like a guardian angel, giving me a sign that all was well, that I did not have to worry about anything. Then I went back inside the station and sat down quietly on the white plastic chair, sinking into deep meditation. It is bewildering to think that some of my deepest spiritual, heart-wrenching experiences happened in broad daylight, sitting on a white plastic chair in the busiest bus terminal in Montreal, one of the largest cities in North America. The name has significance, even if the rest does not.

To shed light on this experience, I again draw upon Rudolf Steiner, speaking about the forces that make up the human being.

---

56 Steiner, *Building Stones for an Understanding of the Mystery of Golgotha*, quoted in Kühlewind, *Wilt Thou be Made Whole?*, pp. 91–92.

During the course of Earth's evolution, the forces of the hierarchies penetrated into humankind from below; those forces that, particularly during the Lemurian epoch but continuing also afterward, streamed into human beings and cooperated in their formation. These forces are recognized by conventional science, as well as by spiritual science, as in their nature working through the Earth. Everywhere on the Earth's surface, wherever one goes, these forces are present....

The influences that resulted in the lion species did not begin to work on the Earth until the approach of the Atlantean time and during that time, and these influences reached Earth as if driven outward from its center toward its surface. But the influences active during the Lemurian time—and that also affected human beings—are connected with what worked as formative forces on our ruminants, influences that esotericism summarizes as the influence of the *bull*. All this began at that time to exercise an influence upon human beings, working into their formation as if from the depths of the Earth toward its surface.

You must not be shocked when I say that, if nothing else had worked upon human beings, they would have resembled the bull in their external form.... But, little by little, other forces working from within the Earth outward laid hold of the human organization.... In esotericism, these influences are summarized with the name *lion*. These forces enter Earth's evolution somewhat later. If the earlier forces had not been present, if only those forces had worked on human beings, their appearance would have resembled that of the lion.

The forces that were now to unite with these came from without, from the periphery....

We can point to certain creatures in our environment upon which the bull forces and the lion forces from within the Earth have little influence—on the contrary upon which the forces working into the substance of the Earth from cosmic space are almost exclusively active. They are the creatures belonging to the bird kingdom.... In the case of all creatures in which reproduction takes place in this way, but especially in members of the bird kingdom, forces streaming in from cosmic space are predominantly at work. In esotericism, these forces are comprised under the name *eagle*....

In the case of mammals, wherever we turn our clairvoyant gaze, we find the astral body very strongly developed, but in the case of the birds the most outstanding feature that meets the clairvoyant eye is the etheric body. For example, it is the etheric body, stimulated by cosmic forces coming in from space that brings to expression the feathers, the plumage. The plumage is formed from without, and a feather can manifest only because the forces that work down upon the Earth from cosmic space are stronger than the forces coming from the Earth....

It is quite different for creatures covered with hair. Forces working upward from the Earth, forces working in the opposite direction from those in the feathers of the birds, are predominantly at work in hair, and hair cannot become feathers, because in the case of animals and human beings, forces coming from cosmic space affect their hair very little.... If we take such paradoxes seriously, we discover certain fundamental secrets in the constitution of our world.

What streamed into the subconscious from cosmic space since the time of Atlantis, even into its baser elements, now at the Baptism by John in the Jordan had begun to flow into humankind's higher, more purified parts. That is a most significant event. These forces from cosmic space, which since the time of Atlantis have worked continuously upon the formation of the Earth and of humanity, began to stream in the purest way not only into the unconscious part of the human being, but in such a way that they can influence consciousness. That is why a pictorial image, one of the great symbols that have come down to us through occult and religious scriptures—the symbol of the dove that we find in the Gospels—had to appear....

That this cosmic stream should flow into the conscious part of the human being is essential to the perfection of humanity upon the Earth. In the picture of Jesus of Nazareth on the banks of the Jordan, with the dove hovering over him, we have in fact the expression of the Mystery that had now been brought to a certain conclusion.

Why was this cosmic influx able to transform itself into that Christic power, the Christ impulse that, as it continues to work further upon the Earth, will permeate the human being completely? As human beings inwardly receive this impulse, we will increasingly feel the truth of St. Paul's words "Not I, but Christ in me." In contrast to the other three currents that were present as the outcome of earlier evolution, this new influence, which is the purest stream from above, will take hold of human beings, will encompass them to a greater and greater extent, and will liberate them increasingly from what binds them to the Earth.[57]

The appearance of this Dove working peacefully on my soul has been an incredible meditation for me all these years. Looking at it from another perspective, if we do not have the influence of this dove-Christ power, what are we going to become? When we go deeply into the meditation, we realize that there is no time to waste, if we are to transform and work on ourselves. Who do we want to become? Who do we allow to influence us?

Georg Kühlewind's book *From Normal to Healthy* presents a clear masterful analysis of what influences us and how we can separate ourselves from these unwanted "energies," or influences.

> The human attempt to experience one's inner mental activity leads us in two directions, each of which brings us to the border of our field of consciousness. In the direction of the sources of our abilities, we come to the region we called the superconscious. And if we examine our power over our own conscious life—what we can and cannot do—we come very soon to a limit where it is clear that autonomous habits, passions, and impulses work themselves into consciousness and often have a determinative influence there. These influences are felt as either desirable or undesirable and this feeling can switch back and forth with regard to a single impulse. But in each case, consciousness has to admit: "There is nothing I can do about it," or in other words, "It is not I who wills it."
>
> It is apparent without further comment that all our mental problems stem from this region. It is harder to realize that the antidote, the solution to the problems, must come from the other side, from the superconscious. We must cultivate these superconscious powers and so shift our conscious life in the direction of liveliness and presence. This is to enrich its abilities, its power. To substantiate this insight, we will now consider the formation and the origin of the subconscious.
>
> Small children have no mental habits and are not egotistical: the feeling of an "I" arises when they begin to address their physical bodies as "I." The process of learning to speak and think reveals a subsequently

---

57 Steiner, *Wonders of the World, Ordeals of the Soul, Revelations of the Spirit*, pp. 154–156, 160. (trans. revised).

forgotten facility for attention that makes possible the first, wordless understanding. It also reveals the independence of this capacity for speaking and understanding from corporeality. Corporeality is inherited. But heredity has nothing to do with learning to speak and therefore, with learning to think. Any child can learn any language with equal facility.... This is highly significant, because speaking is a physiological as well as mental event: the speech organs themselves are subject to heredity, but their functioning is not. From this we may conclude that the forces or energies needed for functioning and for imitating are *free energies....*

The "I"-oriented free energies are word energies: they serve not only talking and thinking, but also cognition, creation, and everything in the realm of the word....

Because a human being is an "I"-being, we have command, from the very start, over *free, superfluous energies*. As an "I"-being, we have no finished form; we are teachable, not simply trainable, and we can determine our own course. Therefore reality does not have the same predetermined effect on us that it has on animals, which behave according to type; they react to the environment and to circumstances. Human beings do not react, if we are behaving in *human* fashion, instead, we perceive, consider, and decide. In animals, "perception" (not perception in the human sense) leads seamlessly into "action" (not action in the human sense). We can *think* after perceiving. In general, we do not *have* to; we *can*, because we have superfluous energies with which to cognize and make new beginnings.

Because we have no completely formed, closed-off character, because we have free energies, we are also faced with the problem of what to do with those energies that increase throughout life. In other words, what that part of reality we do not consciously perceive will do with *us*. This problem was solved by early humankind through traditional paths, cults, religions, membership in communities—for example, the initiatic rites through which youths were accepted into the society of adults. The superfluous energies were not felt as *one's own*; there was no sense that one produced one's own thoughts, and apart from a few chosen ones, no one said (and no one could say) "I think" or even "I." Energies for thinking and cognizing were felt to be superhuman or divine. Therefore, they could be kept under control by "religion," which pulsed through all lived experience. The energies themselves *were* the reality of religion, which was not something special alongside the reality of life, but was the very kernel of reality. In the age of the consciousness soul, in which we now live, nearly everything traditional that could be effective as a means of controlling this problem has been lost. Human beings say "I," "I think"; we have to deal with our free energies on our own. Or we could say that we carry the responsibility for the effects of the world energies that stream toward us, of which we are not conscious.[58]

The "I" gives; the ego takes.

Egoism is not only socially destructive, but also a disease for the individual. Human beings have the use of free word energies. It would be healthy for us to use these *as* word energies—that is, a healthy life would be a creative life. Not everyone has to be a poet, sculptor, or scientist; everyone who radiates peace and warmth or love and evokes these qualities in others is creative....

Egoism means that our attention is divided; a large portion is directed toward oneself, to the effect and consequences of one's activity, and not toward the activity itself, the matter at hand. Stage fright is a typical symptom; artists or lecturers are concerned with themselves—will it go well? Will it be a success?—and not with the work itself. For this very reason, the work fares badly, as well. Creativity is possible only in a state of concentration—loose and not cramped but concentrated. Everything that disturbs one's concentration detracts from creativity. Awareness is us ourselves; it is the "I." If we are concerned with ourselves, as in egoism, we cannot realize our healthy, creative existence. Creation is a pleasure, the greatest of all pleasures.

Egoism always has pretensions, desires, and longings. These repeat themselves and do not really want to be satisfied permanently. Desire itself is a confirmation that I exist, and every normal feeling, even feelings of suffering, are self-confirmations. We would rather suffer than have no feelings at all. Unsatisfied desires seem bad to us, but satisfaction when it comes lasts, at best, only a short time, and it is really *meant* to last only a short time. The repetitive nature of desires, the attachment to one form of sensation, shows how *unword-like* they are; they seek

---

58 Kühlewind, *From Normal to Healthy*, pp. 63-64, 67, 69–70 (trans. revised).

nothing new (a bar of chocolate always offers the same taste). Repetitive compulsion shows what is animal-like in human beings (animals themselves have no harmful desires)....

Subconscious (unaware)	Superconscious (aware)
finished	unfinished
habit	capacity
repetition	improvisation
preformed	form-free
association	thinking
emotion	feeling
instinct	I will it

The left-hand column plays a far greater role in human life than does the right-hand column. Yet, all that is specifically human is to be found in the right-hand column.[59]

These are the words of a true Master.

We took this long detour to explain the magnificent encounter with the dove, but many secrets live in that experience. Knowing about the lion, the bull, and the eagle added to my understanding of the forces that make up our selves. The gentle energies of the dove symbolize the higher self and are the freed energies of which Kühlewind speaks, the creative energies that raise us above the animal world of instincts.

A while later, yet another bewildering experience came upon me. I entered another state of consciousness in which all was light—not ordinary light but a substantial, spiritual light both peaceful and unearthly. I do not know how long I remained there, probably a split second in earthly time, but it offered a taste of eternity. I was perfectly conscious of where I was, what I had entered. I felt a great deal of peace and a general lack of concern. I observed this timeless, nonspatial experience, and when it was over I glanced at the date posted on a

---

59 Ibid., pp. 72–73, 79.

board and said with complete conviction to myself, "This is the first day of my new life; I am born right now." My logical, intellectual mind was still working, and it asked how that could be. "This is not year zero; this is 1979 and I am twenty-nine years old," but there was no logic to it. This was my day of birth, and that was that.

> If you go back to the ancient mysteries of which I have spoken, which were centers of education, religion, and art, you find that festivals relating to the seasons of the year were celebrated there. In spring, they would always have the festival of resurrection, as they called it. Nature does rise again at Easter time. People would say to themselves that the human soul can celebrate its resurrection just as nature can. Nature has the Father. In spring its forces are renewed. In ourselves as human beings, if we take proper care and work on ourselves, the powers of soul are renewed. The main aim in the ancient mysteries—the aim of those who actually knew, those said to have wisdom—was for the soul to gain a kind of "spring experience" in human life. This was a spring experience in which one might say of oneself that everything I have known before is really nothing; now I am like a newborn. It can happen in life that a moment comes when we feel as if new-born, born again from the spirit. This may sound strange to you, but throughout the East, in Asia, people were divided into those born once and those born twice.... Once-born people were born through the powers of the moon and remained like that all their lives. The others, the twice-born, had been instructed in the mysteries, had learned something, and knew that human beings can make themselves free, they can act out of their own powers.[60]

Here is another beautiful passage about this profound experience.

> We may call the refashioning of the astral body indirectly through meditation and concentration by the ancient name *catharsis*, or purification. Catharsis, or purification, seeks to discard from the astral body all that hinders it from becoming harmoniously and regularly organized, thus able to acquire higher organs. The astral body is endowed with the seeds of these higher organs....

60 Steiner, *From Beetroot to Buddhism*, pp. 108–109 (trans. revised).

Once this catharsis has taken place and the astral organs have been formed in the astral body, all this must be imprinted on the etheric body. In pre-Christian initiation, this was done as follows. After students had gone through the appropriate preparatory training, which often lasted for years, they were told that the time had come when the astral body had developed far enough to have gained astral organs of perception. These could now become aware of their counterpart in the etheric body. Then students were subjected to a procedure that is today (at least for our cultural epoch) not only unnecessary, but also not really feasible. They were put into a lethargic condition for three-and-a-half days. During that time, they were treated in such a way that not only did the astral body leave the physical and etheric bodies, which occurs every night in sleep, but the etheric body was also lifted out to a certain degree. They took care that the physical body remained intact so that the students would not die in the process. The etheric body was then liberated from the forces of the physical body that affect it. It became, as it were, elastic and malleable. When the sensory organs that had been formed in the astral body sank down into it, the etheric body received an imprint from the whole astral body. When the hierophant returned the students to a normal state, after the astral body and "I" had been reunited with the physical and etheric bodies (a procedure the hierophant understood), then the pupils experienced not only catharsis, but also what is called illumination, or *photismos*. They were then able not only to perceive all the physically perceptible things in the world around them, but could also employ spiritual organs of perception, which means that they could see and perceive the spiritual. Initiation thus consisted essentially of these two processes, purification, or catharsis, and illumination, or *photismos*....

Consider the words *know thyself* in Greek; they do not mean that you gaze into your own inner being, but that you fructify yourself with what flows into you from the spiritual world. "Know thyself" means "fructify yourself with the content of the spiritual world."

Two things are needed for this; we must prepare ourselves through catharsis and illumination and then open our inner being freely to the spiritual world. In this connection, we may compare our inner nature to the *female* aspect and the outer spiritual to the male. The inner being must be made susceptible of receiving the higher self. Once this has happened, the higher human self flows into us from the spiritual world. You may ask: Where is this higher human self? Is it within us in a personal sense? No, it is not there. On Saturn, Sun, and Moon, the higher self was diffused over the entire cosmos. At that time, the cosmic "I" was spread out over all humankind, but now we have to allow it to work on us. We must allow this "I" to work on our previously prepared inner nature. This means that human inner nature, the astral body, must be cleansed, purified, ennobled—subjected to catharsis. If that is done, the outer spirit will flow in to illumine us. This happens when we have been so well prepared that we have subjected our astral body to catharsis, thereby developing inner organs of perception. The astral body, in any case, has progressed so far now that, when it dips into the etheric and physical bodies, illumination, or *photismos*, results. What actually occurs is that the astral body imprints its organs upon the etheric body, making it possible for the human being to perceive a spiritual world around us. This makes it possible for the inner being, the astral body, to receive what the etheric body is able to offer it, or what the etheric body draws from the entire cosmos, or cosmic "I."

At the moment of illumination, this cleansed, purified astral body bears within it none of the impure impressions of the physical world, but only the organs of perception of the spiritual world. In esoteric Christianity, this is called "the pure, chaste, wise Virgin Sophia."

By means of everything received during catharsis, the student cleanses and purifies the astral body so that it is transformed into the Virgin Sophia. And when the Virgin Sophia encounters the Cosmic "I" (the universal "I," which causes illumination), the student is surrounded by spiritual light. In esoteric Christianity, this second power that approaches the Virgin Sophia is called (and called today) the "Holy Spirit."

Therefore, according to esoteric Christianity it is correct to say that, through this process of initiation, the Christian esotericist attains purification and cleansing of the astral body. We make our astral body into the Virgin Sophia and are illuminated from above—you may call it "overshadowed"—by the "Holy Spirit," the cosmic, universal "I." Those who are thus illuminated, who, in other words, according to esoteric Christianity have received the "Holy Spirit," speak in a new, different way.[61]

---

61   Steiner, *Isis Mary Sophia*, pp. 68–70, 72–73 (trans. revised).

The reader will remember that, after looking at the date for a while in the train station, I got up and proceeded to bless everyone there, lots of women, children, and old men. I went to them and blessed them all, just like that. I was very much aware that what I was doing made no logical sense, and I saw that my actions were totally out of the ordinary, but I proceeded anyway. I had to. I felt that I had received so much peace and love that I had to give it back to whoever was around, which was everyone in the Montreal bus terminal. As I was crossing the room, I saw a young man from the Vipassana course. He did not disturb me and went on his way. This happened about one week after the course had ended.

It is as though a veil of secrecy is drawn over the way, in ancient civilizations, those who sought a deeper religious life and knowledge than one could find in the popular religions were able to satisfy their spiritual needs. An inquiry into how those needs were met leads us directly into the obscurity of the secret cults. The individual seeker there disappears from our view for the moment. We see that the public forms of religion cannot give what the seeker's heart desires. One acknowledges the gods but knows that the customary ideas about the gods do not resolve the great enigmas of life; one seeks wisdom that is carefully guarded by a community of priest-sages. The struggling soul seeks refuge in their community. If sages find one who is ready, they will lead that individual by stages to higher insight, in a way concealed from the outsider's view. The process is not disclosed to the uninitiated. Such a seeker seems entirely removed for a time from earthly life, transported to a hidden world.

Standing again in the light of the day, such seekers are completely changed. We see those for whom no words can be sublime enough to express the meaning of their experience. It seems, not just symbolically but also in some existential sense, that they have passed through death and awakened to a new and higher life. And there is a conviction that no one who has not undergone a similar experience can understand what such individuals have to say....

Plutarch mentions the terror of the initiand, and compares that person's situation to a preparation for death. A special mode of life was one of the requirements for a subsequent initiation. The senses had to be brought under the control of the spirit; to that end, they employed fasting, isolation, ordeals, and certain meditative techniques. The stable realities of ordinary life had to lose all value, and the whole orientation of perception and feeling had to be altered completely. The implication of such exercises and ordeals cannot be in doubt; the wisdom to be presented to the initiand would work properly on the psyche only after one had worked to transform the world of the lower senses. The initiand had to be guided into the life of spirit, and behold a higher world order....

Where is God? Such was the root question of the soul of the *mystes*. God is not existence; but nature exists. God must be discovered in nature, where he lies enchanted in his grave. The *mystai* understood that "God is love" in a special higher sense. God has gone to the utmost lengths of love. He has sacrificed himself in infinite love, poured himself out, dismembered himself into the manifold phenomena of nature. They live, but he is not alive in them; he slumbers in them, but comes to life in human beings who are able to experience the life of God within themselves. If human beings are to attain this *gnosis*, however, they must release it creatively within themselves. Looking into their own being, they find the divine as a hidden creative power, not yet released into existence. Within the soul lies the place where the spellbound God may return to life.

The soul is the mother who can receive the divine seed from nature. If the soul allows herself to be impregnated by nature, she will give birth to the divine. Out of the marriage of the soul with nature, the divine is born, no longer a "hidden God" but something manifest, alive—palpably alive and moving among humankind. In human beings, the spirit has been released from enchantment; yet it is the offspring of the spellbound God. He is not the great God who was, and is, and shall be, yet he may in a certain sense be taken as a revelation of him. The Father remains at rest in the unseen. The Son is born to human beings out of their own souls.

Initiatory knowledge is thus an actual event in the cosmic process. It is the birth of a divine child—a process just as real as any natural process. The great secret of the *mystai* was precisely this—that they release the divine child creatively within themselves. First, however, they must be prepared to recognize it. The uninitiated know nothing of the Father of the divine child. The Father slumbers under a spell. The child seems to be born of a virgin, the soul giving birth to him without impregnation. Whereas all her other offspring are begotten by the world of the senses and have a father who can be seen and touched in perceptible existence, the Son of God is uniquely begotten of the eternal, hidden Father himself....

There is a "burning" process, a consuming fire, in the vision of the Eternal, when it acts upon our customary notions about the world. The spirit dissolves thoughts that derive from the senses, evaporates them, as a destructive fire....

[Empedocles said,] "When, set free from the body, released you rise to the ether, You become divine, an immortal, escaped from the power of death."

Looking at human life from this perspective, the prospect of initiation into the magic circle of the Eternal becomes a real possibility. Forces that would not unfold under purely natural conditions of life must certainly be present in human beings, and if they remain untapped their life will pass away unfructified....

The powers and beings that the initiates in the ancient mysteries sought to find within themselves remain unknown to anyone whose horizon is bounded by received ideas. The *mystai* did not hold back from the great question; they inquired into their own spiritual nature and into powers and laws beyond those of lower, natural existence.

In our ordinary sensory-based life of thought and what may be inferred from it, we worship gods of our own making or, when we discover this, are driven to disclaim them. The *mystai*, however are aware of their god-making, and they understand the reasons why they do so. They have won through, as we should say, to the underlying laws that govern the process of making gods.[62]

These beautiful words of Rudolf Steiner reflect what I was feeling within my soul. After blessing everyone in the room as though it was a normal thing to do, and knowing perfectly well in my "logical mind" that my actions were, to say the least, out of the ordinary, I spoke with a young woman and her child. She was from a little town that I knew in southern Quebec. I then returned to my seat and waited for person who was to provide my ride, whom I thought should be coming quite soon. I meditated some more, and then another experience came over me. This was not as peaceful as the previous one. I felt that

---

62 Steiner, *Christianity as Mystical Fact*, pp. 1–2, 14, 19, 23, 43 (trans. revised).

I had been completely *transfigured*—that is the word. Half of me was in light and the other was dark; I was made up of both, and that was unnerving and upsetting. While this was happening, I remember thinking, *Why can't I be all light? Why is one side dark? I can't change it; both light and dark are present.*

[Heraclitus said,] "The connectedness of things is a tension between opposites, just as in a bow or a lyre."

How much lies concealed in this metaphor! Tension in one direction is balanced exactly by tension in the other, resulting in a unity and harmony of forces. There are high and low notes; yet their contradictions are resolved in the musical scale. Heraclitus's thought extends the analogy to the spiritual world: "Immortals are mortals, mortals immortal; living the ones' death, dying the others' life...."

It is all too easy to misunderstand Heraclitus, for example, when he calls war the father of things—but only of things, not of the Eternal. If there were not contradictions in the world, if there were not the most diverse conflicting tendencies, there would indeed be no becoming, no transitory things. Yet diffused through this contradictoriness and revealing itself there is not war, but connectedness. For though there is war in all things, for that very reason the mind of the wise should flame up over things and bring them into connectedness.

Here we encounter one of Heraclitus's great insights. It is from such a viewpoint that he develops his answer to the question of individual identity. For the human being is composed of the warring elements into which the Divinity is poured.... Moreover, they become aware of the spirit, the *Logos*, which stems from the Eternal. For such people, however, the spirit comes to birth out of the clash of the elements. Indeed, it is the spirit that brings the elements into equilibrium....

It is the spirit, the *Logos*, that works in human beings. But it does so in a special way; out of the temporal. The uniqueness of the human soul consists in this: a temporal being is active and powerful in the same way as an eternal being, and can be likened both to a god and to a worm. Human beings are placed between god and animal....

Plato has recourse to myth when he comes to speak of the soul's life. At the juncture where he leaves the transitory world to seek the eternal core of the soul, concepts deriving from the senses and from the thinking based upon them no longer apply. The *Phaedrus* is devoted to the theme of the eternal in the soul, and the soul is described as a chariot with two horses, each many-winged, and a charioteer. One of the horses is docile and intelligent, the other headstrong and wild. When the chariot encounters an obstacle on its path, the head-strong beast seizes the chance of impeding the reliable one and defying the charioteer. And when the chariot reaches the point of ascending the celestial steep in the wake of the gods, the intractable horse throws it into confusion. Whether the chariot can surmount these difficulties and reach the realm of the suprasensory depends on their relative strengths and, thus, whether the good horse can gain mastery. The soul, however, can never raise itself to the divine without some sort of a struggle. Some souls rise higher in their pursuit of the eternal vision, others less high.

Those souls who have attained the transcendent vision are kept safe until the next cycle, while those who have seen nothing but were thwarted by the unruly horse must enter a new cycle and try again. The cycles here designate the several incarnations of the soul—one cycle standing for its life as a particular personality. The unruly horse and the intelligent horse stand for the lower and the higher aspects of human nature; the charioteer for the soul, which aspires to "divinization," as in the Mysteries.[63]

Sitting there, I was faced with all my unresolved darkness which I would have to work on, and most importantly I had to accept the fact that I was not finished with the endless work of transforming myself. With all the incredible experiences, this one made me forget them all—to face the fact that one must go on. And now, when I face difficulties, I always remind myself to go on and keep working no matter what. By doing this I do not get stuck, but remain forever in movement between light and dark. Illumination came and went, and now I had to be back on Earth and face the transformation of the darkness that remained.

My ride came while I was still deeply absorbed in this transformation of light and dark experiences within my soul, which had just given birth to a child—Me. As soon as I stepped into the car, I panicked. The car was going too fast, and I could feel elemental beings everywhere. But that subsided, and somehow I got used to this state of being as we drove on.

---

63   Ibid., pp. 18–20, 47 (trans. revised).

This picture reminds me of a modern "flying sadhu" going into an altered state of consciousness at seventy miles an hour, holding on for dear life, perhaps in an airplane. One needs to keep a sense of humor somehow.

> Living one's self into the etheric body seems like flowing out, as it were, into cosmic space, during which one is continually conscious of going out into infinity in all directions from one's body as a central point. Experience in the astral body, however, appears as springing out of oneself into the astral body. It is at this moment that one begins to feel outside one's physical body in such a way that everything in the physical body that was called one's self is now experienced as something external, existing outside. One is inside something else....
>
> In the life of the senses, we are confronted with substances, forces, objects, processes, and so on. We are also confronted with beings and, in addition, beings of the other kingdoms of nature.... We are confronted in particular by our own fellow beings.... But when we are seeing into the spiritual world while in the astral body, we can no longer make this distinction. In the spiritual world we are confronted only with beings, but there is no such thing as the so-called course of nature in contrast to those beings. Everything to which you are guided... every thing you meet, is *being*. Wherever there is anything, it is being, and you cannot say as you do in sensory life that there is an animal and here the external substances it is going to eat. There is no such duality there; everything that exists is being.[64]

Before we can follow the spirit as it continues its journey, we must first look at the territory it is entering. This is the world of the spirit, and it is so different from the physical world that everything we have to say about it will seem sheer fantasy to those willing to trust only their physical senses.... Our language, which for the most part serves only the purposes of sense-perceptible reality, is not exactly richly endowed with expressions that can be applied directly to the "land of spirit beings," so it is especially important to take much of what is said here as no more than indications. Because everything described here is so different from the physical world, this is the only possible way of depicting it at all. Because of the inadequacy of our language, which is intended

---

64 Steiner, *Initiation, Eternity, and the Passing Moment*, pp. 89–91.

for communication in the physical world, the statements made here can correspond only crudely to actual experience in the spiritual field.

It must be emphasized above all that the spiritual world is woven from the substance that constitutes human thought—"substance," of course, in a very figurative sense. But thought, as it manifests in human beings, is only a shadowy image or phantom of its real being. A thought appearing by means of a human brain corresponds to a being in the land of spirit beings as a shadow on the wall corresponds to the actual object casting the shadow. But once our spiritual senses have been awakened, we actually perceive the thought being itself, just as our physical eyes perceive a table or a chair. We are surrounded and accompanied by thought beings. Our physical eyes perceive a lion, and our sense-oriented thinking perceives the *idea* of the lion merely as a phantom, a shadowy image. But in the land of spirit beings, the idea of the lion is as real and visible to our spiritual eyes as the material lion is to our physical eyes. The comparison we used in conjunction with the soul world is also pertinent. Just as people who were born blind but have had their sight restored through operations suddenly perceive their surroundings as having the new qualities of color and light, those who have learned to use their spiritual eyes perceive their surroundings as filled with a whole new world of *living* thoughts or spirit beings....

Quite understandably, people who trust only their outer senses will deny the existence of this archetypal world and insist that archetypes are only abstractions that the intellect works out by comparing sense-perceptible phenomena. Such people cannot perceive at all in the higher world; they are aware of the world of thoughts only in its shadowy abstractness. They do not know that individuals capable of spiritual vision are as familiar with spirit beings as they themselves are with their dogs or cats, and that the reality of the archetypal world is actually much more intense than physical sense-perceptible reality.[65]

↓

It was a beautiful end-of-summer day; the apples were ripening on the trees; the Sun was going down slowly for the evening. I suddenly looked at Lake

---

65   Steiner, *Theosophy*, pp. 122–124 (trans. revised).

Champlain and had the feeling, *This is it. I am definitely dying. I will be dead within the hour.* I asked my driver to take me to the next hospital, which was a small clinic-hospital. Convinced I was dying, I went to the emergency room. A Hindu doctor was in attendance and I explained to him that I had just been to a meditation center. He left me lying in a room by myself, probably so he could talk to my driver.

As I lay there, I remember thinking to myself, in a kind of conversation in thought, *Please do not do anything to my mind.* I was terrified of possibly losing everything I ever thought was important, of giving it up. I kept thinking that, whatever happens, my mind must remain intact. *I have studied and read so much; you can't take all that away from me. I like my intellect and I do not want to lose all that knowledge.* I was horrified, and to make it worse I was in a clinic. I had to trust that all would be taken care of, but I had to let go of that strong intellectual streak. Time passed ever so slowly, and then somehow I found myself trusting the beings who were up there (in the spirit world) watching me. I went through the experience, did not die, and did not lose my knowledge. Soon I felt better. I was given some pills and went home.

> In literature, wherever you find initiation mentioned, the mystery of death, so closely concerning all humankind, is touched upon in one way or another. Such records allude to how, at a certain stage, the initiate has to experience, in a somewhat different form, the nature of passing through the gate of death…. The experiences that one must go through while ascending into spiritual worlds are like the experiences people must go through when crossing naturally from life in the physical body to the wholly different sheath found between death and a new birth….
>
> In our life of the senses, what we call "our world" is really only a gathering of all that flows in through the sensory gateways. Then we have the instruments of our understanding, our feeling and willing, with which to work on what meets us in the outer world. Cravings and desires, efforts, states of satisfaction and dissatisfaction, joy, disillusion, and so on arise within one's soul. If we were to envisage the whole compass of what people recognize as themselves, it is all this….
>
> On reaching the boundary between sensory existence and spiritual existence, we have to alter our concepts; we must leave behind all

thoughts of ugly and beautiful, true and false, good and bad. Such concepts will assume a whole different significance.... From this we can get some idea of how we must change ourselves if we wish to enter those worlds.... How much of all that we know can we take with us across the boundary where the Guardian of the Threshold stands?... How much of all that we live through and experience in sensory existence, in our impulses, desires, and passions, in feelings, ideas, and concepts of our understanding and judgments can we take with us across the boundary where the Guardian of the Threshold stands? It is in the first stages of initiation when one discovers that, of all that constitutes the human being, nothing can be carried with us. It is neither an exaggeration nor a paradox but the literal truth to say, of all that can be mentioned as belonging to human sensory existence, we can carry nothing at all into the spiritual world; everything must be left behind at the boundary where the Guardian of the Threshold stands....

Everything must be laid aside; it must remain behind and be discarded for the simple reason that it is not suited to the world we must enter. Just as our physical body is not adapted for a bath in 900-degree molten iron, what we call "our self," with all that we love in ordinary life, is ill-adapted for the spiritual world. It must be left behind; if it were not left behind, we would experience something resembling the effect of a bath of molten iron on a physical body. We would be unable to bear it and be destroyed....

"If I am now to lay aside all that I am, all that I can talk of in the life of my senses, what, at long last, actually remains of me? Is there anything left of myself to enter the spiritual world if I have to cast myself aside?" It is a fact that, of all that we recognize as our self, human beings cannot take anything with them into the suprasensory worlds. All that we can take is something...that is in us without our knowledge, lying in the depths of the soul as the hidden elements of our being. These must be so strong that, out of them, we can take all that we will need into the spiritual worlds when we must lay aside what we know.[66]

The experience of leaving everything behind was an experience of death, the death of all that I treasured. But I did not die. As Rudolf Steiner explains, all must be left behind at the elementary stages of initiation. This is only the

---

66 Steiner, *Initiation, Eternity, and the Passing Moment*, pp. 69–73 (trans. revised).

very beginning of an endless road. Goenka was correct when he said, "Go on, there is more to come. You cannot get stuck in one place and think this is it. Go on." And I still go on. There will always be someone who is far superior, and is there to teach us, or show us. Often our children are there for that.

Here, one can look at this death experience from another perspective: death in the sensory world means awaking into another world—rebirth into the eternal world. Steiner talks here about Plato's *Timeus*.

> To discover the maker and Father of this universe is indeed a hard task, and having found him it would be impossible to tell everyone about him. (Timeus)
>
> The *mystai* understand the force of the word *impossible*. It points toward the inner drama of the Godhead. For them, God is not revealed in the materially comprehensible world, where he manifests only as nature, in which he lies under a spell. He can be apprehended, as was taught in the mysteries, only by one who awakens the divine within. That is why he cannot be made intelligible to everyone....
>
> The father made the universe out of the world body and world soul. He mixed the elements, in harmony and perfect proportion, elements he himself brought into being by pouring himself out, giving up his separate existence. Thus, he produced the world body. Stretched out upon it, in the form of a cross, is the world soul, the divine presence in the world. It suffers death on this cross so that the world can exist. And Plato, therefore, calls nature the "tomb" of the divine—not a tomb in which something lay dead, but the tomb in which lay the Eternal, for which death is nothing but the opportunity to demonstrate the omnipotence of life! Hence, for humanity the right way to view nature is to undertake the rescue of the crucified world soul, which should rise, released from death, released from the spell that binds it. Where can this happen except in the soul of an initiate? Thus, wisdom takes on its proper meaning in a cosmic setting; knowledge is the resurrection, the liberation of God....
>
> Manifestation is the resurrection of God from the "tomb." Within this development, the human being appears.... However, this single and uniquely created world would not be perfect if it did not contain among its images an image of its Creator himself. That image can arise only from the human soul; it is not the Father himself, but the Son, the living

child of God in the soul who is of like nature with the Father, to whom humanity can give birth.[67]

↓

Slowly, my life returned to normal, and I put all these soul and body upheavals far behind me. I kept my meditation practice, sitting one hour in the morning and one hour in the evening. In this way, Goenka said, one remains clean of all the defilements we encounter during the day.

Goenka would always tell us that, here, you learn how to die. You must die to live, and if you have not died, you are not living. Well, as far I was concerned I had just died, but it seemed backward; I had been born, and then I died.

Nevertheless, with all this dying and birthing of my soul, my physical body became pregnant, not as an unconscious act, but as a planned conception. Or, more truthfully, the child wanted to be born in February, and he was born the following spring. I gave birth to a son in 1981, a son who, I must say, is far more intuitive and talented than I will ever be; he perceives the world with incredible clarity. Goenka always said one should purify one's soul-mind-body before becoming pregnant, as it is extremely good for the child. With all the upheavals i had gone through, I am not so sure. Looking at both my son and daughter now, however, I think it must have been good for them.

After realizing that I have darkness in me that I cannot get rid of, I learned that, no matter what, I must live with it and wash it. Many of my québecquois friends used to joke about the retreats and the concept of washing—washing a lot of dirty linen, washing their "souls" clean. I would call R, and often he would laugh about how much dirty linen he had acquired throughout his incarnations. He was a lawyer, and in the winter he spent one month in intense meditation and attended ten-day courses in the summer. We would all laugh about how anyone could be so dirty and how we would run out of soap, and we would say in québecquois French, "Chalice. Tabernacle. Hostie Toastie," my

---

67   Steiner, *Christianity as Mystical Fact*, pp. 36–37 (trans. revised).

favorite irreverent saying in québecquois. Even though we would go through hell inwardly, there was always room for joking, laughing, and lightheartedness about our laundry, our dirty linen.

We all know we have to face and change our inner darkness and not be afraid of it and sometimes even laugh about it. Here is a crude example: One year when my son and daughter were older, my husband had spent a few weeks in the Bahamas, often meditating, he said. Then he came home and proceeded to have a brief "afternoon delight" affair. So we endlessly teased him about his "meditation" experiences and how deeply he had meditated and become thoroughly balanced and so on. We made fun of what was a painful situation for all of us, one that ended in our separation. But we laughed it off, and still do. We can't be so morbid about our weaknesses, painful as they may be.

I went back for a full ten-day course in 1983. I needed a break from my disastrous situation in Iran—a failing marriage and the difficulties of living under an impossible political system. I gladly flew to Bombay and spent a month in India. I took the train to Igatpuri, the headquarters for Goenka's Vipassana centers. Goenka was teaching, and my québecquois friends took care of my young son for the duration of the ten-day course. The meditation center was situated in a beautiful village with all the simple accommodation one needed. There were people from all over the world coming to meditate, so it was very lively, with wonderful food and quiet. Goenka always told us that when we meditate we change the weather of a place. Steiner explains such phenomena in detail.[68]

I was happy to be in a quiet place to face an uncertain future as a single mother with a son, finishing a teaching contract in Tehran with six months remaining, and searching for a teaching job in the US. I could not abandon the children I was teaching, and I had to stay put until June. My husband continued his affairs, his drinking, and was living a bachelor's life. He had been a doctor in the Iran–Iraq war, and that brutal, devastating experience

---

68 In the works of Rudolf Steiner, these phenomena are explained in many of the lecture cycles from various points of view. See, for example, *The Occult Movement in the Nineteenth Century*.

had changed him forever. I had a wonderful circle of French, Persian, and American friends and enjoyed skiing, hiking in the mountains of northern Tehran, horseback riding, picnicking in small gardens enclosed within high dirt walls, and swimming in the Caspian Sea. No matter how bad things got, I always enjoyed myself. A part of me had been made as strong as a rock. A mountain.

I was ready for another round of meditation. This time, the retreat did not cause such upheavals on the soul level as did the earlier one. It was gentler. I developed more capacities as I deepened my meditation and concentration. To my surprise, I discovered that I could communicate with others without using words at all. In India, these capacities are called *siddis,* and some people undertake meditation just to develop such capacities. Goenka, however, always warned his students never to do that. He taught that we should do our meditation, and if something develops, fine, but it should not be the goal of meditation. Meditating to develop capacities would be wrong, unethical, so I never paid much attention to any of those *siddis* but just went on with the exercises.

I am reminded of my Karate class, in which we would do many exercises to master the body and discipline the mind. The master would say to the students who were obsessed with strength and power and who wanted to use their brute force to break boards with their forehead or hands, "Why do you bother coming here? Just stay home and practice hitting your hand on a surface over and over again. Then you will break the board. There is no need to come here and acquire discipline. If you want pure strength, just hit." A karate Master does not teach brute strength.

One of the first things to occur when an esoteric student begins practicing the exercises is that the light of the lotus flowers intensifies; later the flowers will also begin to rotate. When this happens, it means that the person is beginning to have the ability to see clairvoyantly. These "flowers" are the sense organs of the soul. Their rotation indicates that we are able to perceive the suprasensory realm. Until we have developed the astral senses in this way, we cannot see anything suprasensory.

The spiritual sense organ, which is situated near the larynx, enables us to see clairvoyantly into the way of thinking of other soul beings. It also allows us a deeper insight into the true laws of natural phenomena, while the organ located in the region of the heart opens clairvoyant cognition into the mentality and character of other souls. Whoever has developed this organ is also able to cognize certain deeper forces in plants and animals. With the sense organ situated near the solar plexus, we gain insight into the abilities and talents of other souls and see what role animals, plants, minerals, metals, atmospheric phenomena, and so on play in the household of nature.

The organ in the vicinity of the larynx has sixteen "petals," or "spokes"; the one near the heart, twelve; and the one near the solar plexus, ten.[69]

Some of the capacities of which I became aware in myself were reading someone's thoughts, awareness of other beings, hearing the music of the spheres, smelling an aura, speaking to someone's heart, having visions of future calamities, and being at one with the elements, flowers, animals, and metals. But again, I never paid much attention to these things or became attached to their manifestations. I continued with the work. Rather than being excited about these capacities, I was surprised by them, and since I did not understand what was happening, they did not have much meaning for me. Some meditants get stuck on them and lost their way or simply forgot the purpose of the path. The Bodhisattva path leads to liberation so that we can help our brothers and sisters and be of service.

For those who want to know more about this path, there are books to read and meditations to be practiced. Five minutes a day is a good beginning. Of course, there are hundreds of Vipassana classes all over the world, and one can also do a ten-day course. But as Western human beings, I believe the safest path is the one described by Rudolf Steiner. One can ascend to the top of the mountain by different routes. The high cliffs are the shortest route, but only expert mountaineers should attempt that. There are much longer and safer routes available, and it is wise to choose those, as one will not fall off cliffs and get hurt in the process. I must say that I have fallen

---

69   Steiner, *How to Know Higher Worlds*, pp. 110–111 (trans. revised).

off the cliffs several times, and yet I attempted more ascents—solo, with no ropes. This picture comes to mind: I was climbing the Mt. Everest of inner journeys, but I was unaware that it was an ascent. I was there in blessed ignorance just for the climbing, in some respects a kind of Parcival Fool.

"Yoga of Light"

For readers who are considering the practice of some kind of meditation, perhaps my experience will contribute to a decision about which technique to pursue. I have followed both Eastern and Western approaches, as this book relates, and have gained personal insights into both.

When undertaking the practice of Vipassana meditation, one uses the tip of the nose where the breath goes in; it is called *anapana* in Pali, for concentration. Then one proceeds to use the entire body for further concentration, always observing the sensations coming in and penetrating more deeply within the body. That is the technique; it is always the same movement throughout the body, using one's own flesh, bones, and muscles as objects of concentration. We observe what happens and learn not to react to anything, whether good or bad, thereby gaining complete self-control in the process. This leads the meditant to experience whether one is ripe for development of the lotus flower, a well-known image in Eastern traditions.

There is another way to meditate that was introduced by Rudolf Steiner and developed further by many talented students of his work, some of whom teach it today. Steiner explains that, as modern Westerners, we must not use our body at all. We must use thoughts. He calls this the "Yoga of Light." In the practice of older methods of meditation such as the 2,500-year-old Vipassana, which had been preserved in the mountains of Burma and reintroduced to India by my teacher Goenka, we use our bodies as a focus. Now our Western bodies are different, and we have other techniques more appropriate to our development in the Western world.

Before describing some of my experiences in the practice of the Western path, however, I will mention one capacity that I enjoy thoroughly. I can pick up a book, read one sentence of it and know instantly in my heart whether it is truthful or not. There is no thinking involved. The words instantly give away their secret: *Yes, this is authentic. No, this is not. Yes, this book speaks from a living experience. No, this book is still stuck in someone's head and intellect with no life, just words.* Or, the words become lost in sentimental gushy nonsensical emotion, drowning the reader in a pool of unclear distorted feelings. Other times, the words can be truly beautiful, but unfortunately there is nothing behind them, just bubbles.

The more I work with Rudolf Steiner's writing, the more they become alive and powerful, and the less I can read material like newspapers, which give me a headache. I have the same discernment when I listen to an authentic speech, whereby a person speaks from personal treasures of experiences. Then I enjoy it; it speaks the truth and I feel the honesty and beauty of the words. If someone speaks a pack of lies, or speaks about things they have not experienced, then the words feel cold, abstract, and painful and I usually walk out or work inwardly on my patience. A real experience is to listen to political speeches and see the ugly forms, the beings, that come out of that experience.

An activity now begins in connection with which it is important to consider distinguishing between true and false images. This must be called *thinking of the heart.* . . . In ordinary life, we feel that we think with the head. This is, of course, a pictorial expression, for we actually think with the spiritual organs that underlie the brain. Nevertheless, it is generally accepted that we think with the head. We have quite a different feeling about the thinking that becomes possible when we have made some progress. The feeling then arises that the process that had been located thus far in the head is now located in the heart. This does not refer to the physical heart but to the spiritual organ that develops in the area of the heart, the twelve-petalled lotus flower. This organ becomes a kind of organ of thinking in one who achieves inner development, and this thinking of the heart is very different from ordinary thinking.

In ordinary thinking, everyone knows that reflection is needed to reach a particular truth. The mind moves from one concept to another and, after logical deliberation and reflection, reaches what is called "knowledge." It is different when we want to recognize the truth connected with genuine symbols or emblems. They exist before us like objects, but the kind of thinking we apply to them cannot be confused with ordinary brain-thinking. Whether they are true or false is directly evident without any reflection being necessary as in the case of ordinary thinking. What can be said about the higher worlds is directly evident. As soon as the pictures are before us, we know what we have to say to ourselves and to others about them. This is the nature of heart thinking.

There are not many things in everyday life that may be compared with heart thinking, but I will say something that may make it comprehensible. There are events that bring the intellect virtually to a standstill. For example, suppose an event confronts you like a flash of lightning and you are terrified. No ordinary thought occurs between the event and the terror. The inner experience, the terror, can stop the mind. That is a good expression for it; people feel what has, in fact, happened. Similarly, we may fly into a rage at the sight of an act we witness in the street. Again, it is the direct impression that evokes the inner experience. If we begin to reflect about that event, we find that in most cases we form a different judgment of it.

Such experiences that arise when an action or inner state of mind directly follows the first impression are the only experiences in everyday life that may be compared with those of spiritual investigators when they speak about their experiences in the higher worlds. If we begin to reason and apply much logical criticism to those experiences, we drive them away. Furthermore, when ordinary thinking is applied to such cases, it will usually produce something false....

Those who want to undergo higher development must also undergo training in logical thinking for a certain time and then disregard it to pass on to heart thinking. In this way, they retain a certain habit of conscientiousness regarding the acceptance of truth in the higher worlds. Those who have undergone such training will not consider every symbol to be a true *Imagination* or interpret it arbitrarily; rather, they will have the inner strength to move toward reality, to see and interpret it correctly. Thorough training is necessary because we must have an immediate feeling as to whether something is true or false. To put it precisely, this means that in the higher worlds our thinking must have been developed enough that we can determine truth or falsity spontaneously, whereas in ordinary life we use reflection.

A good preparation for such direct sight is another quality that must be acquired and is present only to a very small extent in ordinary life. Most people will cry out if, say, they are pricked by a needle or if very hot water is poured over their heads. But how many really feel anything akin (I expressly say *akin*) to pain when a foolish or absurd statement is made? Countless people can tolerate this quite easily. However, those who want to develop the immediate feeling of a thing being true and another false, in such a way that the Imaginative world plays a part in the experience, must train themselves so that error causes them actual pain and that truth encountered in physical life brings gladness and joy.

To acquire this quality is an exacting process, and it is connected with the effort involved in preparing for entry to the higher worlds. To be indifferent to truth and error is clearly more comfortable than to feel pain when faced with error and joy when faced with truth. There is plenty of opportunity today to feel pain over the foolishness contained in many books. Part of the training for thinking of the heart is feeling pain and suffering in the face of ugliness, falsehood, and evil, even when it is only external and not actually inflicted on us, and feeling pleasure over beauty, truth, and goodness, even when we are not personally concerned.[70]

In his marvelous work, *How to Know Higher Worlds*, Steiner discusses the development of the twelve-petalled lotus flower in the region of the heart; again, one must carefully study the text.

A seer who has developed this sense organ can describe—for every way of thinking and natural law—the particular shape in which the thinking or law expresses itself. For example, a vengeful thought has an arrow-like and jagged shape, while a kind thought often has the form of a flower beginning to blossom, and so on. Thoughts that are firm and meaningful are symmetrical and regular; concepts that are unclear have wavy, almost frizzy outlines.

Quite different perceptions come to light through the twelve-petalled lotus flower. These may be roughly characterized in terms of warmth and coldness of soul. Seers, endowed with this sense organ, feel soul warmth or coldness streaming from the figures perceived by the sixteen-petalled lotus flower....

---

70 Steiner, *Macrocosm and Microcosm*, pp. 151–153, 156–157 (trans. revised).

Developing the twelve-petalled lotus flower gives us profound insight into the processes of nature. Everything growing and maturing radiates soul warmth, while everything undergoing death, destruction, and decay has the quality of soul coldness.[71]

Here are some of the many attributes which contribute to the thinking of the heart that one must practice: control of thought, control of actions, perseverance, tolerance, faith that moves mountains, and equanimity. The main thing here, however, is valuing the thinking of the heart, not our intellect. Unfortunately one does not acquire this thinking overnight, and it requires a little effort every day in the form of meditation practices. It reminds me of walking along the stony banks of wild river streams that flow from glaciers, where one can see how a huge granite boulder has been made smooth by the action of the water. One can contemplate the centuries of power by watching the action of the water flowing down on the rough granite. Five minutes a day of practice has that same kind of power to develop the thinking of the heart.

Today's path of knowledge must be entirely different. We have seen how one way, yoga, tried to reach thinking indirectly, through breathing, so as to experience such thinking in a way that it is not perceived in ordinary life.... We cannot take this detour via breathing. We must try, therefore, to transform thinking by other means, so that through that transformed thinking we can attain knowledge that will serve as a kind of extension of natural knowledge. Thus, if we understand ourselves correctly, we will start today, not by manipulating thinking indirectly via breathing, but by manipulating it directly and by doing certain exercises to make thinking more forceful and energetic than it is in ordinary consciousness.

In ordinary consciousness, we indulge in rather passive thinking that adheres to the course of external events. To follow a new, suprasensory way of knowledge, we place certain readily comprehended concepts at the center of our consciousness. We remain within the thought itself....

Today, we go straight to thinking by cultivating meditation, by concentrating on certain subjects of thought for extended periods. In the realm of the soul, we perform something comparable to building a

---

71 Steiner, *How to Know Higher Worlds*, pp. 119–120.

muscle. If we use a muscle repeatedly in continuous exertion, whatever the goal and purpose, the muscle must develop. We can do the same with thinking. Instead of always submitting, in our thinking, to the course of external events, we bring into the center of our consciousness, with a great effort of will, clear-cut concepts we have formed ourselves or have been given by an expert in the field, and in which no associations can persist of which we are unaware. We shut out all other awareness and concentrate only on the one subject.... One person takes weeks, another months, to achieve it. We eventually accomplish a process that is the opposite of what yogis went through when awareness learns to rest continually upon the same content so that the content itself becomes a matter of complete indifference, and we devote all our attention and all our inner experience to building up and spiritually energizing our mental activity. In other words, we tear our thinking away from the process of breathing.

Today, this still seems absurd and fantastic to people. Yet, just as yogis pushed their thinking into the body, linking it to the rhythm of their breath, and in this way experienced their self, or inner spirituality, likewise we release thinking from the remnant of breathing that survives unconsciously in all our ordinary thinking.... By these means, we gradually succeed in not only separating the thought sequence from the respiration process, but also making it quite free of the physical body. Only then do we see what a great service the so-called materialistic—or rather, the mechanistic—outlook on life has rendered to humankind. It has made us aware that ordinary thinking is based on bodily processes. From this, the incentive can arise to seek a kind of thinking no longer based on bodily processes. However, this can be discovered by only building up ordinary thinking as described. By doing so, we attain thinking that is set free from the body, thinking that consists purely of soul processes. Thus, we come to know what once had a semblance nature in us—as only images to begin with, but images that show us life free of our body.

This is the first step toward a way of knowledge suited to modern people. It brings us, however, to an experience hidden from ordinary awareness. Just as Indian yogis linked themselves in their thinking with the eternal rhythm of respiration, as well as with their spiritual self that lives in the breathing rhythm—just as they moved inward, we go outward....

Yogis sought to move *into* the human substance and reach the self; we seek to move *out* to the world rhythm. Ascetics of ancient times suppressed the body to express spiritual experience and allow it to exist independently. The modern way of knowledge is not inclined to asceticism; it avoids all arts of castigation and addresses itself intimately to the very life of the soul. Both modern ways, therefore, place people wholly within life, whereas the ways of asceticism and yoga drew people away from life....

As modern people, through certain mental exercises we manage to remove thinking from its normal state of passive surrender to phenomena of the outer world and to what seem inwardly to be memories but are also connected with the outer world. We transcend that kind of thinking through our serious, patient, and energetic practice of meditation exercises, repeating them again and again. Depending on our predisposition, it may take one person years, another not as long. However, all can note, as they reach the crucial point, how their thinking has gone from what I have called dead and abstract thinking to inwardly vital thinking, in tune with the rhythm of the world....

Compare the vitality of your experience of colors perceived through the eyes and the sounds you hear through the ear to the pallor of your experience of thought in ordinary consciousness. By energizing your mental life...you can gradually give the mere life of thought and concept the same intense quality as the life of the senses has.[72]

The correct path for people today is to transform, through meditation and concentration, the otherwise merely logical connections between thoughts into something of a musical quality. Meditation today should always begin with an experience in thought, an experience of the transition from one thought into another, from one mental picture into another.

The yogis of ancient India passed from one kind of breathing into another, but people today must attempt to project themselves into a living experience of, for example, the color red. Thus we remain within the realm of thought. We must then do the same with blue and experience the rhythm red-blue, blue-red, and so on, which is a thought-rhythm. But it is not a rhythm that can be found in a logical thought sequence, but thinking that is far more alive....

---

72 Steiner, *The Tension between East and West*, pp. 26–28, 32, 41 (trans. revised).

The goal of all modern exercises in meditation is to separate thinking entirely from breathing. This does not tear thinking away from rhythm; as thinking becomes separated from the inner rhythm of breathing, it is gradually linked to an outer rhythm. By freeing thinking from the breath, we let it flow, as it were, into the rhythm of the external world. Yogis turned back into their own rhythm. Today, people return to the rhythm of the outer world. In *How to Know Higher Worlds*, you will find that one of the first exercises shows how to contemplate the germination and growth of a plant. This meditation works to separate thinking from breathing, allowing it to plunge into the growth forces of the plant itself.

Thinking must pass into the rhythm that pervades the external world. Once thinking becomes truly free of the bodily functions, the moment it has torn itself away from breathing and gradually unites with the external rhythm, it dives into the spiritual in individual objects and not into the physical qualities of phenomena.

We look at a plant; it is green and its blossoms are red. Our eyes tell us this and our intellect confirms it. This is the reaction of ordinary awareness. We develop a different consciousness when we separate thinking from breathing and connect it with what exists outside. Such thinking longs to vibrate with the plant as it grows and develops its blossoms. This thinking follows how green passes into red in a rose, for example. Thinking vibrates within the spiritual that lies at the foundation of each single object in the external world.

This is how modern meditation differs from the yoga exercises practiced in very ancient times. There are naturally many intermediary stages; I chose these two extremes. Yogis sank, as it were, into their own breathing process; they sank into their self. This caused them to experience the self as if in memory. They remembered what they had been before they came down to Earth. We, on the other hand, pass out of the physical body with our soul and unite with what lives spiritually in the rhythms of the outer world.[73]

In lonely thinking [brooding] lies the luciferic attraction, whereas there is the ahrimanic element in mere listening or in any other kind of perception. However, one can maintain the middle path and move between the two, so to speak. It is neither necessary to stop short at abstract,

---

73 Steiner, *The Human Soul in Relation to World Evolution*, pp. 112–114 (trans. revised).

introspective thinking, whereby we shut ourselves away in our own souls like hermits, nor do we need to devote ourselves entirely to seeing or hearing the things our eyes and ears perceive. We can do something more; we can make whatever we think so inwardly forceful that our own thought appears before us like a living thing. We can immerse ourselves in it just as actively as we do in something heard or seen outside. Our thought then becomes as real and concrete as the phenomena we hear or see. That is the middle way.

In mere thought, close to brooding, Lucifer assails the person. In mere listening, whether as perception or accepting the authority of others, the ahrimanic element is present. Once we have strengthened and aroused our soul inwardly so that we can hear or see our thoughts while thinking, we have arrived at meditation. *Meditation is the middle way.* It is neither thinking nor perceiving.... People live in this divine, flowing stream when they meditate, living in their thoughts in such a way that they become as alive in them as their perceptions of the outside world. On their right are mere thoughts; on their left is the ahrimanic element, mere listening; they shut out neither, but understand that they live in a threefold state, for indeed life is ruled and ordered by number. They understand, too, that between that polarity, this antithesis of the two elements, meditation moves as a river.[74]

During the first few years that I studied the work of Rudolf Steiner, Anthroposophy, we lived in Buffalo, New York, where I joined Bruce McCausland and his study group. The Aurora Group had decided to read Rudolf Steiner's *Philosophy of Freedom*, and we each took turns preparing one chapter and presenting it to the group. I remember being given the book, and I attended meetings for three weeks, not being able to read it or even to become remotely interested in it. I glanced at the first paragraph, and then closed the book. I was absorbed in Steiner's lecture courses, but had no interest in that written work. Then came my turn to prepare and present it. During that week

---

74 Steiner, *Secrets of the Threshold*, pp. 89–90.

I worked furiously on the preceding three chapters and the one I would present. Then something happened.

I had never been exposed to such writing. There was not a single "warm" word; it seemed nearly devoid of adjectives. It was very mysterious writing, and its effect on me was instantaneous. At night, or whenever I was working on it, I was literally living in a different world. The way Rudolf Steiner had written this masterpiece makes you feel the other world. The pure, clear-cut writing moved the reader to perceive something else, which was, of course, the intent. One thought came after another with utter precision, no distraction for a wandering mind to follow. There was no way back to the thought before another came, and there was no room for fanciful daydreaming. It was like a Zen activity in the *dojo*, with the master tapping you softly on the shoulder with the stick to get you back on track. There was no wandering thought here. It was a cold world, like a diamond, clear as crystal. I was taken aback by its primal power. I had read many books, but this one was by far the most powerful I had ever experienced.

> What then did *The Philosophy of Freedom* set out to do? The necessary task was to show that if people are unable to find moral impulses when they stand outside of nature, because through the senses they can reach only natural laws, then they must go out of their self. They can no longer remain within the confines of the body. I had to describe this first going out, when one leaves bodily nature behind. This first going out is accomplished in pure thinking, as described in *The Philosophy of Freedom*. Here people do not project their self into the environment by means of instinctive clairvoyance; they leave the body altogether. They transfer their consciousness into the outer world. And what do they attain there? They gain moral intuition, because they have reached the very first delicate degree of clairvoyance—or you may wish to use the subjective term I used then, *moral imagination*. In this case, people go out of their self to find the spiritual within the technical (the spiritual is, after all, within it), where it is first found—in the realm of morality.
>
> However, people do not recognize that what *The Philosophy of Freedom* describes is the very first degree of the new clairvoyance. This is not

recognized, because people still think that clairvoyance means plunging into the obscure and unfamiliar. Here it is only the familiar that is sought; here one goes out with thinking that has become free of matter. This thinking sustains itself, so that the world is grasped in a purely spiritual way for the first time through this self-sustaining thinking....

Mystics find too much emphasis on thinking in *The Philosophy of Freedom*. According to them, it is just too full of thoughts. Others, such as rationalists and scientists and even modern philosophers, can make nothing of it for the very reason that it leads into a realm of spiritual sight where they do not wish to go. They want to remain within the realm of outer sight, even when their subject is philosophy. The whole approach and content of *The Philosophy of Freedom* fulfils the obligation placed on modern humanity.[75]

The Philosophy of Freedom was not written with the same intent with which most books are written today. Nowadays, books are written simply to inform the reader about the book's subject, so that the reader learns the book's content.... This was not my primary intention in writing *The Philosophy of Freedom*, and thus it will not be popular with those who read books only to acquire information. The purpose of the book is to cause readers to engage their thinking activity directly on every page.

In a sense, the book is a kind of musical score that one must read with inner thought activity just to progress as a result of one's own efforts, from one thought to the next. The book constantly presupposes the reader's mental collaboration. Moreover, it presupposes what the soul will become in the process of such mental exertion. Those who have worked through this book with their own inner activity of thinking and cannot say that they have gained self-knowledge in a previously unknown part of their inner life have not read *The Philosophy of Freedom* properly. Readers should feel that they are being lifted out of their usual thinking... into thinking that is independent of the senses,... fully immersed, so that one feels freed from the conditions of physical existence. Those who cannot admit this to themselves have, in fact, misunderstood the book. Readers should be able to say to themselves, *Now I know what pure thinking actually is because of the inner thought activity I myself have expended.*

---

75 Steiner, *The Human Soul in Relation to World Evolution*, pp. 77–78 (trans. revised).

The strange thing is that most Western philosophers completely deny the reality of the very thing that my *Philosophy of Freedom* seeks to awake in the souls of the readers as real.[76]

Because I studied languages (French, Latin, German, Spanish, Italian, and Persian) and made a living with them for many years, I cannot resist analyzing, in my simple way, one little paragraph (taken at random) from this most amazing book. Here, I have used the newest translation of *Philosophy of Freedom*, now titled *Intuitive Thinking as a Spiritual Path: A Philosophy of Freedom*.

This is the moment to move from thinking to the being who thinks. For it is through the thinker that thinking is linked to observation. Human consciousness is the stage where concept and observation meet and are connected to one another. This is, in fact, what characterizes human consciousness. It is the mediator between thinking and observation. To the extent that human beings observe things, things appear as given; to the extent that human beings think, they experience themselves as active. They regard things as *objects*, and themselves as thinking *subjects*. Because they direct their thinking to what they observe, they are conscious of objects; because they direct their thinking to themselves, they are conscious of themselves, they have *self-consciousness*. Human consciousness must necessarily at the same time also be *self*-conscious, because it is a *thinking* consciousness. For when thinking directs its gaze toward its own activity, it has before it as its object its very own being, that is, its subject.[77]

Examining this passage from the perspective of language, we suddenly become aware of something: in addition to the articles, conjunctions and prepositions, the words are mostly verbs, nouns, and pronouns, with only essential adjectives and almost no adverbs. Little is added to the action words, the verbs, and the nouns. As we read, we are kept very tightly on this level of *being* and *action*.

The verbs in this passage are: *is, move, thinks, is, is, is, meet, are, is, characterizes, is, observe, appear, think, experience, regard, direct, observe, are, direct, are,*

---

76 Steiner, *The Boundaries of Natural Science*, pp. 106–107 (trans. revised).

77 Steiner, *Intuitive Thinking as a Spiritual Path*, pp. 51–52.

have, must, be, is, directs, has, is. The nouns are: *moment, thinking, being, thinker, thinking, observation, consciousness, stage, concept, observation, fact, consciousness, mediator, thinking, observation, extent, beings, things, things, extent, beings, things, objects, subjects, thinking, objects, thinking, self-consciousness, consciousness, time, consciousness, thinking, gaze, activity, object, being, subject.* Pronouns are: *this, who, it, one another, this, what, it, they, themselves, they, themselves, they, what, they, they, they, themselves, they, themselves, they, it, it, it, that, its.* Adjectives are: *linked, human, connected, human, human, given, human, active, thinking, their, conscious, conscious, human, same, self-conscious, thinking, its, its, own, its, its, very, own.* Adverbs are *necessarily, also.*

When we read all 200 pages of this remarkable text, we can see how it affects us, since it is composed primarily of action words. There is nothing to stop us, nothing in the sentences where we pause to wonder. We are made to thinking actively at all times, thereby entering another realm, that of *action, life, aliveness.* In other words, we enter the *spirit world*, not the world of passive, brain reflection. This is the point of this difficult book.

In my own writing, I admit to meandering greatly, but I always return to the point. In this book, I deliberately offer these diversions to give the reader a bit of a rest before going back to the difficult, steep, thorny ascent of understanding. But I always reread *The Philosophy of Freedom* once or twice a year just to sharpen my mind, to teach myself to stay with the subject and not wander around it with too many diversions, disciplining it to become like a sword penetrating the truth. It can be painful.

Steiner tells us that if we want to communicate with departed souls, we should communicate only with verbs, action words, because that is what they understand. When sending prayers, use only verbs like being, becoming, loving, and not other words.[78] That is a meditation in itself. So if you have not picked up this remarkable book lately, or ever, now is the time—one sentence at a time.

Whoever reads my *Philosophy of Spiritual Activity* will find that it is based entirely on the theory of knowledge that holds: for people, reality

---

78 See Steiner, *Staying Connected*, chapter 12, "The Language of the Heart."

is attained by human effort in the activity of thinking. *Thus human knowledge is the gateway into the actual experience of reality....*

In *The Philosophy of Spiritual Activity*, I set up in its place the transformed "I," which having raised itself into the spiritual sphere begins to *love* virtue and practices it, because it loves it in its own individual being.[79]

We can also look at "active thinking" from another perspective: What actually happens when we think? Steiner's insight awakens within us something extremely powerful. It is all about warmth and heat. We enter the activity of thinking from the side of physics. The heat, the warmth element, is what unites, bridging the heavens with the Earth.

Of everything in the universe, of all properties of being in the universe, one such property is easier to study than others if we set aside the biases of modern science; it is the element of *heat....*

In this particular heat...in what we possess as our own heat, and in what separates itself from all other universal warmth as our own warmth organism—we have our inmost corporeality, our inmost bodily field of activity. We are unaware of this because it escapes ordinary observation that the element of soul and spirit dwelling in us finds its immediate continuation in the effect it has on the heat within us.... When we see someone before us, we also have an enclosed space of heat before us that is warmer than its environment. Our soul and spirit element lives in that increased temperature, and the soul and spirit in us is indirectly conveyed, by means of the heat, to our other organs....

If we truly investigate the idea of the human being, we find that the thinking that asserts itself in the head is connected closely with the activity within conditions of heat and warmth. If we observe this interaction of thoughts in this enclosed space of heat, it becomes clear that something like cooperation takes place between thought activity and heat activity.... Suppose we have a fluid substance; we bring it to the boiling point, then it evaporates and changes into a more rarefied substance. The same process takes place far more intensely in human thinking, whose effect on metabolism in the human head is to make all substance fall away like a sediment and be expelled, so that nothing remains of it but mere picture.

79　Steiner, *The Redemption of Thinking*, pp. 109–110 (trans. revised).

I will use another image to clarify matters. Suppose you have a vessel containing a solution. You cool it down, which is also a heat-process. A sediment collects below, with a finer liquid remaining above. This is also the case with the human head, but here no substance whatever is collected above, but only pictures; all matter is expelled. This is the activity of the human head; it forms mere pictures and expels what is matter. This process takes place, as a matter of fact, in everything that may be called our transition to pure thinking. All material substance that has been active in our inner life falls back into the organism, so to speak, and only pictures remain. It is a fact that, when we rise to pure thought, we live in pictures. Our soul lives in pictures; and these images are the remains of all that has gone before. Not the substance, but only the pictures remain.

What I have described to you can be followed right into the thoughts themselves, for this process takes place only at the moment when thoughts change into only images. Initially, thoughts live, as it were, in corporeal and embodied form. They are permeated by substance, but as pictures they separate themselves from this substance. If, however, we go to work in a truly spiritual-scientific way, we can easily distinguish pure thought—sense-free thought that has separated itself from the material process—from all thoughts belonging to what I have called "instinctive wisdom of the ancients."

The nature of this instinctive wisdom of the ancients was such that it did not filter out matter in this way. This filtering away of matter and substance is a result of human evolution. Although not observed by external physiology, it is a fact that the thinking of earthly humanity before the Mystery of Golgotha was generally united with matter, and that when the Mystery of Golgotha intervened in the life Earth's evolution, humanity had evolved to the point where it could separate matter from the inner process of thought, and matter-free thought became possible.

Please do not think this unimportant. It is actually one of the most important things of all that humankind in its evolution has become freed of corporeal thinking, that thoughts have changed to pure images. Thus, we may say that, up to the time of the Mystery of Golgotha, bodily pictures lived in human beings, but after the Mystery of Golgotha, material-free pictures lived in human beings. *Before* the Mystery of Golgotha, the universe affected human beings in such a way that they could not attain body-free, matter-free pictures. *Since* the Mystery of Golgotha, the universe has withdrawn. Humankind has been transposed to an existence that takes place only in pictures....

Descartes was still floundering, and instead of saying "I think, therefore I am not," he said the opposite of the truth: "I think, therefore I am."

When we live in pictures, we really *are not.* When we live in mere thoughts, it is the surest sign that we are not. Thoughts must be filled with substantiality. So that human beings might not continue to live in mere pictures, so that inner substantiality might exist again in human beings, the being who entered through the Mystery of Golgotha [Christ] intervened....

Throughout the world of nature, the conversion and transformation of forces and energy prevail. Matter is cast out by pure thought only in human beings. The matter that is actually cast out of the human being by pure thought is also annihilated; it passes into nothingness. The human being, therefore, is a place in the universe where matter ceases to exist.

If we reflect on this, we must think of all earthly existence as follows. Here is the Earth, and on the Earth is humankind; matter passes into human beings. Everywhere else, it is transformed. In human beings it is annihilated. The material Earth will pass away as human beings gradually destroy matter. Someday, when all earthly substance has passed through the human organism, having been used for thinking, the Earth will cease to be a planetary body. What humankind will have gained from the earth will be images. These, however, will have a new reality; they will preserve a primal reality. That reality is the one arising from the central force that entered human evolution through the Mystery of Golgotha.... Without the mystery of Golgotha, the Earth would be reabsorbed into the universe at the end of earthly evolution, and only images without reality would remain. What makes them real, however, is the fact that the Mystery of Golgotha was present within human evolution, giving these pictures inner reality for the life to come. Through the Mystery of Golgotha, a new beginning becomes possible for the Earth's future existence....

Christianity will not be understood until it has penetrated all of our knowledge, right into the realm of physics, until we understand how, even in physical existence, Christ's substantiality works within world existence. We cannot understand Christianity until we can say: Precisely in the domain of heat a change is taking place in human beings that results in matter being destroyed and a purely picture existence arising out of matter; but through the union of the human soul with the Christ substance this picture existence becomes a new reality....

Today, people generally look upward into abstraction; we have our thoughts up there, and we look down into physical materiality. But we do not recognize the inwardly stirring heat or warmth between these, which has, at least for human instinct, a physical as well as a soul aspect. We can develop warmth for others morally—soul warmth, which is the counterpart of physical warmth. This soul warmth, however, does not arise through a physical change.... But how does it arise? I might say that here it gives palpable evidence of itself. Why do we speak of "warm" feelings? Because we feel, we experience, that the feeling we call "warm" is an image of outer, physical warmth. Warmth percolates into the image. And what is only soul warmth today will play a physical part in a future cosmic existence, for the Christ impulse will live in it. What is simply an image of warmth today in our world of feeling will live, become physical, when earthly warmth has disappeared, in what is Christ substance, Christ nature.[80]

I included this long quotation because understanding what actually happens within us when we think properly and exert some force with our thinking is complex. As we read *Intuitive Thinking as a Spiritual Path: A Philosophy of Freedom*, and as we meditate, we generate heat within us as warmth and love, and in that substantiality, the Christ force lives and brings to life the dead, abstract, cold images. In Christ's words: "I am the way, the truth, and the life" (John 14:6). If this does not happen, we simply have no future, because there are no beginnings. In this case, Descartes might be right, "I think, therefore I am," or more likely, "I think, therefore I am dead."

I spend a lot of time reading, studying, living into one course of lectures after another, and plunging myself into Steiner's works, his Anthroposophy, or wisdom of humanity. When I was thirty-nine years old, at the very beginning

---

80 Steiner, *Mystery of the Universe*, pp. 205–209, 210, 212, 213, 216 (trans. revised).

of my discovery of this marvelous work, I remember enthusiastically telling a friend at High Mowing in Wilton, New Hampshire, where I was teaching, that I was going to read all of his books. I had no inkling of the dimension of Steiner's work, the hundreds of books and published lecture courses, and it is no wonder the person looked at me and seemed to be thinking, *Good luck!* I could not understand this attitude at the time, but sometimes ignorance is a blessing. If I had known the magnitude of Steiner's colossal body of work, I might never have begun.

⟱

One summer, I spent a few weeks with my young daughter at the Rudolf Steiner Institute in Maine, where I studied with Dennis Klocek. I saw in the Rudolf Steiner Institute's catalogue that he was teaching projective geometry, as well as a course on plants, and I decided I must attend. I had previously done a lot of work with projective geometry on my own, using *Sunspace*, the beautiful book by Olive Whicher. I fell in love with the beauty of that book and did all its exercises in large notebooks. I loved its simplicity and plunging and living into the forms. At university, I had started to major in both mathematics and literature. I loved the clarity of mathematics, but my professor was not gifted with imagination, so I quit mathematics and continued with literature. Now I was happy to pursue mathematics in this lively form again, and to this day I still pick up my ruler, pencil, and compass, and enjoy these beautiful forms.

The first day of the class, I was not sure that I wanted to repeat exercises that I had previously done on my own, and I went up to Dennis and announced rather arrogantly (though not intentionally), "Dennis, I have done all that stuff already, is there anything new?" He looked at me, and said "Well, think about it. There is always something new."

So I stayed in the class and once again experienced something new. Under his masterful teaching, I discovered much more that I had missed. After that experience, I told myself that I would never again assume that I know something, because if I had written off all those exercises, I would have missed the next level. Dennis, who now teaches at Rudolf Steiner College in Sacramento, has become one of my favorite teachers, someone whom I love and highly respect. He is one of the few who knows much but never stops inquiring, because there is always another level to reach.

I discovered what Dennis already knew, that by making the platonic solids in clay and paper, the exercises became gates through which to enter the spiritual world. Our class was a meditation and everyone was spellbound by the powers inherent in these exercises. A few years later, when I read Rudolf Steiner's *Autobiography*, I understood why he had the most amazing experiences while practicing geometry in school. It is the most wonderful gift to our children in the Waldorf schools when they experience it, as it is for adults to study it alone or in a group. The platonic solids are:

cube, or hexahedron (six faces)	EARTH
tetrahedron (four faces)	FIRE
icosahedron (twenty faces)	WATER
octahedron (eight faces)	AIR
dodecahedron (twelve faces)	ETHER

We enter the elemental world as we move our consciousness from one platonic solid to another. As we form one shape and morph it into another, we move our attention from one consciousness to another—from earth, to fire, to water, to air, and backward—it is fascinating and rewarding, and of course very lively.

His other class was about the plant world. I have always been an avid gardener and am a trained herbalist, and I have my hands in the dirt for at least five months out of the year, so that class also spoke to my heart. He taught us how to see the different cosmic and earthly forces active in the plants, and much more. This was not the study of dissecting things in fragments of knowledge, but an active participation in life and becoming—Goethean science.

As the session grand finale, we built contraptions out of the platonic solids and went outside to work on clouds. Everyone was exhilarated and spellbound as we dissolved cloud formations and built clouds. Dennis is an expert weatherman, and has an internet site that is both educating and exiting.[81]

Here we see meditation at its best, in nature, observing how the cosmos and the Earth work in harmony. These are healthy, safe ways to meditate, whether through botany, platonic solids, colors, projective geometry, or "new alchemy," of which Dennis is an expert.

Rudolf Steiner College has a serious spiritual science program. Students who enter are prepared for "entrance into the spiritual world." Dennis always makes his students very much aware of what is at stake. One of his comments to young men and women (and the not so young) is, "If you enter the spiritual world unprepared, you will be a plaything for the beings who are waiting there. So you better build your hut." As far as I am concerned, it is one of the best programs for students who are serious about entering the "modern path of initiation." Young people now need to be initiated, but not in the wrong ways such as through drugs, risk-taking activities, or unhealthy living. They need programs such those at Rudolf Steiner College, where they can learn properly how to practice meditation and learn what it is they are getting into by fooling around with meditation. They need to realize the seriousness of meditation, as I have tried to show in this book.

There is another kind of meditation I have practiced all of my life, because it has been there for free—nature as a teacher, or simply the Earth. Most people know this meditation and walk in nature and partake in nature's beauty in every season, and it has been one of my own ways of meditating. I have spent countless hours working in my flower, herb, and vegetable gardens, observing the plants growing, greeting the different plants every day, and learning something from them. It has been a fascinating study and has brought me enormous joy and love for the plant world. The simple act of watching a beautiful, delicate poppy unfold in the wind, unfolding slowing under my gaze, is a gift. Observing the insect world, birds, and farm animals teaches us something if we are awake.

It is a meditation to watch the seasons and live by them. I often spend time in high mountains and enjoy the purity of the winter landscapes. The bare

---

81   See, for example, Klocek, *Climate: Soul of the Earth.*

white snowy scenes offer a return to simplicity, to the hard work of keeping warm by splitting wood, and learning how to live with very little. Skiing in white-out blizzard conditions is a real joy. It makes one realize how small we are. I have lived that way for many years, and I would not give up the "snow-ice" experience for anything. I have also enjoyed the ocean in all its magnificent glory, its awesome cleansing and rejuvenation powers, and have learned much from its infinite depth. When we live with the elements, we have access to an entrance into the spiritual world that is both safe and awesome.

There is a path followed by the Russian sages, the *staretz*, or spiritual fathers, which is called *Hesychia* (from the Greek personification of tranquillity and peace). It is a tradition of the Christian contemplative tradition, practiced for hundreds of years across Russia. In this tradition, one repeats a mantra such as *"Kyrie eleison"* (Lord, take pity on me), thousands of times in a day. They live in deep total silence at Mt. Athos in Greece.[82]

French writer Jean-Yves Leloup described meditations he practiced when he was a young man in many of his wonderful books such as *Writings on Hesychasm*. Jean-Yves was taught by Father Seraphin at Mt. Athos in Greece.

> Meditate like a mountain—sit down like a mountain
> Meditate like a poppy, learn to flower
> Meditate like the ocean
> Meditate like a bird
> Meditate like Abraham
> Meditate like Jesus
> Now you can go.

Hesychasm is born directly out of the Christian tradition. It is based on the Christ. Without the Christ there is no possibility of divinization, or becoming godly. Christ's incarnation establishes communion between God and Man. "God became Man so that Man can become God."[83]

Here are some meditations from this wonderful text:

---

82   See, for example, the anonymously written *The Way of a Pilgrim*, which records a first-hand experience of practicing the Jesus Prayer, "Lord Jesus Christ have mercy on me."

83   Leloup, *Writings on Hesychasme*, p. 100.

Faire quelque chose sans amour, voila ce qui rend l'homme impur, introduire de l'amour dans tous nos actes, c'est ce qui les transforme et les purifie du dedans, comme le feu, disent les anciens alchemists.

Ancient alchemists said, "To act without love, that is what makes a person impure; to introduce love into all our actions, that is what transforms and purifies one from within like fire."

Dieu cherche parmi les hommes un lieu pour son repos.
God looks among men for a dwelling in which to rest.

When do we realize our hearts are pure? When we know that all people are good; when no one seems soiled; then we are pure of heart.

I have the word *love* on my lips, but I do not taste it in my heart.[84]

This brings me to another meditation I have practiced for a long time. In the early 1990s, I attended an anthroposophic conference where René Querido gave a talk. I approached him and asked him if he knew of a good meditation for a beginner to practice. I still considered myself a beginner; technically I was not, but that was my attitude then and now; always go on; you know nothing; always start with nothing. René Querido suggested I meditate on the first verses of St. John's Gospel, which at the time I thought was strange for a meditation. Months later, I joined Kühlewind's group, which worked in a very special way with St. John's Gospel.

> By continually meditating upon passages of the Gospel of St. John, students of Christian initiation are actually in a condition to reach initiation without the three-and-a-half-day continued lethargic sleep. If students allow the first verses of the Gospel of St. John, from "In the beginning was the Word" to the passage "full of grace and truth" to work on them every day, this text becomes a very powerful meditation. The words contain power. John's Gospel is not there simply to be read and understood with the intellect; it must be fully experienced and felt inwardly. It is a force that aids and works for initiation.[85]

---

84 Ibid., p. *115.*

85 Steiner, *Isis, Mary, Sophia,* pp. 70–71.

John's Gospel belongs to the most profound writings of the world, but it must be read correctly; that means that we must not in the least believe that reading alone is sufficient. It is a book of life. Above all, you must be clear about the fact that the first words are not written merely to be read or for philosophical speculation. They are written for meditation. We need, however, to have them properly translated, not in the usual translation....

Meditation consists of an inner immersion in certain formulas, sentences, or words. But meditation that represents an important means of development is not a mere philosophical or intellectual absorption in what the esoteric teacher gives—it is rather a living into the content, even into the sounds. If you were to reflect on a sentence given to you by a teacher, you could bring forth only thoughts that you already have. But you are supposed to receive something new—that is what it is all about. Meditation sentences are sentences that are meant to open doors to the spiritual world for you. They are based on centuries of experience. One knows that every letter, every phrasing has an effect on the soul. Hence, you must meditate on the first sentences precisely according to the letter.[86]

It took me a few years to begin. I meditated for a whole year on the first few words, and lived with the words twice daily for fifteen minutes or more each time, from January until the following January. It was an awesome experience to live within those powerful words and to discover a tiny bit of what is hidden in them and to learn how the words become alive in oneself, opening new doors and new knowledge.

The most important thing is to infuse our feelings into the words so that they become more than a word and alive within ourselves. Just the few words "In the beginning" have become a treasure for me, a fountain of rejuvenation from which everything comes.

> What exists and what does not exist is made of empty attention, which therefore neither exists nor does not exist.[87]

Now back to Kühlewind's meditation. During the weekend retreat, as we sat in a circle, participating in the meditation which Georg Kühlewind

---

86 Steiner, *The Christian Mystery*, pp. 162–163.
87 Kühlewind, *The Light of the "I,"* p. 66.

had prepared for us, he lead us carefully and slowly to the spiritual world. He had us experience hovering into the spiritual world, the entrance into the spirit world, with a masterful stroke. Slowly we would enter into the peaceful "I am," not as a fiery entrance into an unknown world, but as a soft tasting of the world beyond. He designed special exercises for us to use in order to handle the entrance to the threshold. He also had an unusual way of presenting something of incredible significance. He always talked about the "robe," and in later years, at one of the weekends, he spoke about "hot ballooning." I never laughed so hard.

I am forever thankful to have participated in these retreats. I am reminded of another precious moment when all of us sat in a circle and introduced our-selves. We said where we were from and what we were doing and so on. I never knew what to say on these occasions, because I always did dozens of things—I am a gardener or something like that, or a housewife—and one person said, "I am a lover." I thought that was wonderful, just letting everything go. But here is one example, out of hundreds, of these exercises:

> Imagine an image; hold it for a short time...then let it fade away by ceasing to address it with the inner gaze. After letting associations enter, recall the image. Repeat these two movements several times....
>
> Once we attain a certain degree of intensity, which is impossible to define, our attention begins and continues to grow by itself, without our care and effort. Attention is then directed healthily toward one thing. To be one-pointed is attention's original and healthy nature.
>
> We can now have two further experiences. First, we can feel our-selves identified with the object, with its function or idea.
>
> Second, at the same time, or by slightly more growth, our attention can experience itself flowing into the theme, bringing about the theme, but still in a form-free state.
>
> *This experience we call the "I am" experience.* It is the universal heal-ing medicine. It is a feeling of identity with an ever-deepening being that wills itself. It provides certainty, creativity, and solidity, and dissolves what comes from egotism. From it, the knowledge arises that nothing can happen to me (the one who is experiencing this): I am safe, completely

independent of circumstances, opinions, successes, or failures. I have found my spiritual roots.[88]

Georg Kühlewind was a master. He wanted to make sure that students enter the spiritual world fully prepared, unlike the way I had done. With him, it was a controlled ascent, with everyone fully in charge through the continuous practice of well-defined, carefully orchestrated exercises, taking us across the threshold and then back. He was a real artist, unrecognized by most at this time, but perhaps this will change in the future.

I would call Kühlewind's way of meditation the Western Zen path of meditation. I enjoyed it because it does not involve much talk but plenty of silence. Participants would usually use words sparingly, meaningfully, and thoughtfully. We would concentrate on a couple of words at a time, such as:

"Pick up thy bed and Walk."
"Let thyself be whole."
"Light is form-free."
"Light is beyond words."
"Love speaks."
"I am always in the beginning."
"that "
"is"

And one of my favorites, "True attention is Love."

---

88   Ibid., pp. 36, 38–39.

FULL CIRCLE

We have made a complete circle, but I have not finished the story. In this book of many tales, I have wandered around Eastern and Western worlds, and I am still wandering—only now they are both joined, which is the way such a journey should end. I started with one-pointedness, and I end with one-pointedness. I had the good fortune of working with one Master of the East, Goenka, and one Master of the West, Dennis Klocek, and a Master of the Middle, Georg Kühlewind, and one of the greatest masters and seers of them all, Rudolf Steiner.

We all have our own Master and helpers in our own journeys. I am very fortunate that I am still working with all these incredible human beings, in body or in spirit. Perhaps you can describe or write your own journey and learn as much about it as I have as I wrote about my awkward journey. I must thank the reader for traveling on this journey with me. Some passages have not been easy to experience or understand. But if you have gone through the pain of trying to understand them, then you can now appreciate these little meditations and start you own journey into meditation, whichever way you choose, the Eastern or the Western way. Georg Kühlewind said, "Understanding is not-understanding; it stops when *something* is understood." [89] So therefore, there is no end; it is a circle, not a spiral.

Following this detailed account of upheavals of my soul, we return to my last journey to India, just a few weeks before writing this. Having mentioned Benares, Rishikesh, and Bodh Gaya, I will tell of my journey to the snow kingdom of Sikkim and more about the holy city of Benares, seat of *siva* worship.

The Himalayan ranges extend over almost 1,500 miles in length. Mount Everest, towering upward over 29,000 feet on the border of Nepal and

---

89 Kühlewind, *The Light of the "I,"* p. 64.

Tibet.... The word *Himalaya* comes from Sanskrit words: *hima*, meaning "snow," and *alaya*, meaning "home"—the home of snows. I would
like to make you aware that the Himalayas are not merely the home of
snow, but that they have also been a stronghold of yogic wisdom and
spirituality for millions of people, regardless of their religious beliefs.
This ancient and rich tradition still exists there today as these unique
mountains continue to whisper their spiritual glory to all who have an
ear to hear.[90]

After spending a week in Benares, the place I had chosen to relive these
experiences and write, I developed a sinus inflammation, like everyone else,
because of the extreme pollution on the plains. I decided to flee to the North.
I abandoned all my plans, left my suitcase full of books at the hostel, and took
the all-night train heading northeast toward Darjeeling. The journey took
more than thirty-five hours instead of the usual eighteen, but we all sat or
slept in our berths and rode patiently. I was thoroughly entertained, as usual,
by all the pandemonium in the train and the many people who came and went
and are always fascinated by a Western woman traveling alone. They always
ask: Why are you alone? Are you married? Aren't you afraid to go off into the
Mountains? Why? What is your religion? Do you like ours? I have fun reply-
ing and asking them the same questions in return. I am then a diplomat from
the Western world, a real diplomat, except that I do not get paid for it.

During the first part of the journey, there was a beautiful, sensual woman,
a type I have never seen before, with beautifully henna-painted hands, a sign
that she was a newlywed. She had long dark curly hair that gracefully framed
her exquisite face, with its voluptuous lips and dark gazelle eyes. She had a
beautiful *sari*, and her breasts were spilling out of her low-cut blouse. She
looked like my idea of a favorite in someone's harem. She was sexual, sensual,
and utterly seductive. I am sure no man could resist a desire for this most
unusual young woman. She was uneducated and wore a lot of gold on her
wrist. This unique, Eastern beauty seemed to be at ease with her sensuality.
She was nothing like the dry model of the West. Her husband slept with her
on the berth opposite mine. I was amazed to see that no one paid any attention

---

90   Swami Rama, *Living with Himalayan Masters*, p. 3.

to this voluptuousness, though this woman typified what the Muslim world fears, causing them to hide women behind veils.

The journey went on, and I could hear the loud conversations of men on cell phones, and there were long stops in the middle of nowhere when the train had to change course. Someone had bombed the tracks. That kind of news is never published, which is probably a good thing.

Finally, I arrived at my stop and took a little three-wheeled taxi to town, where I applied for a visa to enter the kingdom of Sikkim. I joined ten other people as we piled into a jeep to drive on the dangerous dirt road to the capital, Gangtok. The road wound through canyons and climbed up into the foothills of the Himalayas. On one side of the road, cliffs rose to mountains, and on the other the roadside fell straight down to a wild river. One small mistake and a person would disappear. We endured six hours of wild driving, I with a handkerchief on my mouth and nose because of the dust flying into the old jeep. My companions in the jeep were women who had been shopping in India, old men, workers, and young students with cell phones. Some looked Tibetan, some were dark-skinned Hindus, and all were very friendly to me.

I arrived in the capital, which is perched among several hills, a very prosperous city from the look of it, where people of three distinct groups mingle: the Tibetan, Chinese, and Hindus. I settled in a tall building where most backpackers stay and enjoyed walking around this very active, full-of-life city. I roamed the small streets where cars navigated its ups and downs and hairpin turns. I wondering how these cars could even function; they were like goat carts. The main attraction was the main street that, like bazaars of the Middle East, was full of people walking around, a sign of a lively economy with interchange and commerce taking place. Young girls strolled about in Western or traditional clothes, giggling and using cell phones, and there were old cowboy-outfitted Tibetan men who were yak herders with huge whips, matrons shopping, old men sitting on benches talking, Muslim men, Hindu women in *saris*, traditional *Sikkim*-dressed men and women, Tibetan women shopping or selling their arts and crafts, Hindu businessmen, hippies from all over the world, mountain climbers and trekkers from Italy, tourists from England, and more. They all mingled in this beautiful old city full of Buddhist temples; shrines; monasteries;

schools; shops with merchandise from China, India, and the United States; Hindu clothes to die for; and excellent food, cakes, and cappuccinos.

I visited several temples and walked through uphill gardens. In one garden, I heard a lovely young woman dressed in military uniform ask, "Aunty, can you join us for a picture?"

She was in a group of giggling young girls from India who were on a trip, all dressed in uniforms with their long beautiful black hair in braids. So we took pictures, all of them wanting a picture of me with them. I proceeded to walk with them for the next several hours. They had escaped the village life, where they would have had two or three children by now, and joined the army. I loved their reverence for older people. My new name in India is Aunty. All the older women are called Aunty, which is such a lovely term.

I first heard about this ancient city Gangtok when, in my twenties, I read all the books of Alexandra David-Neel, my favorite adventurer of this part of the world. I translated from the French her journals to her husband whom she abandoned to travel the world to report on the ancient traditions of the East. Her great wealth of stories fascinated me; I wanted to live such a life. So when I escaped Benares, I chose this little kingdom east of Nepal that I had never visited before. North of Sikkim is Tibet, in the west is Bhutan, and south is India. This path through Sikkim is one that Alexandra David-Neel chose when she escaped into Lhasa, the Forbidden City, dressed as a monk one hundred years ago.

During breakfast at the hostel I overheard a conversation between a couple of Israeli backpackers who were going trekking, and I paid close attention: trekking, mountains, walking. I had not planned on it, but there I was, so trekking I would go. I had brought my hiking shoes and backpack just in case. As I said before, I was supposed to stay put in Benares and write this meditation book, but my mind was elsewhere. I was in the middle of new beginnings and I needed to walk once again and forget about words for the time being.

After walking up and down the many hills of this big city, I took a jeep down to the Eastern part of Sikkim. Ten of us piled into the jeep very early one morning and drove through the same scenery, but worse now, up and down the mountains. No sooner did we arrive on top of one mountain than we had to go down another one, and this continued all day. There were pot holes as big as tires and water flowing from the mountainside onto the road. We stopped every now and then at roadside tea houses for food. There were small farms on every hillside, growing all sorts of food for animals and human beings, each farmed by hand—barley, wheat, millet, spinach, cabbages, two-foot-long white daikon radishes, salad greens, squashes, and more. Here people are left in peace because the terrain is difficult to tame.

Finally I arrived in the small town of Pelling, further south and closer to Nepal, where I stayed in a small hotel for backpackers. This cozy place was full of travelers and offered good Tibetan soups, breakfast, and stunning views of the Himalayas. I got up at 5:00 a.m. and took pictures of the view from the terrace, rejoicing in the magical sunrise, its colors kissing the over-25,000-foot peaks in the distance, the golden roof of the world.

It was still early in the morning when I walked throughout the little mountaintop town to a beautiful old monastery and was fortunate to partake in a Buddhist celebration there. Monks old and young were present. I sat by the wall on small pillows the entire morning, entranced by the readings and chanting of sacred 2,500-year-old Buddhist *sutras*. Voices resonated in the old monastery with the cacophony of ancient instruments being blown or struck, a noise that at times was not peaceful at all but very loud. I wanted to experience it to the fullest, so I sat cross-legged and listened to the wild sounds echoing throughout the old three-storied buildings. The walls were decorated with old *tonka* paintings of demons peeking out, wild tongues hanging out, furious mating—all enough to scare anyone out of their wits. But in the end, all this is within ourselves, and there is no sense in being afraid. One must face fear and change it, transform it. The monks included me in their rituals while other tourists came in and out. I sat quietly and meditated, thankful just to be allowed there among them, part of their ancient rituals.

They gave me part of their offerings. I was the only woman in the large room, but it did not matter. When I bowed and left, my body still reverberated with the wild sounds of the unusual musical instruments. If you let yourself flow with the sounds, they definitely broke the veil between this world and the other. It went on for hours, sounds that come from another world—not earthly, nor paradise either, but full of grotesque figures.

Trekking the Himalayas in Sikkim, India

I walked back slowly to the hotel and joined a young Australian Vietnamese girl, Michele, who wanted to trek. We decided to trek together for ten days. One could not go alone. The next day we departed, once again in a jeep, and this time they told me the road would be really bad. It was—pot holes, more rivers running through the road, mud slides—but we finally got to the village of Yoksum where all the trekkers depart to access the highest elevations into Nepal, Tibet, and China.

The town was full of life, with yaks, horses, and ponies coming back from the mountains or loading for another expedition. We stayed in a lovely hotel which had hot water and took our last shower for the next 10 days. The town was as it had been hundreds of years ago. In the evening we sat cozily at a local open-air tent restaurant and ate our dinner in the company of worn out trekkers dressed in worn-out clothing, from everywhere around the world, old and young, excited about past journeys and planning new ones, sharing their precious moments on the road.

The next morning after an excellent breakfast we joined our hired team. We were completely surprised to learn that for just the two of us, there was one chef-cook-guide, one assistant cook-porter, one yak herder, one porter, one more younger guide who would walk with us at all times so we would not get lost, and two lovely black yaks. We were given warm sleeping bags, and I was given two walking sticks. After a couple of hours of packing into huge baskets the cooking gear, fresh eggs and other foods that the two yaks would carry on their backs, we were off.

Michele had never gone walking or trekking, but she ran ahead of me: she is twenty-one and I am sixty-one. I had an adopted daughter for the next few weeks. I felt fortunate to partake in this unplanned agenda. I generally do not plan much when I travel, but just let things happen. Rare occasions arise when I do schedule things, like writing in India, but sometimes things turn out much more exciting than the original plan.

Finally I was getting a taste of what Alexandra David-Neel had spent her whole life doing. No wonder she felt ill and morose whenever she returned to Europe and could not wait to escape back to these Himalayan kingdoms. I had

already trekked for months at a time in western and eastern Nepal, but then I
was alone carrying my own things; now I felt completely spoiled.

There was magic in these tallest, most majestic mountains of Mother
Earth, where holy men came to retire in the highest caves hidden above 15,000
feet. I was walking on ancient paths, passing lovely villages full of flowers, fruit
orchards, vegetable plots, and small millet fields. They were like Swiss villages
with small cozy homes. Michele, whose looks were much appreciated in this
place, said she could settle here. The guides constantly told her she looked
Nepalese, and they love the special beauty of the Nepalese women.

> Writers dare say that the Himalayas are economically disappointing,
> having few mineral deposits and being unable to support enterprises
> on a large scale. I agree with them: economically these mountains are
> not rich. They are spiritual mountains and provide for renunciates, not
> for the materially wealthy. Those who have tried to explore the riches of
> the Himalayas from an economic viewpoint have met with disaster...
> Himalayan villages have not received their share of modern education,
> technology, and medicine, even though the Himalayas are the reservoirs
> for the drinking and irrigation waters for the whole of India... However,
> the Himalayan inhabitants prefer things to remain as they are. "Leave
> us alone without exploitation; just be grateful and respect us from a dis-
> tance" are the words I hear from many villagers of the Himalayas.
>
> The economy of the villages is supported by the nearby tiny terraced
> fields, where barley, wheat, lentils are grown. Livestock include buffaloes,
> sheep, cattle, ponies, goats.[91]

The first day we spent climbing. When I say climbing I mean climbing
7000 feet in one day, relentlessly putting one foot in front of the other. But we
were living in the magic of the scenery, beautiful pink blooming trees, orchids,
birds, snowy peaks, green tropical forests, rocky paths smoothed by hundreds of human feet, moss, waterfalls, edible fruits, and suspended bridges.
Climbing was hard work, but the magic of the scenery made the day pass
without too much physical pain. We had lunch given to us on higher ground,
the cook prepared some hot tea for us, and from then on we felt absolutely

---

91 Swami Rama, *Living with the Himalayan Masters*, pp. 16–17.

spoiled. I thought I did not want to come back to the West. I was ready to just go on, to Tibet, China, Nepal, and across the entire mountain range. Behind us was a group of fifteen Italians who had just flown in to trek for ten days and then return home. They were all very fit older men and women, and they kept us company during the entire ten days. They had at least twelve yaks and an army of cooks, porters, and guides. They were also ready to laugh, sing, and have fun at all times and we thoroughly enjoyed them. We could feel why the sages flock here and remain.

That gentle and amiable sage of the Himalayas had only one entrancing theme: Love—for nature, love—for creatures, and love—for the Whole. The Himalayan sages taught me the gospel of nature. Then I started listening to the music coming from the blooming flowers, from the songs of the birds, and even from the smallest blade of grass and thorn of the bush. In everything lives the evidence of the beautiful. If one does not learn to listen to the music of nature and appreciate her beauty, then that which impels man to seek love at its fountain may be lost in the remotest antiquity.... This gospel of nature speaks its parables from the glacial streams, the valleys laden with lilies, the forests covered with flowers, and the light of the stars....

When one learns to hear the music of nature and appreciate her beauty, then his soul moves in harmony with its entire environment. His every movement and every sound will surely then finds its due place in human society. The mind of man should be trained to love nature before he looks through the corridor of his life. Then a revelation comes peeping through with the dawn. The pain and miseries of life disappear with the darkness and the mist when the sun rises....

When one learns to appreciate fully the profundity of nature in its simplicity, then thoughts flow spontaneously in response to the appeals of his delicate senses they come in contact with nature. This soul-vibrating experience, in its full harmony with the perfect orchestra of melodies and echoes, reflects from the sound of the ripples of the Ganges, the gushing of the winds, the rustling of leaves, and the roar of thundering clouds. The light of the self is revealed and all the obstacles are removed. He ascends the top of the mountain, where he perceives the vast horizon. In the depth of the silence is hidden the source of love. The eye of faith alone can unveil and see the illumination of that love. This music resounds in my ears and has become the song of my life.

This discovery of the sages binds the whole of humanity in the harmony of the cosmos. Sages are the sources from which mankind receives knowledge and wisdom to behold the light, truth, and beauty which show the path of freedom and happiness to all. They make humanity aware of the mere shadows and vain illusions of this world. With their eyes the unity of the entire universe is best seen.

"The truth is hidden by a golden disc. O Lord. Help us in unveiling so that we can see the truth." The gospel of Love as taught by the Himalayan sages makes the whole universe aware of the fountainhead of light, life, and beauty.[92]

This beautiful passage from this treasure-book reflects the mood that everyone was in as they ascended higher and higher into the mountains. We walked all day in serene scenery, climbing ever higher into the distant land of the eternal snows. We slept on the floor of old dilapidated stone buildings, and the crew cooked three full vegetarian meals a day with nothing but a small kerosene stove, with no wood and only raw materials: onions, ginger, garlic, cauliflower, cabbage, bananas, and apples. They made porridge, coconut cakes, chapatti, hot ginger tea, masala tea, lemon dessert, spaghetti, and many curries. These wonderful cooks-chefs-porters cooked as if by magic, and we fell in love with their smiles, frankness, joviality, endurance, and toughness. Every day unfolded with other magic as well, as we beheld snowy plateaus, wild noisy streams splashing on enormous boulders fallen from the glaciers, all varieties of bushes in flaming reds of autumn, green fir trees, and subtly colored mosses on massive granite rocks. We crossed rivers and ravines by narrow foot bridges that seemingly floated in the wind, and we took small, narrow paths where one had to climb up steep sides to let the yaks and ponies go by with their heavy charges. We stopped and picnicked by wild waters and enjoyed calm views of the peaks. At night, after a long day, we ate on small tables set for us with table cloths and candles. We always had warm tea and a sumptuous dinner. After getting amoebic dysentery on the Indian plain and losing weight, I was happy to be eating well or, as Michele said, stuffing ourselves.

---

92   Ibid., pp. 5–6.

Every morning, the helper cook gave us each a small container full of warm water to wash with. Trekkers in long underwear and Italians alike, we were out half naked in the freezing weather, washing ourselves as best we could in the early morning hours while the sun's rays hit the mountain peaks. Then we would pack the animals and continue for another day of climbing until we finally reached 14,000 feet. We were given ginger tea, which helped for an hour or two with the headaches that we all had. Some had to go back down because of altitude sickness. We finally arrived at the high plateau and climbed even higher, leaving all the porters and animals in the high valley. At 16,000 feet, in the moon-like landscape of ancient rocks, ice, ice lakes, ancient stones carved with mantras, and flags floating in the icy wind, we saw wild sheep on the cliffs looking for food. We descended another way, thus making a beautiful circle amidst these ancient peaks.

On the way down, I noticed a party of twelve going up, crossing our path with their yaks, and I saw a pale-faced, blue-eyed man having a very difficult time climbing. He was with his beautiful Indian wife. That night, the couple came to the place we were staying, and we learned that he had altitude sickness and had to turn around. He had been extremely ill, but the next day he felt better and we had a lovely chat. We shared our food because their party had gone on to the peak. He was an engineer on vacation from Germany with his Hindu wife who was a scientist—more friends for me to visit in Germany.

On the last day, the crew went on ahead of us, and by noon they had set up the little tables again, with a full-course Indian meal at the foot of a large tumbling waterfall. Here they all tidied up, washed, brushed their teeth, and went into the icy waters before reaching the village. Michele and I just ate, watching the rushing waters, saying thank you again and again.

We reached the small town and took our first hot shower, somewhat back to civilization again. We rode by jeep back to the monastery town of Pelling, and I booked myself into a deluxe but surprisingly affordable hotel for two days. The view from my room was a horizon of high snowy peaks, and I enjoyed a fireplace for warmth and a few wonderful people for companionship. As I was walking along the winding narrow road of the town, I saw a man with wild white hair on a motorcycle. He stopped to ask where to stay and I showed him my hotel. There I heard his stories of touring India on this motorbike. His name was Pierre, and he had fascinating tales about his journeys from one end of the Himalayas to the other. Thank goodness for such a free spirit; our society cannot tame them. Earlier I had met an amazing woman from Paris who had given up her job as a pharmacist to travel the whole world for a year. She had just flown in from Tajikistan, where she had gone on a wild horseback riding adventure on the tundra and there had met the love of her life, a German airline pilot. Traveling is fantastic; one meets the most amazing human beings. So that evening I invited this young woman, Pierre, and the abbot of the monastery for tea. They stayed for dinner. Entertainment in these sacred, remote places is magic.

There was also a newlywed couple from Bombay wearing regal Muslim clothes. The lady was beautiful—not the seductive beauty of the woman on the train, but a beauty only known to the East. She was a teacher and highly intelligent, and her husband was as handsome as she was beautiful. We all chatted until it was time for us to get some rest.

The next day I rented a jeep with the Muslim couple from Bombay to go to the Airport, a six-hour ride across the mountains. I flew to Calcutta and took another flight back to Benares for the continuation of my trip. Finally, after all these years, I had tasted Alexandra David-Neel's world. And I was ready for more. Once one has the travel bug, there is no ignoring it. Or are we the "ravens"? Some of us have to go to the far corners of the Earth to bring back some news, real news.

The trip back to Benares was quite an ordeal. I took an airplane to a city where I had to spend the night, and then a train to Benares the next morning. I arrived late and had to hire a rickshaw to take me into the city to find a hotel. I spent at least two hours wandering by rickshaw from hotel to hotel. The whole city was full, extremely full, and that was a terrible position to be in. There were no women in sight, only men, but as I am not given to being fearful, I kept going on, asking for help from strangers. They told me that there was a huge computer conference going on and there were no rooms to be had. Then I remembered that the train station had rooms to let to foreign tourists, and I went back there and pleaded with two attendants to give me a room. By now the station was full of people, whole families sleeping on the floor, one on top of the other. I thought that perhaps I would have to sleep next to them on the floor, with rats running among us. There must have been thousands of bodies sleeping on top of their bundles. I pleaded again with the old guys and they gave me a room.

It was by far the dirtiest room I have ever been in. I later learned that these rooms are rented by the hour to men for sexual encounters with other men. I settled in this atmosphere and tried to sleep. Of course I could not, with the dirt, the stench, the noise, the flimsy lock, and the unclean aura of the place—not the accommodation I was used to. I wrapped myself in my shawl as best I could, spread some clothes on the filthy foam mattress, and waited for morning. At least I had a room. When one travels as I do, these are the moments that invariably come and one must endure them. Tomorrow, all will be forgotten, as indeed it was the next day as I left on the train.

After the fresh air in the mountains, I was ready to spend a few more days in Benares to meet up with friends. I especially enjoyed a restaurant owned by a German woman, which was outdoors on a terrace high up on the banks of the river, a favorite of travelers. There one could lounge on foam mattresses and enjoy the view of the wide flowing river down below. I did more shopping for Indian clothes, bought some books, and took rides on the river early and late in the day.

I witnessed the dead wrapped in silks, brought from all parts of India, transported in the narrow city streets on the shoulders of young men twenty-four hours a day, bound for the *ghats* after being anointed on the seven chakras with sacred oils. One of the young brahmans circulating and chatting among the foreigners at the *ghats* shared this knowledge:

first chakra, honey:	bee
second, curd:	cow
third, butter:	cow
fourth, rose:	plant, five-pointed star
fifth, sandalwood tree;	aromatic wood
sixth, jasmine;	flower
seventh, lotus oil;	flower

We see that the highest chakras are anointed with gifts of the bees and sacred cows. At the heart is the "universal rose." The lowest chakras are anointed with oils of sacred scent. What an amazing science! If one wants to study aryuvedic medicine, plants, or flower essences, Benares, or Varanasi, is a good place to go.

I watched as many as ten bodies burning at the same time and the intense activities of the cremations rites, which were well-ordered amidst total chaos. Goats and their twin kids munched on flower garlands from off the bodies, cows wandered everywhere, and dogs meandered in between the funeral pyres, quietly and peacefully. Everything had a meaning even though it looked like the biggest mess I have ever witnessed. There were the men who sold the wood to the family members so that the body could burn; the thin, poor men who worked on the funeral pyres in underwear arranging the logs; and the men who hung around in the water after the rest of the body was thrown in the river. The latter dove and picked up any jewelry found on the remains of the bodies. There was a boat with a body on top which would not be burned, per-haps that of a pregnant woman. She would be dropped into the Ganges with a stone attached to her. Sometimes, the stones are not attached correctly and the bodies float amidst the boats. The families stand by, the husbands and the sons with shaved heads. They recite prayers and we observe it all from afar, trying not to disturb. If one thinks how many souls are going to the higher world from this sacred city, one must feel its impact. I see it as a huge entrance into the spirit world. They say that the funeral pyres never stop, and have never stopped, for thousands of years, and *Agni*, the purifier energies, are present everywhere.

> With the conception of *Agni*, the divine fire, we are very close to the core of the doctrine and its esoteric, transcendent foundation. In fact, *Agni* is the cosmic agent, the principle of the universe, par excellence. "It is not only the terrestrial fire of lightning, and the sun. Its true domain is the unseen, mystical heaven, temporary dwelling place of the eternal light and of the first principles of all things. Its births are infinite, whether it bursts forth from the piece of wood in which it sleeps like the embryo in the womb, ...

"Soul of heaven and of earth, of Indra and Vishnu, with Agni, it forms an inseparable couple; this couple that lighted the sun and stars."

The conception of *Agni* and *Soma* contains the two essential principle of the universe, according to esoteric doctrine and all living philosophy. Agni is the *Eternal Masculine*, the creative intellect, pure spirit; Soma is the *Eternal Feminine*, the soul of the world, or the ethereal substance, womb of all the visible and invisible worlds before the eyes of the flesh, and finally nature, or subtle matter in its infinite transformations. And the perfect union of these two beings constitutes the supreme being and essence of God.

From these two major ideas springs a third and no less fecund one. The Vedas make of *the cosmogonic act a perpetual sacrifice*. In order to produce all that exists, the supreme being sacrifices himself; he divides himself in order to emerge from his unity....

The fire sacrifice with its ceremonies and prayers, the unchangeable center of the Vedic cult, thus becomes a reflection of this great cosmogonic act....

As for the immortality of the soul, the Vedas confirm this with unmistakable clarity. "There is an immortal side to man; that is the one, O Agni, which you must warm with your rays and quicken with your fires. O Jatavedas, in the glorious body, formed by you, carry it to the world of the godly." The Vedic poets not only indicate the destiny of the soul, but are also concerned with its origin. "Where were souls born? There are those who come to us and return, who return and come back again."[93]

Benares is one of the liveliest cities I have ever lived in. All of India is alive, we know, but this city is in a league of its own. I lived daily with the funeral pyres and fires during the festivals, and ever-present tiny hand-made lights with small candlewicks lit by the worshippers that float by on these sacred waters by the thousands. The lively children with their fully awake eyes seem to know you; everyone looks at your soul, at who you are—not what you look like physically, but who you truly are.

---

93 Schuré, *The Great Initiates*, pp. 60–63.

The Eagle, the Lion, and the Holy Cow

Here I must speak about the ever-present holy cow, especially in the very narrow passages of ancient Benares, Veranasi. At first I had to overcome the stench of it all, but after a while I noticed that the streets do get cleaned, and the manure disappears for a couple of hours before it, of course, reappears. The gentle cows and bulls wander in the tiny streets. Benares is the farmyard of these holy animals; they are fed the refuse of the city. People put down uneaten food in plastic bags and the cows eat whatever is left over. I learned that often the cows get very ill from eating the plastic bags which then become stuck in their long stomachs, and a team of foreign veterinarians operate on them regularly. The bulls try to mate in the middle of the path, and everyone goes on with their business as if nothing is happening. Children pass by, the holy sadhu gently pets the hump of the grey cow, or the businessman in his suit pats the head of a soft doe-eyed cow on his way to work, and deeper inside the city one notices that under the tall buildings, in the basements, there are small barns where the cows are kept and milked. I heard that all cows wandering in the city are owned by someone. Where I was staying, one cow was tied to a rope and her calf was having its breakfast. There is also a small milk market where the locals come with milk cans and pick up milk in huge containers that have been driven there by bikes, rickshaws, or trucks. The very large milk cans are enveloped in iced heavy cotton bags to keep the milk cool. Everyone waits in a long queue for the milk. It's a city where the milk is still delivered. Benares is really a village, and one can get everything in this very simple way. What a gift! In Wisconsin, where I used to live part of the year, one of our wonderful farms has been closed down because the large companies that own the lawmakers want to own the right to sell milk in packages. That is where we are in the great sophisticated West. Where is the progress?

As mentioned before, I spent quite a long time traveling in India in my twenties from west to south, to east and north, for many months at a time. I observed the cows and was fascinated. But it was many years before I read what Rudolf Steiner had to say about the deep significance of this sacred animal in India. As usual, it is complex and not to be read as information, but as substance to meditate upon. In order to understand the veneration and love for the cow, we must use "thinking of the heart," and not our intellect.

Earlier, as I was relating my experience of the dove, you will recall that I explored the insights of the dove-eagle-bird kingdom and the lion and cow-ox kingdoms. Now I would like to return to that and look deeper into these connections.

> When we look back into ancient periods of humankind, we find everywhere that the present "I" developed from such a group-consciousness, a group "I"; ... There are four main types of group soul, four archetypes. ...
>
> When the mineral beings began to assume their present form, human beings emerged from invisibility. The neophyte saw it in this way: Surrounded by a kind of shell, human beings descended from the regions that are now regions of air. They were not yet as physically condensed when the animals already existed in the flesh. Humans were delicate airy beings, even in the Lemurian [pre-Atlantian] epoch, and they developed in such a way that a clairvoyant picture reveals the four group souls. On the one hand, something like the image of a lion, on the other the likeness of a bull, above something like an eagle and below, in the center something similar to a human being. ... Thus human beings come from the darkness of the spirit land. ... These four group souls developed from the common god-human who descends. From time immemorial, this stage has been symbolized in the form represented by the second of the seven "occult seal pictures."[94]

If we contemplate these matters today and realize again that human beings are actually born from the whole nature, that we bear the whole nature within us, that we bear the bird kingdom, the lion kingdom, the essential nature of the cow in us, then we have the individual aspects of what is expressed in the abstract sentence: The human being is a

---

94 Steiner, *The Apocalypse of St. John*, pp. 49, 50 (trans. revised).

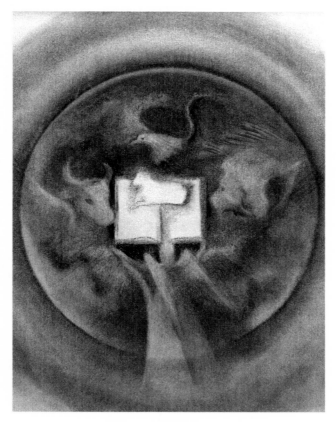

The charcoal rendering by Dorothea Sunier-Pierce of the second seal, showing the Eagle,
the Lion, the Cow or Bull, and the Human Being, with the Lamb of God in the center.

microcosm. We are indeed each a microcosm, and the macrocosm is in us; all the creatures that live in the air, all the animals on the face of earth, whose special element is the air that circulates there, and the animals whose special element is below the surface of the earth, in the forces of gravity—all these work together in human beings as a harmonious whole. Thus, the human being is a synthesis of eagle, lion, and ox or cow.[95]

Not only is the human being composed of these three—eagle, lion and cow—but also the eagle stands for the head or the thinking system; the lion for the breathing heart, or the feeling system; and the cow for the digestive/

---

95   Steiner, *Harmony of the Creative Word*, p. 12 (trans. revised).

metabolic system, or the will. Another insight for someone who travels extensively around the globe is that the Western world, the Americas, are under the influence of the great eagle. I observe that very easily as I cross the US continent at least once a year. In the Dakotas and barren Wyoming I always see eagles perched on the posts of fences along the highway keeping vigil, quietly looking for rabbits. Everywhere in the US, the eagle is as a symbol.

> If one contemplates the eagle with real understanding as it soars through the air, it appears as though it bore in its plumage a memory of what was present at the very inception of earth. The eagle has preserved in its plumage the forces that still worked into the earth from above. It can be said that in every eagle we see past millennia of the earth; with its physical nature the eagle has not touched the earth, or at the most only for the purpose of seizing its prey, and in no way for the satisfaction of its own life. To fulfill its own life, the eagle circles in the air because it is indifferent to what has developed on the earth, because it takes joy and inspiration from the forces of the air, because it actually despises the life of the earth and wishes to live in the element in which the earth itself lived when it was not yet earth, but, in the beginning of its evolution, was still imbuing itself with heavenly forces. The eagle is the proud creature that would not partake in the evolution of the solid earth, which withdrew from the influence of this solidifying process and wished to remain united only with the forces which were there at the inception of the earth.[96]

We have in our minds the picture of the great native chiefs of the plains, American Indians, with stunning headdress made of eagle feathers. In India, the world of the Hindus, we cannot be surprised that their eagle is the holy cow. In Europe, Germany in its center has the lion as its cow. One can also see this influence in literature, with the great lionhearted heroes such as Richard *coeur de lion* for example. And there is Georg Kühlewind, a big warmhearted thinker from Hungary in the heart of Europe. In Steiner's lecture cycle *Harmony of the Creative Word*, which is a masterpiece, one can read about these profound insights into humanity and the world:

---

96   Ibid., p. 33 (trans. revised).

Let us now turn our attention from everything we perceive as the bird kingdom up in the air, and from everything that lives in the circulation of the air in the immediate environment of the earth—the lion, for example. Let us consider the ox or cow. I have frequently spoken of the pleasure to be gained from watching a herd of cattle, lying replete and satisfied in a meadow, and from observing the process of digestion that is again expressed in the position of the body, in the eyes, in every movement.... It is really marvelous to see how the animal raises its head, how in this lifting there is a feeling that it is all heaviness, that it is not easy for a cow to lift its head, and there is something rather special going on. Seeing a cow in the meadow disturbed in this way, we must say to ourselves: This cow is amazed at having to raise its head for anything but grazing. "Why am I raising my head? I am not grazing, and there is no point in lifting my head unless it is to graze."... You cannot imagine a lion lifting its head the way a cow does. This is in the shape of the head. And if we observe the animal's whole form further, we see that it is indeed what I may call a complete digestive system. The weight of the digestion burdens the circulation to such a degree that it overwhelms everything to do with the head and breathing. The animal is all digestion. It is truly marvelous, if we observe with the spiritual eye, when we turn our gaze upward to the birds, and then down to the cow....

A cow becomes beautiful in the process of digestion. Seen in its astral aspect, this digestive process has something infinitely beautiful. In the light of ordinary mundane notions, crude ideas of perfection, the business of digestion is the lowest of the low. Yet one is proved utterly wrong in this, once a higher point of view is achieved and one sees the digestive process in the cow with the spiritual eye. It is beautiful; it is magnificent; it is something of a tremendous spiritual nature....

If we now want to look for similar phenomena in human beings, something that corresponds to a one-sided development in the cow, or the physical embodiment of a certain astral element, we find it in human digestive organs and their continuation into the limbs—interwoven harmoniously with whatever else is there. The things I see in the eagle high in the air above and in the animal that rejoices in the surrounding air, just as the lion does, and in the animal connected with earth forces that come from below ground and are active also in the digestive organs—in other words, if I do not look up to the heights but into the depths, entering the nature of the cow with understanding—I find all three configurations united as one, harmonized and balanced in the human being. I find the metamorphosis of the bird in the human head, the metamorphosis of the lion in the human chest, and the metamorphosis of the cow in the digestive system, and the limbs—once again utterly metamorphosed, completely transformed....

When these things are researched and rediscovered through a modern science of the invisible, of the spirit, one gains that great respect for ancient instinctive clairvoyant insight into the cosmos, of which I have often spoken, respect for the grand vision that human beings consist of eagle, lion, and cow or ox which together, harmonized in true proportion, form human beings in their wholeness....

When the human head looks for what accords with its nature, it must gaze upward to the bird kingdom. The human chest—the heartbeat and breathing—must, if it desires to understand itself as a mystery of nature, turn its gaze to something like the nature of the lion. And human beings must try to understand their metabolic system through the constitution, or organization, of the ox or cow. In the head, however, human beings have the vehicle for thoughts, in the chest the vehicle for feelings, and in the metabolic system the vehicle for the will. Thus, in our soul-nature, too, we are an image of the thoughts that move through the world with the birds and find expression in the bird's plumage; of the world of feeling that encircles the earth, which is to be found in the lion in the balanced life of heartbeat and breathing. These latter are toned down in human beings, but nevertheless represent the quality of inner courage....

Mahatma Gandhi is a man who certainly directs his activities entirely toward outer affairs, but nonetheless represents something like an eighteenth-century rationalist among the Indian people and in relation to the ancient Hindu religion. The remarkable phenomenon is that he has nevertheless retained veneration of the cow in his enlightened Hinduism.

Things such as these, which have persisted so tenaciously in more spiritual cultures, can be understood only when we are aware of the inner connections, when we truly know the tremendous secrets that lie in the ruminating animal, the cow. Then we can understand why people come to venerate a sublime astrality in the cow that has, as it were, become earthly, and only in this respect more lowly. Such phenomena enable us to understand religious veneration of the cow in Hinduism, whereas a whole collection of rationalistic and intellectualistic concepts brought to bear on this subject will never help us to understand it.[97]

Steiner mentions the forces active in the depths of the earth, forces streaming from the planets of Venus, Mercury, and Moon. I am going into the details, because it is important to have those images in my mind (and in yours as you read this) in order to live truly with what the East is. I had already read and reread and lived with these imaginations for years, and as I was traveling, breathing the air of Hinduism and the people, I wanted to reach, to understand, what Steiner meant. To drive on empty highways and see the eagles flying, or to witness a beautiful-eyed cow sitting on a pile of refuse, tranquilly chewing its cud after having dined on a bucket of curried rice and vegetables, are certainly experiences. I do not think I will meet a gentle lion sitting in the Black Forest of Germany, unless I look for it in the big heart of a gentle human being, which is what it means.

> By turning our minds toward the Sun's cosmic activities in conjunction with Mercury, Venus, and Moon, we come to the region containing forces taken up by ... the cow.... There, we have what the Sun cannot do on its own, but what it can do only when its own forces are conducted to Earth through the planets nearest to Earth. When these forces are all active, when they not only stream through the air, but also penetrate the Earth's surface in various ways, then they work upward from the Earth's depths. And what thus works from the depths belongs to the sphere that we see outwardly embodied in the organism of the cow.
>
> The cow is the animal of digestion. It is, moreover, the animal that accomplishes digestion so that in its digestive processes is an earthly reflection of something supra-earthly; its whole digestive process is permeated with astrality that reflects the entire cosmos in a wonderful, light-filled way. There is ... a whole world in this astral organism of the cow, but everything is based on gravity; everything is organized so that the Earth's gravity works there. You have only to consider that a cow needs to consume about an eighth of its weight in food each day. Human

---

97 Ibid., pp. 10–14 (trans. revised).

beings can be satisfied with a fortieth part and remain healthy. Thus the cow needs Earth's gravity to fully meet the needs of its organism. This organism is designed for the gravity of matter. Each day, a cow must metabolize an eighth of her weight. This binds the cow and its material substance to the Earth; yet through its astrality, it is at the same time an image of the heights, of the cosmos....

The cow is the object of much veneration for those who follow the Hindu religion. Hindu say to themselves: The cow lives here on Earth; but because of this fact it creates in physical matter, subject to gravity, an image of something supra-earthly.

It is indeed the case that the human being's organization is normal when harmony is established between these three cosmic activities that manifest in a one-sided way in the eagle, lion and cow—when human beings are the confluence of the activities of eagle, lion and cow or bull.[98]

↓

While walking the narrow, filthy back streets of Benares, I became aware of a feeling that sometimes overwhelmed me. I tried to put words to that feeling: Here I am in this city, like no other city, and I feel like I am living in the bowels of the Earth. People are everywhere, sitting on the ground without much separating them from Mother Earth, amid the chaos of the wandering cows, bulls, and calves. The cows all walk gently, minding their own business as if they were in a meadow rather than in the middle of a big city.

It was certainly overwhelming to be in the Earth's bowels. This picture that I repeatedly envisioned reflects my understanding of deep insights given by Rudolf Steiner. India, the bowels of the Earth, teems with life, the will.

Veneration of the cow goes much deeper into the psyche of Eastern people than it does those in the West. They are living with incredible powers everyday as a fait accompli. To them, living with such powers is a reality. We can see it as an ocean of people walking in the chaotic streets with no apparent order. We can feel the power of Will, teeming with life, which no intellect can master. Organizing a city like Benares is absolutely impossible because of the lively forces embodied in the Hindu people. But the work is

---

98   Ibid., pp. 25–26 (trans. revised).

accomplished as if by some miracle and the city functions in its own way, a way that baffles the Westerner from Eagle Country. Westerners ask, "How does this work?" Easterners will it.

I was exhausted for the first few days. My mind reeled, moving fast-forward with plans about how to improve this or that, as I continued my Western intellectual habit to fix things. It finally stopped from exhaustion, from trying to figure out how to help this giant, lively wave of people. One leaves thinking behind.

No wonder my French intellectual friend Christine loves it; she can at last feel the pulse of will, something the French have lost. The French are imprisoned in their thought towers, taking anti-depressants or undergoing shock therapy to resuscitate them from their dead, deadly thinking. That wonderful gift from Descartes—the dualistic mentality of "I think, therefore I am"—is strangling a whole nation. Here Christine had found a new home where she could truly live exuberantly, passionately, devotedly. Through life and will, she broke the shackles of intellectual, cold, dead thoughts.

But now comes something even more difficult to approach. When a country or a human being is one-sided in character, trouble begins. In the US, we plainly see the influence of the eagle culture, as I call it, or the New Age culture. At a supermarket, dozens of magazines offer ways to reach the heights— to meditate, speak with spirits, or conduct all sorts of ceremonies. There are Native American ceremonies and sweat lodges; Buddhist, Tibetan, Hindu, Sufi rituals; or ceremonies led by shamans from Mexico or Peru that include drumming, music, or fire-walks. Others might stem from mainstream religions, such as monastic and born-again Christianity, Jewish mysticism, healing, vision quests, or channeling. And let us not forget the drug culture of antidepressants, pill-proscribing psychiatrists, and cavernous drugstores, or those who get lost in the sex and porn culture. We do not want to feel the pain of being on the Earth, so we follow the eagle's appeal to reach the heights. The land of the soaring eagle forgets the Earth, while India listens to the appeal of the cow and the Earth where we are born, where we are supposed to work.

If the alluring call of the Eagle were to seduce the West so that it would succeed in spreading its way of thinking and attitude of mind over the whole Earth, binding itself up in a one-sided way in this kind of thinking and attitude, then in humanity as a whole there would arise an urge to connect directly with the suprasensory world, as this once was in the beginning, at the outset of Earth evolution. People would feel an urge to extinguish what human beings have won for themselves in freedom and independence. They would come to live only and entirely in that unconscious will that allows the gods to live in human muscles and nerves. They would revert to primitive clairvoyance. Human beings would seek to free themselves from the Earth by turning back to the Earth's beginnings....

The voice of the grazing cow that says, "Do not look upward; all power comes from the Earth. Learn to know all that lies in the Earth's activities. You will be the lord of the Earth. You will perpetuate the results of your work on Earth." Yes, if humankind were to succumb to this alluring call, it would be impossible to avoid the danger I have mentioned—the mechanization of the earthly civilization. The astrality of this animal of digestion wants to make the present enduring, make the present eternal....

The call of what lies in the heaviness of the cow sounds upward from the depths, like a rumbling, muffled roar.... But, although the East is primarily exposed to this alluring call of the cow because of the ancient veneration of the cow in Hinduism, if this allure were actually to take hold of humankind so that what arises from it gained mastery, then the influences emanating from the East would produce a civilization that, spreading through Central Europe and the West, would hinder progress and give rise to decadence. The demonic Earth forces would work on earthly civilization in a one-sided way. What then would actually happen?

The following would happen. In the course of recent centuries, technology, an outer life of technology, has developed under the influence of materialistic science.... The forces of nature are active in technology in their lifeless form.

[An] independent physicist said, "Anything that can be measured is real; anything that cannot be measured is not real." The ideal, in this view, is for everything that exists to be brought into the laboratory and weighed, measured, and enumerated.... Number, measure, and weight are therefore meant to become the foundation of all civilization.

As long as people use only their ordinary understanding to apply measure, number, and weight, matters are not particularly bad. People are certainly smart, but they are still a long way from being as smart as the universe. And this is why things cannot become particularly bad so long as, compared to the universe, people go about their measuring, weighing, and counting in an amateurish way. However, if today's civilization were to be transformed into initiation, things would indeed be bad if this attitude of mind remained. And this could happen if Western civilization, which stands entirely under the sign of measure, number, and weight, were to be flooded by what might well come to pass in the East—namely, that through initiation science people might fathom what actually lives spiritually in the organism of the cow. If you were to penetrate into the organism of the cow, burdened with earthly heaviness, with this one-eighth of its weight in food, with all that can be weighed, measured, and counted, if you were to learn what is being organized spiritually within the cow by this earthly gravity, if you came to understand the whole organism of the cow as it lies in the meadow digesting, and in this process of digestion manifesting wonderful revelations from the astrality of the universe, you would also learn how to make what can be weighed, measured, and counted into a system with which you could overcome all other forms of civilization and impose on the whole globe a civilization that would do nothing but weigh, count, and measure, making everything else disappear....

What would be the result? Well, the way in which people construct machines, for instance, varies greatly according to the nature of the machine in question; at present, machines are still imperfect and primitive, but everything tends toward the gradual development of a kind of machine that depends on oscillations, in which oscillation, vibration, and sequential motion produce the machine's effect.... However, if machines can be constructed that function together in the way that can be learned from the distribution of food in the organization of the cow, then the oscillations produced by machines on Earth, these small earthly oscillations, will be such that what is above the Earth will oscillate in harmony with what is happening upon the Earth; then the movements of our planetary system would be compelled to oscillate in harmony with the Earth's system, just as a string tuned to a certain pitch vibrates in sympathy when another one is struck in the same room.

That is the terrible law of oscillations sounding in unison that would come to pass if the alluring call of the cow so seduces the East that the East would then be able to penetrate completely the unspiritual, purely mechanistic civilization of the West and Center. It would then become possible to create on Earth a mechanistic system engineered to match precisely the mechanistic system of the universe. Everything connected with the activities of the air, the environment, and everything connected with the activities of the stars, would be purged from human civilization. What human beings experience—for instance, through the cycle of the year, and what people experience through living together with the sprouting, budding life of spring, with the fading, dying life of autumn—all this would lose its significance for them. Human civilization would resound with the clattering and rattling of oscillating machines and with the echo of this clattering and rattling, which would stream down to Earth from the cosmos as a reaction to this mechanization of the Earth.[99]

India's population is growing very quickly; it will soon surpass China's population. One can read in the local newspapers that the Indian nation wants to become a superpower, to have the powers ascribed to the West. Many Indians are infatuated with technology, and brilliant engineers are educated in India. As one walks the wide avenues of any Indian city, among its masses of people playing with technology, one wonders where it will all lead. Already there are major technological centers in India where Westerners come to work and make money. We see modern technology alongside 3,000-year-old ways. The alluring call of the cow is not a fantasy.

Here are the Mantras that Rudolf Steiner gave to meet the challenges of these three alluring calls:

> [**West**]
> Learn to know my nature.
> I give you the power
> To create a universe
> In your head.
> Thus speaks the Eagle....

---

99   Ibid., pp. 32, 28–31 (trans. revised).

[**Center**]
Learn to know my nature.
I give you the power
To embody the universe
In the radiance of the encircling air.
Thus speaks the Lion....

[East]
Learn to know my nature.
I give you the power
To wrest from the universe
Measure, number and weight.
Thus speaks the Cow....

I must learn
Your power, O Cow
From the language
Which the stars reveal to me

I must learn
Your Power, O Lion
From the language
Which, through year and day,
Surrounding life engenders in me.

I must learn
Your Power, O Eagle
From the language
Which earth-sprung life creates in me.[100]

This is what the Hindus have to say about the sacred cow, *Gau Mata*:

There are different types of animals all over the world. Among them a cow (Gau Mata), occupies the most important and valuable place in the Indian Psyche. She is the backbone of Indian culture. She is regarded as the most sacred animal in India and its value cannot be denied by any country of the world because her milk has been scientifically proved that it is not only milk but also medicine and ambrosia. According to

---

100 Ibid., pp. 27–28, 36.

the religious scriptures, she grants the four objectives of life—Dharma, Artha, Kama, and Moksa. During the inception of the creation, the Vedas, Agni (fire), a cow and Brahmins came into existence. The relation between Indian civilization and a cow is inseparable. According to the Mahabarata, Brahma, Siva, Asvani Kumar, the Moon, the Sun, Parvati constellation, Laksmi, the Sea, the Sky abide in different parts of the cow. The tri-world is situated on her back. She possesses *Sattva Guna*, happiness, honesty, light righteousness, to the most possible extent. It is very surprisingly and curiously interesting that laksmi belongs to the cow dung and the Ganga to urine. It is notable that the cow dung drives away goblins or ghosts.

The cow represents the greatest amount of miraculous power flowing from the fountain invested with unlimited power.[101]

In biodynamic farming, developed under the direction of Rudolf Steiner's indications, the cow is a most important animal in making special field preparations to keep the forces in the soil.

> I must learn
> Your Power, O Cow
> From the language
> Which the stars reveal to me.

---

101 Upadhyay, *Hindu Gods and Goddesses*, pp. 230–231.

Language of the Heart

These passages contain a very powerful meditation. Whether we live in the East or the West, we are at a point in our civilization in which much is being decided. Our actions have effects which have immense significance for the Earth. Whether we get lost in the land of the eagle, or become chained to the land of the cow or lion, our own actions will have power if we become more conscious of what we are doing.

There is one more picture which I would like to share. That is the beautiful face of Thich Nhat Hanh, a Vietnamese Monk. His face is a meditation in itself because I can recognize the love, compassion, equanimity, and peacefulness of this human being. There is nothing in that human face which reflects untransformed emotions. It is fully transparent and sends love to the world. One of my meditations when dealing with negativity is to look at this peaceful face, and I become enthusiastic with the knowledge that on this Earth it is possible, amidst all the chaos, to attain such peace. If this human being reflects it, I too can work on myself and reflect that peace.

This reminds me of a story about my family when we were in a museum in Buffalo. There was a performance by Tibetan monks; they were building a colored sand mandala. I brought my two children (eleven and five) to the event. We all enjoyed the process, which lasted several hours. My son, whom I had been home-schooling for a few months, had just finished studying the life of Buddha, so it was relevant to spend time with these monks. As we observed the building of the mandala, my son said to me, "Mom, these monks have beautiful faces; they look so kind and peaceful, don't they? They are different from regular people."

I replied, "Yes," and went on to talk about Buddhism and the Buddha so that he could understand the direct effect of meditation on someone's life. Later, we all went out to eat. The Tibetan monks, wearing their dark-red robes, piled into my car with the children and other friends, and we had a wonderful afternoon. But the most important part was what my son could see. With these beautiful, smiling, free, compassionate human beings, my son saw—actually saw—what happens when one leads a sacred life. That was the most wonderful gift of the day, better than any religious speeches, books, or preaching.

Thich Nhat Hanh's work is to bring back the feeling that to become a Buddha is not something foreign to our nature, but something that is feasible.

This is the great insight of the Mahayana [greater vehicle]: everyone can become a Buddha. What Siddharta achieved, all of us can also achieve, whether we are a man or woman, no matter what social class or ethnic group we were born into, or whether we practice as a monastic or as a layperson. We all have the capacity to become a fully enlightened Buddha. And while on the path of becoming a fully enlightened Buddha, we are all bodhisattvas....

The Sanskrit word *kshanti* is often translated as "forbearance," or "endurance," but this does not convey the true meaning of this *paramita*. Forbearance implies that you have to suffer a little bit in order to be able to accept something. If we look at the Chinese character for *kshanti*, in the lower part is the character for "heart," and in the upper part there is a stroke that looks like a knife, something sharp that is a little bit difficult to handle. This is a graphic expression of its true root meaning, "all embracing inclusiveness." If our heart is large and open enough, we can accept the sharp thing and it will not bother us. Something that seems unpleasant or disturbing only feels that way when our heart is too small. When our heart is large enough, we can be very comfortable, we can embrace the sharp, difficult thing without injury. In fact, it allows us to escape the kind of suffering we experience when our heart is too small. When our heart is big enough, we won't suffer.

The Buddha offers us a very beautiful illustration of this principle. Suppose you have a handful of salt and you pour it into a bowl of water and stir it. Now the water in the bowl is too salty to drink. But if you throw that handful of salt into a river, it will not turn the river salty and people can continue to drink the water. When you are only a bowl of water, you suffer. But when you become the river, you don't suffer anymore.

If our heart remains small, we may suffer very deeply from all the difficulties we encounter in life—heat, cold, floods, bacteria, sickness, old age, stubborn people, cruel people. But through the practice of *kshanti* we can embrace everything, and we won't have to suffer. A small heart cannot accept too much—it cannot take in and embrace everything, every difficulty that arises. But a heart that is expansive and open can easily accept everything, and you no longer have to suffer. Perfecting the practice of *kshanti* consists of continually making your heart bigger and bigger so that it can accept and embrace everything. That is the power and the miracle of love.[102]

I think it is relevant to introduce here the six auxiliary exercises mentioned by Rudolf Steiner in various books, exercises that I practice regularly as part of my discipline. His subtle exercises (there are many) show that in the West, thanks to Rudolf Steiner, we have our own "new" tradition and practice which is safe, detailed, and based on ancient initiation practices.

To a certain extent the six auxiliary exercises serve as preparation for the actual esoteric exercises. In those who devote themselves to these auxiliary exercises with the proper earnestness and enthusiasm they will create the fundamental soul constitution necessary in order to derive the proper fruit from occult exercises.

1. *Control of thought*: For at least five minutes daily, one should take time to reflect on an object as insignificant as possible, in which one has no interest from the outset. One should logically connect everything one can think about the object. It is important that it be an insignificant object, for it is precisely the control that one must then exert on oneself to abide with it that awakens the slumbering faculties in the soul. After a time, one notices in one's soul a feeling of solidity and confidence. Now, you must not imagine that this feeling overwhelms you with surprising power. No, this is a very fine, subtle feeling that you must listen for. Those who claim that they absolutely cannot sense this feeling within are most like those who go out to find a very small, delicate object among many other objects. Indeed, they do seek, but only superficially, and then they can't find the small object because they overlook it. One must listen very quietly, and then one senses this feeling; indeed, it appears

---

102 Thich Nhat Hanh, *Peaceful Action, Open Heart*, pp. 18, 255–256.

primarily in the front part of the head. If one has felt it there, then one pours it into the thoughts in the brain and into the spinal cord. Gradually one then comes to think that rays are going forth from the forebrain back into the spinal cord.

2. *Initiative in action*: For this exercise one must choose an action that one thinks up for oneself. If, for example, one takes as an activity the watering of a flower . . . then one is doing something entirely useless. For the action must arise from one's own initiative; i.e., one must think of it oneself. Then, with this exercise a feeling soon makes itself noticeable, something like this: "I can achieve something," "I am more diligent than before," "I feel the need to be active." Actually, one feels this in the entire upper part of one's body. One then tries to let this feeling flow to the heart.

3. *Superiority to pleasure and pain*: For example, one feels oneself starting to cry. Then it is time to do this exercise. One forces oneself with all one's might not to cry now. The same holds for laughing. When laughter comes, one tries not to laugh but rather remain calm. This does not mean that one should not laugh anymore but one must take oneself in hand and become master over laughing and crying. And if one has overcome oneself a few times then one soon senses a feeling of calmness and equanimity. One allows this feeling to flow through one's entire body, by first pouring it out from the heart into one's arms and hands so that it radiates out through one's hands into one's deeds. Then one lets it stream to one's feet and at last to the head. This exercise demands serious self-observation; one should carry it out for a least a quarter of an hour each day.

4. *Positivity*: One should know how to find the kernel of goodness in everything bad, how to find the beautiful in everything ugly and also the little spark of divinity in every criminal. Then one gets the feeling as if one were expanding out of one's skin. It is a feeling similar to the feeling of becoming larger that the etheric body has after death. If one senses this feeling, then one lets it radiate away from one through the eyes, ears, and the entire skin, but mainly through the eyes.

5. *Openness*: One should keep oneself flexible, always be capable of taking in something new. If someone tells us something that we consider improbable, nevertheless there must always remain a little

corner in our hearts where we say to ourselves, "This person could be right." This does not need to make us undiscriminating; we can always check the facts. Then a feeling overcomes us as if something were streaming toward us from outside. This we draw in through our eyes, ears, and our entire skin.

6. *Balance*: The five previous feelings should be brought into harmony by giving each of them an equal amount of attention. These exercises do not need to be done for one month each. It is just that a period of time has to be indicated. What is most important is that these exercises be done precisely in this sequence. Those who do the second exercise before the first derive no benefit whatsoever, for it is just the sequence that is important. Some even think they must begin with the sixth exercise, with harmonizing. But can anything be harmonized when it doesn't exist? For those who do not wish to do the exercises in the proper sequence, the exercises are useless....

> More radiant than the Sun,
> Purer than snow,
> Subtler than the ether,
> Is the self
> The spirit of my Heart,
> I am this self,
> This self am I....

The spirit in my heart: We have only really understood something when we have grasped with our heart. Intellect and reason are merely mediators for the heart's understanding. Through intellect and reason we penetrate to divine thoughts. But once we have really taken hold of the thought, then we must learn to *love* it. Gradually we learn to love all things. This does not mean that we should give our heart without discrimination to every thing we encounter. For our experience is at first deceptive. However, when we make an effort to understand a being or a thing down to is origin in the divine, then we also begin to love it. If I have a depraved human being standing in front of me, then in no way should I love his or her depravity. Through such an act I would only be in error and would not help the person at all. However, if I reflect on how this person has come to his or her depravity, and if I help the person leave it behind, then I am helping that person, and I myself struggle through to the truth. I must seek everywhere to find *how* I can love. God is present in all things, but his divinity in any particular thing I must first seek it. It is not the external aspect of a being or thing that I should love straightaway, for this can be deceptive and I could easily love the error. But Truth lies *behind* all illusion, and we can always love truth. And if the heart seeks the love of truth in all beings, then there lies the "spirit in all heart." Such love is the garment the soul should always wear. Then the soul itself weaves the divine into things. ...

It is not a matter of meditating on many sentences, but of letting a little live again and again in a soul that has become still.

During the meditation itself, one should speculate very little, but rather quietly allow the content of the sentences to work upon one. But apart from the meditation, during free moments in the course of the day one should return to the content of the sentences and see what reflections one can draw from them. Then they become a living power that sinks into the soul and makes it strong and vigorous. For when the soul unites with eternal truth, it lives in the eternal. And when the soul lives in the eternal, then higher beings have access to it, and can let their own power sink into it.[103]

I would like to mention an encounter I had with Father Thomas Keating at his monastery in Colorado in the land of the eagle a few months after my return from India. It was in the late spring, when St. Benedict's Monastery (in Snowmass, Colorado) was surrounded in the green splendor of soft mountains, aspens, and pines. The monastery has a delightful chapel called Our Lady of Snowmass in which, following the tradition of the Trappist-Cistercian monks, one can pray and meditate. A few monks live there in harmony with nature, praying, meditating, working the land, and living a Christian life as thousands of people did centuries ago across Europe. It is a little oasis that I thoroughly enjoyed. Father Keating speaks to the heart of contemporary human beings, and his retreats are enormously popular. His practice is called Centering

---

103 Steiner, *Esoteric Lessons, 1904–1909*, pp. 190–191, 34, 36–37.

Prayer. I have not practiced it, but I would like to bring some of my insights into what I perceived about Father Keating, the beauty of his big heart, and of course something about meditation and the chapel, which is located at the center of the other buildings at Snowmass and is where the monks pray.

The men there live among men; no women are allowed in their compounds. But a woman can rent a space in the other buildings scattered around the large property. It is not forbidden for women to come to pray and meditate at the chapel—unlike Mt. Athos, Greece where no females are allowed at all, not even female animals. Here the monks live a spiritual life, and meditation is more than a part—it is their whole life. The beautiful stained-glass window that depicts Our Lady of Snowmass looks down on the believers in the chapel and sends her protective love to all.

My insight is that all these men develop within themselves a space for Mary, the Mother of God. As I looked more and more deeply into Father Keating's face, it dawned on me that he was a man who had become Our Lady of Snowmass, and all the Monks there were, in fact, becoming Our Lady, too. They had become what they prayed to. After forty, fifty, or sixty years of praying, these men had become the Big Heart, Mary. They had worked on transforming their lower selves, had embraced the feminine within themselves, and had given birth to the Mother of God within. It was a revelation to me, to see this tall, masculine man who had become such a beautiful Madonna within himself. He was definitely a virile man, but his heart was a Madonna—deep, encompassing the whole world, full of understanding, love, and compassion for all.

While the world underwent a sexual revolution, these monks were accomplishing, thanks to their devotion to the Madonna, Mary, Mother of God, what most sexually confused men and women were looking for. They had united their female and male aspects within, and thereby had no need to live as female if they were male or male if they were female. They had gone beyond our sexist society within themselves. Theirs was no longer a question of proscribed roles—I am a male, I am a female, or I am a male with female tendencies, or female with male tendencies—which they needed to live out. They had come to an understanding deep within themselves of what it is to be male and female, without the fear of being misunderstood in our uncreative, dry society.

In their hearts they had become Mary, Mother of God, or were on their ways to becoming Mary. Within themselves, they had performed the Alchemical Wedding we often hear about, whereby we are no longer one or the other but have both within. We are complete human beings, whole and wholesome, rather than one-sided, too much of this or that. That is one of Kühlewind's meditations and the title of one of his books, *Wilt Thou Become Whole?*

The little monastery is a small center for alchemy of the soul, uniting Heaven and Earth.

> In a couple one observes that the husband and the wife often end up looking like each other as they get old, in the same way when one lives by and with constant prayer in the closeness of God, one ends up resembling what one loves. We become what we love.[104]

Father Thomas Keating's writings show that he is a master in Christian meditation. In the particular passages that follow, he shares his deep understanding of the transformation that a Christian soul undergoes when one endured the necessary trials. It has all the familiar symbols that I have already spoken about in my own trials, brought about by my Buddhist practice: the dove, transfiguration, illumination, light and dark, heavenly scent, and more.

Transfiguration 1: The Holy Mountain

> Jesus' going up the mountain to be transfigured points to the transformation that we receive on the spiritual journey after a time of purification. After enduring the inner desert of purification, God refreshes us with transforming experiences. The mountain of the Transfiguration is not just a place of retreat. It symbolizes the experience of spiritual awakening that is the purpose of the practice of contemplative prayer.
>
> The grace of the Transfiguration is not just a vision of glory, an isolated experience of divine consolation, however exalted. Of course, such

---

104 Jean-Yves Leloup, *Ecrits sur l'Hesychasm*, p. 130.

an experience has immense value. But its primary purpose is something greater: to empower us to live in the presence of God and to see the radiance of that presence in all events, people, the cosmos, and in ourselves.[105]

Transfiguration 2: Sleepers, Awake

Let us consider the context of this glorification of Jesus' body. It seems that an inner light that was normally hidden emerged and grew so bright that it saturated his clothes and produced an extraordinary radiance. The divine person of the Word is the source of this light. Jesus miraculously hid this light during his earthly lifetime. We must see the Transfiguration as Jesus' normal state of being since there was nothing inherent to his humanity to limit his glory. Like Moses, who had to veil his face after he came down from Mount Sinai because his face had become so radiant that none of the Israelites dared to look at him, Jesus had to veil the presence of the divine Person within his humanity. Faith penetrates this veil and touches the Eternal Word. The disciples were finally ready.

Remember how, in the Gospel story of Mary and Martha, Mary of Bethany sat at Jesus' feet in complete, undivided attention. As she listened to his word at this ever-deepening level, she was penetrating the details of his humanity and opening to the divine Person who possessed it. This is precisely what we do in contemplative prayer. We let go of the contents of our rational faculties and the limitations of their ways of knowing. Our awareness slips between the cracks of thinking, feeling, and perceiving and fastens on the person of Christ.... The cosmos is the body of Christ in varied forms of expression. As faith grows, the disguises of God fall away and we perceive the divine presence and its activity within and around us all the time.[106]

Transfiguration 3: Resting in God

The Feast of the Transfiguration is celebrated in the church on August 6, but the Transfiguration Gospel is also read on the Second Sunday of Lent. In the context of Lent this text follows the temptation of Jesus in the wilderness, indicating that all ascetical practice, desert experiences,

---

105 Thomas Keating, *Reawakenings*, p. 119.

106 Ibid.

and penances are a preparation for transfiguration. The experience of God (the transmission of the Divine consciousness) is given in the degree that we are prepared to receive it. The period of Jesus in the wilderness followed his baptism in the Jordan where he seems to have been anointed by the Holy Spirit with full consciousness of his divine personhood, as well as his mission. The Spirit led him into the wilderness; he, in turn, led the disciples up this high mountain.

At the river Jordan, the voice from the cloud said, "This is my beloved Son on whom my favor rests." The Spirit descended in the form of a dove and rested upon him. Rest is the sign of divine transmission. It is the interior milieu in which we move toward complete openness to God's presence and action within. It means that we participate in the descent of the Spirit upon Jesus. His consciousness of the Ultimate Reality as Abba, the God of infinite compassion, is extended to us.

In the context of Christ's anointing by the Spirit and his extension of that anointing to each of us, the experience on the holy mountain is of great significance. The practice of contemplative prayer opens us to the gentle but firm invasion of truth, light and love.

The experience of the disciples is a paradigm of the awakening of spiritual attentiveness. The first sign of this development is called by Fathers of the Church, "the divine perfume." Perfume is an analogy of the sweetness of the divine presence. The divine presence, like pleasurable objects to the external senses, is attractive. The attraction of the external senses obviously is different from that of the inner experience of grace that draws us to our inmost center. There is no reflection, no effort, no activity on our part. The attraction rises up because the divine presence is there. As soon as the obstacles that keep it hidden in ordinary life have been sufficiently reduced, the divine perfume slips into the cracks of our defense mechanisms, and a whiff of the sweetness of God's presence is experienced. It is an attraction to something within us that we had not known before, at least not in this degree. God lifts a corner of the veil and the aroma of the divine sweetness escapes. Like the perfume in the house of Simon, which filled the whole house, the divine presence fills our entire being with its delight. The awakening to this presence is signified in this event by Jesus leading the disciples up the high mountain. Even when our time of prayer is a mess, unbearable, boring, going nowhere, this mysterious anointing will not let us go. On some level we feel the attraction for silence, solitude, prayer, and the need to be faithful to the practice.

Christ calls to us throughout all time, "Come to me all you who labor and are burdened and I will give you rest." "Rest" refers to interior quiet, tranquility, the peace of the abyss, the rootedness of being one with the divine presence.

"Rest" implies that we are beginning to experience the mind of Christ, his awareness of the Godhead as infinite mercy, concern for everything that is, and the servant of creation. This rest is our reassurance at the deepest level that everything is okay. The ultimate freedom is to rest in God in suffering as well as in joy. God was just as present to Jesus in his abandonment on the cross as on the Mountain of Transfiguration.

The sense of spiritual touch is a more intimate experience of the awakening of spiritual attentiveness. We observe the frequent reference to touch in Jesus' miracles. He touched the little children and put his arms around them. The hugging of children symbolizes the interior embrace of God in which we are not just attracted to the divine presence, but are in immediate proximity to it.... The touch of Jesus initiates the process of inner resurrection. It imparts health at every level of our being.[107]

Here the "touch" is what we can also call entering the spiritual world, hovering over the spiritual substance after having left the world of physical laws. This is "crossing the threshold," which Rudolf Steiner speaks of in *Spiritual Science*. In Kühlewind's language, it is entering the world of wholeness, of being touched by oneness, being healed by a split-second encounter with the eternal.

This experience we call the "I am" experience. It is the universal healing medicine. It is a feeling of identity with an ever-deepening being that wills itself. It provides certainty, creativity, and solidity, and dissolves what comes from egotism. From it, the knowledge arises that nothing can happen to me (the one who is experiencing this): I am safe, completely independent of circumstances, opinions, successes or failures. I have found my spiritual roots.[108]

---

107 Ibid., p. 127.
108 Kühlewind, *The Light of the "I,"* p. 39.

In Buddhist terms, it is touching upon a deep peace after countless trials and tribulations. The West meets the East, and vice versa. We can choose different paths and there will always be a Master ready to help us when we are ready. But we must always be ready to ask: *What is it that I am practicing?*

A true Master will never mentioned the *siddis* or effects of meditation such as seeing auras or elemental beings or experiencing visions or the ability to read someone's thoughts. If students mention these phenomena or a desire to become rich from acquiring such effects, they will always advise those students to leave immediately. If students even talk about such experiences in a way that increases their egoism—for example, "I can see elemental beings, how about you?" "This person is clairvoyant. I can do that." Students with such an attitude are diverted from the correct path and will not achieve the next level, which is far more important. The true master will say, "Just practice, and ignore it all. The goal is to be free and then to help others be free human beings."

The following translation from Jean-Yves Leloup shows the similarity among the Desert Fathers, Hesychiasts, Russian Staretz, spiritual Fathers, and Father Thomas Keating's Centering Prayer. It illustrates why I was so touched by this wonderful man of prayer and by the other resident monks.

> The experience of the transfiguration compared to the experience of simple love is one of the fundamental characteristics of the hesychiast (peaceful) life; at Mt. Athos following Gregory Palamas, the realism of this Transfiguration experience is taken very seriously, because it is a step on the ladder of our "born again" life, participation in the uncreated light. Mr. Kazantzakis notices that our tendency to "make God human" should be replaced by our making human beings godly, or deify human beings, not humanize God, but deify humankind in its entirety.
>
> Perhaps an example from the history of art can help us understand what could be called "the lost theology of divine energies in our Western world." The body of Christ and the Saints used to be represented by a halo of light, bathed totally in a supernatural light; then this light became a small circle around the face, then a little moon over the head of Christ and the Saints, just as if Grace had left the human body. Grace

was no longer manifested in the body, but was simply hovering lightly in a tiny nebulous crescent above the head.

The pilgrim sees a transfigured world, meaning a world that reveals "the fire of things." The world has not changed, but it is the eyes that have opened through prayers and have become capable of seeing "the glory of Yhwh" within the world body. The glory of God in the Judeo-Christian tradition evokes an experience that bears weight, has a luminous density.... We have lost sight of the vision of a "subtle body of energy" [ether body] of the Earth; we see only the earthly body, the body made of matter. The pilgrim, through the vibration of the heart awakened by vision, has access to this vision that was Moses's vision of the Burning Bush; "He saw the flame in the Bush," and in the flame, fire, and in the flame, the voice of the Other who says "I am" the Burning Bush; "I am" isn't that the experience, the same vision of nature, of energy, of the transcendent essence of its manifestation? Isn't that equally the same experience undergone by the disciples during the Transfiguration. Byzantine sacred writings inform us that their eyes learned to see him "as he is": in his body of flesh, in his body of light, in his relation to "the being" who speaks the words "This is my beloved Son," which can be translated in metaphysical language as: Here is my manifestation, my energy. The apostles now contemplate "the visible in the invisible"; they hear the "name of the unspeakable"; they touch, or rather they are touched, by the "one who lives within the inaccessible light." In this capacity, the Russian pilgrim enters and lives in this experience of the transfiguration, which is the goal of the hesychiast meditation. Finally, that one is happy and something that happiness can reach us: This happiness not only illuminated the darkness within my soul; the outside world, as well, appeared in a new luminous presence, everything called me to love and glorify God; human beings, trees, the plant kingdom, the animal kingdom, everything became familiar to me, and everywhere I found the name of him, Jesus Christ. Sometimes, I found myself so light that I thought I no longer had a body, and I floated gently in the air. Sometimes I would enter within myself; my body would become transparent to me, and I would admire the incredible sacredness of the human body.

We are here in the presence of a spirituality that is fully incarnated, and the problem is not "how I am going to get out of this low world of the flesh, this world of the rotted senses?" Rather, how can we let the flame of the Pentecost come gently down and touch all the elements of our perishable universe; how can we speed up the trans-figuration of the world?...

The path of the Pilgrim is not against social work and reforms or the desire for justice; it simply reminds us that a change in society without a change within the human heart is doomed to failure.[109]

Here is another fascinating story from Swami Rama to end this long tale:

I once went to Assam to meet Mataji, a great lady yogi who was then ninety-six years of age. She was then living next to a famous Shakti Temple called Kamakhya. Everyone aspires to go there but very few are able to visit that place, because it is in a far corner of India. From Cal-cutta I went to Gohati and then on foot to Kamakhya. I reached the temple late in the evening, stumbling in the darkness and stubbing my toes many times. At that time there were three or four small wooden houses near the temple. I was asked by the temple priest to stay on the second floor of the same building in which the famous woman was living. My room had many holes and cracks through which mice and snakes would crawl in. It was terrible, but I was helpless. I would close the holes with pieces of cloth which I found here and there. I managed to live in that room for two months. My experiences there were shocking and surprising in the beginning, but very pleasant toward the end of my stay.

It was the twentieth year in which this old woman had not come outside during the daytime. However, she regularly visited the temple at midnight and at three o'clock in the morning. For the first four nights I remained inside my room, but on the fifth night I came out and went to the temple. It was a moonlit night. When I reached the temple gate I could hear someone chanting mantras inside. It was that old woman sit-ting all alone with an oil lamp burning beside her. When she sensed me outside the north gate she shouted very assertively, "Don't come in. You will kill yourself. I am the Mother Divine. Get out of this place."

I was frightened, but at the same time I was curious to know what was happening inside that small temple. I peeped in and she rushed toward me. She was completely naked—a bag of bones wrapped inside shining skin. Her eyes were glowing like bowls of fire. She shouted, "Go away.—Why are you watching what I am doing?" I bowed with reverence

---

109 Leloup, *Écrits sur l'hésychasme* (trans. the author and editor), p. 136.

and out of fear, thinking she would calm down, but she whipped with her cane and drove me away. I went back to my room.

The next morning this mother teacher called me to her room and began to talk to me. I said, "I need your blessing." She was in silence for a few seconds then muttered my nickname, which was not known to anyone except my gurudeva. She hugged me and put me on her lap. I don't know what happened to me then, but if there is any seventh heaven, I can tell you, I was there.

Stroking me on the head, she blessed me and said, "Although you will find obstacles on the path, all will be crossed. Go with my blessings." But I said, "I want to stay here for some time, "and she consented.

When I asked this mother teacher what she was doing all alone in the temple at three o'clock in the morning, she said, "I do Shakti worship, and I do not want anyone near me at midnight and at three in the morning." From midnight to two o'clock and from three to four-thirty nobody visits that temple.

She permitted me to sit with her for half an hour every evening. When I sat in front of her my whole consciousness would rise exactly as if I were sitting before my master. In my heart I accepted her as my mother teacher. I had many questions I wanted to ask her, but she told me to remain silent. I followed her instruction and received answers to my questions without either of us speaking. This silence was more communicative than any other type of teaching. The most advanced teachers impart their knowledge in silence.

She was a very powerful and yet gentle old woman, with tremendous willpower. I observed that whatever she said would always come true. When someone came to ask her help, she spoke very little and always in a brief sentence. "Go, it will happen." "Bless you." "Pray to the Mother Divine." Then she would go to her room.

When I heard that this mother, whom I called Mother Teacher, did not lie down to sleep, but would remain sitting in her meditation posture throughout the night, I started observing her by peeping through the crack in her door. I spent three days and nights watching her, and found that it was true that she never slept.

One day, I said to her "Mother, if you lie down, I will give you a gentle massage which will help you to fall asleep."

She giggled and said, "Sleep. That is not for me. I am beyond sloth and inertia. I enjoy sleepless sleep, for which I do not need to lie down. One who enjoys yoga sleep, why does she need the sleep of pigs?"

I asked, "What is that?"

She said, "Pigs eat beyond their capacity and then lay themselves down snoring. I wonder how they can sleep so much." She explained to me the whole anatomy of sleep, and asked me if I knew that mechanism in which a human being goes from the conscious state to the dreaming state and then to the deeper state of sleep. She started giving me accurate and systematic lessons. After that I was able to understand the Mandukya Upanishad, which explains the three states of mind—waking, dreaming, sleeping—and the fourth state, Turiya, which is termed as "the state beyond." The Mandukya is considered to be the most important and difficult of all the Upanishads. I filled up seventy pages of my diary taking down the notes as she talked. In her gentle, slow speech, there were no repetitions and no mistakes. She gave a systematic commentary on this Upanishad, which I intellectually understood but I did not understand in reality until I started to practice remaining conscious during these four states.

After two and a half months, the day of parting came. I was very sad, but she said, "Don't be attached to the mother image in my physical body and personality. I am the mother of the universe, who is everywhere. Learn to raise your consciousness above and beyond my mortal self." With tears in my eyes I looked at her and she said, "Be fearless. I am with you." I bade her goodbye and returned to my Himalayan abode. My Master spoke very highly of this old woman. She had lived by that temple area since she was twelve years old and stayed there up to the age of 101, when she left her body.[110]

What do we have in the West to compare with the surrendering of this Lady Sadhu? She had become the Shakti, the divine Mother energy, even though she lived like a pauper and was a "heap of bones." What we have in the West is the other bag of bones, the tall model, the cold beauty, who walks on the stage or the movie set, young and vain, with artificial beauty and nothing in the head but empty thoughts.

---

110 Swami Rama, *Living with the Himalayan Masters*, p. 103.

In the East, the old ancient divine energy, the "heap of bones" female sage, abundant in warmth and love, lives in the heavens sequestered from the world in her dark cave. In the West, the sexual empty-headed superficial beauty lives sequestered from the world as well, in her abstract tower. Are we ever going to make a bridge between the two?

> Wisdom makes a person open and receptive because it is a foundation from which love for all things grows. To preach love is useless.... When wisdom warms the soul, love streams forth; thus we can understand that there are people who can heal through the laying on of hands. Wisdom pours forces of love through their limbs. Christ was the wisest, and therefore also the greatest, healer. Unless love and compassion unite with wisdom, no genuine help can be forthcoming....
>
> We are always surrounded by wisdom because wise beings created the world. When this wisdom has reached its climax it will have become all-encompassing love. Love will stream toward us from the world of the future. Love is born of wisdom, and the wisest spiritual being is the greatest healer.[111]

This old woman sadhu had become such a healer. In terms of our Western "bag of bones" model, here is what happened:

> Human beings had become empty bags because they no longer experienced anything within themselves....
>
> The human being came to be seen as a system of solid parts. In this realm of clearly outlined parts, everything takes place in a mechanical way. One part pushes another; the other moves; things get pumped; it all works like suction or pressure pumps. The body is viewed from a mechanical standpoint, as existing only through the interplay of solidly contoured organs....
>
> Naturally, people began to think that the heart is really a pump that mechanically pumps the blood through the body, because they no longer knew that our inner fluids have their own life and therefore move on their own....
>
> The human being was seen only as a physical body, and that only to the extent that one consists of solid parts. These were now dealt with by

---

111 Steiner, *Isis Mary Sophia*, p. 67.

means of physics, which had in the meantime also been cast out of the human being. Physics was now applied externally to human beings, now no longer understood. Human beings had been turned into empty bags, and physics had been established in an abstract way. Now this same physics was reapplied to the human being. Thus, one no longer had the living human being, but only an empty bag stuffed with theories.[112]

$$\Downarrow$$

The way a society thinks becomes reflected in its population. Our cold, emaciated, bloodless model is one of its reflections. How are we going to infuse this Western, cold model with the Eastern sage, full of love and warmth? One is starving for the other. My journey was my small attempt at bridging one with the other.

Our Earth is one planet; our destiny is to develop love. As I travel on the Earth's paths witnessing the ancient, the modern, the searching souls in different bodies, all searching for the same thing whether poor, rich, young, old, Easterner or Westerner, it becomes obvious that there is only one language. But as Georg Kühlewind points out, we will not speak that language unless we make the effort to learn it. We are no longer being given anything. We must earn it with hard painful work.

This little journey was an effort in making that language comprehensible. One must go through the difficult passages and enter the meaning. I hope that the reader has penetrated a little bit further in understanding the language of the heart. So now I truly end this journey; but of course there is already another journey around the corner.

All the best from an unknower, because as soon as "I think I know," I don't know at all.

> *Yasmājj jātam jagat sarvam, yasminn eva pralīyate*
> *Yenedam dhāryate sarvam, tasmai jnānātmane namaḥ.*

> Archetypal self, from which we have come forth,
> Archetypal self, who lives in all things,

---

112 Steiner, *The Origins of Natural Science*, pp. 109, 111–112 (trans. revised).

To you, our higher self, we return again.[113]

Once we attain a certain degree of intensity, which is impossible to define, our attention begins and continues to grow by itself, without our care and effort. Attention is then directed healthily toward one thing. To be one-pointed is attention's original and healthy nature.[114]

"True attention is love." —GEORG KÜHLEWIND

↓

Satyam jnanam anantam brahma
Anandarupam amritam bibharti
Shantam shivam advaitam
Om, shanti, shanti, shanti

Truth, wisdom, immeasurability
Blessedness, eternity, beauty,
Peace, blessing, indivisibility
Aum, peace, peace, peace.

---

113 Steiner, *Esoteric Lessons*, p. 106.
114 Kühlewind, *The Light of the "I,"* pp. 38–39.

References

Ahir, D. C. *Vipassana: A Universal Buddhist Meditation Technique.* Delhi: Sri Satguru, 1999.

Anonymous. *The Way of a Pilgrim and A Pilgrim Continues on His Way.* Boston: Shambhala, 2001.

Collins, Mabel. "Light on the Path"; see Rudolf Steiner, *From the History and Contents...*

Eck, Diana. *Darsan: Seeing the Divine Image in India.* New York: Columbia University, 1998.

Keating, Thomas. *Reawakenings.* New York: Crossroad, 2000 [1992].

Klocek, Dennis. *Climate: Soul of the Earth.* Great Barrington, MA: Lindisfarne Books, 2010.

Kühlewind, Georg. *From Normal to Healthy: Paths to the Liberation of Consciousness.* Great Barrington, MA: Lindisfarne Books, 1988.

———. *The Light of the "I": Guidelines for Meditation.* Great Barrington, MA: Lindisfarne Books, 2008.

———. *Wilt Thou Be Made Whole? Healings in the Gospels.* Great Barrington, MA: Lindisfarne Books, 2008.

Leloup, Jean-Yves. *Écrits sur l'hésychasme: Une tradition contemplative oubliée.* Paris: Spirituality Vivantes, 1990.

———. *Writings on Hesychasme.* Paris: Spirituality Vivantes, 1990.

Nhat Hanh, Thich. *Peaceful Action, Open Heart: Lessons from the Lotus Sutra.* Berkeley, CA: Parallax, 2008.

Pandit, Harendr Upadhyay. *Hindu Gods and Goddesses: Spiritual and Scientific Approach.* Delhi: Pilgrims, 2004.

Rama, Swami. *Living with the Himalayan Masters.* Himalayan Institute, 1999 [1978].

Schuré, Édouard. *The Great Initiates: A Study of the Secret History of Religions.* Hudson, NY: SteinerBooks, 1989.

Steiner, Rudolf. *The Apocalypse of St. John: Lectures on the Book of Revelation.* Hudson, NY: Anthroposophic Press, 1993.

———. *Approaching the Mystery of Golgotha.* Great Barrington, MA: SteinerBooks, 2006.

———. *The Bhagavad Gita and the West: The Esoteric Significance of the Bhagavad Gita and its Relation to the Epistles of Paul.* Great Barrington, MA: SteinerBooks, 2009.

———. *The Boundaries of Natural Science.* Spring Valley, NY: Anthroposophic Press, 1983.

———. *Building Stones for an Understanding of the Mystery of Golgotha.* London: Rudolf Steiner Press, 1985.

———. *The Christian Mystery: Early Lectures.* Great Barrington, MA: Anthroposophic Press, 1998.

———. *Christianity as Mystical Fact and the Mysteries of Antiquity.* Great Barrington, MA: SteinerBooks, 2006.

———. *Esoteric Lessons, 1904–1909: Lectures, Notes, Meditations, and Exercises.* Great Barrington, MA: SteinerBooks, 2007.

———. *From Beetroot to Buddhism...: Answers to Questions.* London: Rudolf Steiner Press, 1999.

———. *From the History and Contents of the First Section of the Esoteric School, 1904–1914: Letters, Documents, and Lectures,* Great Barrington, MA: SteinerBooks, 2010.

———. *The Gospel of St. John and its Relation to the Other Gospels.* Hudson, NY: Anthroposophic Press, 1982.

———. *Harmony of the Creative Word: The Human Being and the Elemental, Animal, Plant, and Mineral Kingdoms.* London: Rudolf Steiner Press, 2001.

———. *How to Know Higher Worlds: A Modern Path of Initiation.* Hudson, NY: Anthroposophic Press, 1994.

———. *The Human Soul in Relation to World Evolution.* Spring Valley, NY: Anthroposophic Press, 1984.

———. *Initiation, Eternity, and the Passing Moment,* Spring Valley, NY: Anthroposophic Press, 1980.

———. *Intuitive Thinking as a Spiritual Path: A Philosophy of Freedom.* Great Hudson, NY: Anthroposophic Press, 1995.

———. *Isis Mary Sophia: Her Mission and Ours.* Great Barrington, MA: SteinerBooks, 2003.

———. *Macrocosm and Microcosm.* London: Rudolf Steiner Press, 1985.

———. *The Mysteries of the East and of Christianity.* Blauvelt, NY: Garber, 1989.

———. *Mystery of the Universe: The Human Being, Model of Creation.* London: Rudolf Steiner Press, 2001.

———. *The Occult Movement in the Nineteenth Century.* London: Rudolf Steiner Press, 1973.

———. *Old and New Methods of Initiation.* London: Rudolf Steiner Press, 1991.

———. *The Origins of Natural Science.* Spring Valley, NY: Anthroposophic Press, 1985.

———. *Philosophy, Cosmology, and Religion.* Spring Valley, NY: Anthroposophic Press, 1984.

———. *Polarities in the Evolution of Mankind: West and East, Materialism and Mysticism, Knowledge and Belief.* Hudson, NY: Anthroposophic Press, 1987.

———. *The Redemption of Thinking: A Study in the Philosophy of Thomas Aquinas.* Spring Valley, NY: Anthroposophic Press, 1983.

———. *Secrets of the Threshold.* Great Barrington, MA: SteinerBooks, 2007.

———. *Staying Connected: How to Continue Your Relationships with Those Who Have Died.* Great Barrington, MA: SteinerBooks, 1999.

———. *The Tension between East and West.* Great Barrington, MA: SteinerBooks, 1983.

———. *Theosophy: An Introduction to the Spiritual Processes in Human Life and in the Cosmos.* Hudson, NY: Anthroposophic Press, 1994.

———. *A Way of Self-Knowledge & the Threshold of the Spiritual World.* Great Barrington, MA: SteinerBooks, 2006.

———. *Wonders of the World: Ordeals of the Soul, Revelations of the Spirit.* London: Rudolf Steiner Press, 1983.

Whicher, Olive. *Sunspace: Science at a Threshold of Spiritual Understanding.* London: Rudolf Steiner Press, 1989.